Human Development Network

Health, Nutrition, and Population Series

Private Participation in Health Services

April Harding
Alexander S. Preker
Editors

THE WORLD BANK
Washington, D.C.

ISBN 0-8213-5152-4

Library of Congress Cataloging-in-Publication Data has been applied for.

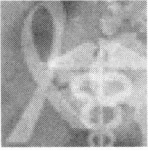

Contents

Appendixes

Tables

Figures

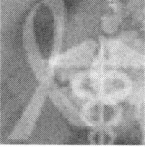

Foreword

Julian Le Grand

Two years ago, I was asked to join a commission being set up by a British think-tank, the Institute of Public Policy Research, on public-private partnerships. The commission was supposed to explore, among other things, the use of the private sector to help provide publicly funded services such as health care or education. As in many countries in both the developed and the developing worlds, this had previously been in large part a no-go area in Britain, where the tradition that only providers who were government owned and operated could be given public money to supply public services was deeply ingrained. Successive British governments had successfully challenged that belief with respect to relatively mundane public services such as refuse collection or street cleaning. But to suggest that the private sector might have a role to play in the provision of services with the political and social prominence of health care and education was blasphemy indeed.

So it was not surprising that, when the commission's report appeared recommending some mild experimentation with the use of the private sector in the health care area, it caused a furor. The fuss began when a draft version was leaked during the election campaign of that year. The commission, and by implication the Labour Government of Tony Blair to whom it was known to be close, was accused of wanting back-door privatization of the health service. When the report was finally published a month after the election (Institute for Public Policy Research 2001), it generated enormous media coverage and, especially from health policy analysts and commentators, some vituperative responses (see, for instance, Pollock and others 2001).

The extraordinary reactions to the report, especially the more hostile ones, are of interest to those policymakers in any country who are involved in the provision of health care—and especially to potential users of this book—because they provide an insight into the likely opposition that policymakers will encounter if they dare to suggest that greater attention be paid to the potential for mobilizing the private sector to serve the public good in the area.

Some of the reactions, especially those involving accusations of privatization, arose from a simple confusion between finance and provision. As this book emphasizes in several places, the use of private providers does not necessarily imply the use of private finance. Publicly financed commissioners can contract with private or nonprofit organizations to provide health care services without compromising the principle of government funding. To recommend private participation in publicly funded health care is not the same as advocating full-scale privatization.

A second line of objection concerned morality. Making profits from health care was regarded as morally wrong. Quite why it should be more morally objectionable to make profits from the provision of health care than in other areas of equal or even greater importance to human welfare where private provision was common, such as food or housing, was never made clear. Also, it quickly became apparent that this was not an issue that greatly disturbed the general public; for them, the important question was the quality and quantity of the service provided, not the moral standing of the provider.

More important than either of these was the objection of impracticality. Public officials knew how to deal with and manage public organizations; but they had little knowledge of the private sector. How could they be expected to deal with sharp, experienced private operators? How should they contract with them? How should the private operators be monitored? How could the internal market be regulated? If the private sector were only small or even nonexistent, how could it be encouraged to grow? More generally, how could the private sector be marshaled to serve the public good—and prevented from exploiting any superiority it might have in information and skills to serve its own ends?

These worries about practicality were compounded by ignorance. Although in fact many countries make effective use of the private sector in key ways to further public aims in health care, there was remarkably little knowledge of their experiences in these areas. Not surprisingly, therefore, there was also no understanding of the lessons that could be drawn from those experiences.

Our commission tried to address these problems, but sadly, found them difficult at best and intractable at worst. That, however, is not a difficulty for readers of this book, because the book has drawn on a wide range of country experience to provide a judicious blend of practical advice and useful information on all these issues. It discusses how to assess the potential for private sector involvement, how to engage in contracting with the private sector for health services, and how to regulate the sector. It also provides advice on what to do when key information is not there: a crucial element of any strategy, especially in developing countries where data and information sources are scarce.

With the decline of ideology, politicians have grown increasingly fond of the dictum "What's best is what works." This book is an excellent lesson on what works in health care—or more precisely, on how to make what works work better, especially with respect to the involvement of the private sector. It should be on every health policymaker's desk.

References

Institute for Public Policy Research (IPPR). 2001. *Building Better Partnerships: The Final Report of the Commission on Public Private Partnerships.* London.

Pollock, Allyson, and others. 2001. *A Response to the IPPR Commission on Public Private Partnerships.* London: The Catalyst Trust.

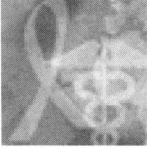

Acknowledgments

The final version of this volume has benefited from our interaction with many individuals. We would like to express our thanks to all for giving so generously of their time. In particular, we thank Elizabeth Smith, Ruairi Brugha, and Anthony Zwi for sharing their material and insights during the preparation of their guide, "Working with Private Sector Providers for Better Health Care." Their generosity and that of their sponsor, the Department for International Development (United Kingdom), meant that we could build on their considerable efforts, rather than duplicate them. The observations and insights of many of our colleagues are captured here, we hope correctly. In particular, we thank Flavia Bustreo, Mariam Claeson, Tonia Marek, and Henrik Axelsson for challenging our thinking and broadening our horizons.

Special thanks must also go to our colleagues who have taken on the significant challenge of operationalizing our ideas: David Peters, Rashmi Sharma, and Abdo Yazbeck from the India health team; and Akiko Maeda and Egbe Osifo from the West Bank and Gaza health team.

We are grateful to Charles Griffin, Peter Berman, Gerver Torres, and Simon Blair for "paving the way" with their early vision and efforts to put the issue of public policy toward the private health sector on the development policy agenda (and keep it there!).

This handbook would not have been possible without the funding of the Development Marketplace, and the active support of Matthias

Meyer, and Jemal-ud-din Kassum, our project's sponsor and mentor, respectively.

The Academy for Educational Development team—Gary Filerman, Robert Taylor, and Susan Taylor—conducted a survey of World Bank health sector staff. This survey contributed greatly to the handbook's structure, content, and operational relevance.

We would especially like to thank Gerard La Forgia, Nicole Tapay, Adam Wagstaff, and Richard Saltman for their helpful comments on the draft report.

The editorial help of Kathleen A. Lynch and the tireless word processing assistance of Sithie Mowlana were critical to the development of the volume. To them we are grateful.

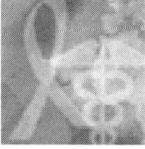

Acronyms and Abbreviations

ABMS	American Board of Medical Specialties
AHA	Australian Hospital Association
AIDS	Acquired immune deficiency syndrome
AMA	Australian Medical Association
AMC	Australian Medical Council
ANAES	Agence Nationale d'Accréditation et d'Evaluation en Santé, France
ARI	Acute respiratory illness
BNHS	British National Health Service
BTO	Build-transfer-operate
CFPC	College of Family Physicians of Canada
CME	Continued medical education
CON	Certificate of Need
COPRA	Consumer Protection Act
CQI	Continuous quality improvement
CRAG	Clinical Resource and Audit Group
DDQA	Data-driven quality assurance
DfID	Department for International Development (United Kingdom)
DHS	Demographic and Health Surveys
DOH	New South Wales Department of Health
DOTS	Directly observed treatment, short course
DRGs	Diagnostic-related groups
ERISA	Employee Retirement Income Security Act

FCPSF	Federal Committee of Physicians and Sickness Funds
GMC	General Medical Council
GP	General practitioner
HHI	Herfindahl-Hirschman Index
HIV	Human immunodeficiency virus
HMO	Health maintenance organization
HSAs	Health system agencies
IMCI	Integrated management of childhood illnesses
JCAHO	U.S. Joint Commission on Accreditation of Health Care Organizations
JCIA	Joint Commission International Accreditation
LMCs	Low- and middle-income countries
LSMS	Living Standards Measurement Survey
MEC	Middle East Crescent
NCQA	National Commission on Quality Assurance
NGO	Nongovernmental organizations
NHA	National health account
NHS	National Health Service
NICE	National Institute for Clinical Excellence
PHC	Primary health care
PHSA	Private health sector assessment
PMA	Provider market analysis
PPP	Public-private partnerships
PPRS	Pharmaceutical price regulation scheme
PPS	Prospective payment system
PRACTION	Private Practitioner Treatment Improvement Intervention
PRO	Peer review organization
PSRO	Professional standard review organization
RACOG	Royal Australian College of Obstetricians and Gynecologists
RBRVS	Resource-Based Relative Value Scale
RCPSC	Royal College of Physicians and Surgeons of Canada
RFP	Request for proposal

SHI	Social health insurance
SPA	Service Provision Assessment
TOR	Terms of reference
TQM	Total quality management
UNICEF	United Nations Children's Fund
UR	Utilization review
USAID	U.S. Agency for International Development
USMLE	U.S. Medical Licensing Examination
WHO	World Health Organization
ZHAC	Zambia Health Accreditation Council

Introduction

Awareness is growing about the importance of the private sector in achieving health sector objectives within developing countries. Recent household surveys from many of these countries indicate private providers play a significant role in health care delivery, even to the poor (Gwatkin and others 2000). Reviews of disease control and child and reproductive health programs have similarly found the private sector to be a necessary, though oft-overlooked part, of these efforts (Waters, Hatt, and Axelsson 2002; Uplekar, Pathenia, and Raviglione 2001; and Rosen 2000).

This recognition is motivating increased efforts to engage the private sector, especially private health care providers, in developing-country health programs. Although most experts agree that ignoring the private sector's large role in the service delivery system is unwise, there is less agreement, and far less knowledge, about strategies for engaging the private sector—such as which strategies work and under what conditions. So far, efforts to engage the private sector have often been poorly documented and almost never rigorously evaluated. Nevertheless, it is critical that health policymakers and analysts glean whatever insights can be gained from these early developing-country experiences. Where relevant, learning from the established mechanisms used in developed countries' mixed-delivery health systems is also critical. Many policymakers will confront a number of predictable challenges as they try to identify and implement strategies to mobilize private providers toward achieving important program or sectoral objectives in their own countries. This handbook is intended to synthesize available information on these topics.

Numerous World Bank clients are among those policymakers struggling to integrate this new perspective on the private sector into health policy and practice in their countries. Bank sector specialists are working to assist them in these efforts. This handbook was developed to help these clients and staff by presenting, in a "user-friendly" manner, whatever practical information is available about methods of working with the private health sector that is relevant for developing countries. The handbook is intended to be a practitioner's guide.

The Task

Countless topics and strategies could be covered in such a guide. We have divided policymakers' tasks into three parts in order to define the scope and structure of the handbook:

- *Assessing* what is going on in the private health sector

- *Selecting a strategy* to engage the private sector in contributing to the programs and objectives being considered

- *Identifying* the appropriate set of *instruments* for doing so.

Assessment

Health sector analytical work frequently focuses on the public sector. When, as is commonly the case, the private sector plays a significant role in health care delivery, this narrow focus undermines the soundness of the analysis and the validity of conclusions and recommendations. Chapter 2 of this handbook, "Conducting a Private Health Sector Assessment," presents guidelines for ascertaining the private sector's current role in delivering health services and for identifying areas where private providers might increase or improve their contribution to government programs and objectives. Thus, this "how-to" chapter is intended to complement traditional health (public) sector analysis with comparable evaluation of the private sector. Such analysis is necessarily the first step of any effort to work with the private health sector.

Although this assessment may lead to a decision to encourage the private sector to expand or take on new tasks in certain areas, the handbook does not advocate private sector expansion, privatization, or working with the private sector for its own sake. Instead, it proposes approaching the private sector from a strategic and proactive perspective—looking for opportunities to utilize or enhance its contribution to social objectives.

Selecting a Strategy

This handbook distinguishes clearly between overall strategies for working with the private sector and instruments for implementing these strategies. Any instrument (such as contracting, franchising, or training) can be used in multiple ways to pursue a range of objectives, and as part of specific strategies toward the private sector. Contracting, for example, can be used to improve current providers' quality of services, or to attract new providers to generate growth of services. Contracting is also a critical element of conversion, where publicly delivered services are transferred to private providers but continue to be publicly funded. To differentiate among these distinct initiatives we categorize efforts to work with private providers according to what they are seeking to do with respect to the private sector. Are they seeking to harness or influence the private sector that already exists? Are they seeking to grow the private sector in a strategic way? Or are they seeking to turn over (convert) public services to private operation?

Harnessing. As noted, most developing countries already have a large private sector in health care, especially in health care delivery. Engaging or harnessing those providers is the first and most obvious strategy to consider for enhancing the private sector's contribution to health policy objectives. Such a strategy consists of taking steps to guide the behavior of identified providers, and takes advantage of the fact that the providers are already delivering services and serving populations that are critical to program or sector objectives. This is a lower risk strategy than others, such as conversion, where public services arrangements are discontinued and handed over to new operators.

Growing. An assessment of the private sector may identify areas where increased private sector activities would further priority objectives such as increasing access to services in specific regions. Policymakers in that situation would want to take steps to encourage private providers to grow their activities in these areas. Similar to "harnessing," this strategy is relatively low risk, because it does not alter existing service delivery arrangements.

Conversion. In certain countries, an assessment of the private sector, combined with traditional analysis of the public (health) sector, will identify public activities that may be productively turned over to private hands. In Central Europe, for example, the transition to social insurance funding arrangements motivated a number of countries to convert their salaried general practitioners to private (self-) employment. Policymakers can use the same instruments to work with the private sector in these instances as under the previous strategies, but they will need to include additional steps to transfer the activities to private entities.

From the wide range of instruments for implementing these strategies, this handbook focuses on two: contracting and regulation. These two mechanisms are the most widely used in developing (and developed) countries, though often with disappointing results. Thus, they are of interest to a large portion of World Bank client governments.

Identifying Instruments

Policymakers must start by selecting their strategy—that is, by deciding exactly what they want the private sector to do. They must then identify the right instruments to get them to do what they want. As noted, most instruments can be used to implement any of the strategies, but contracting and regulation are the tools most often used in both developing and developed countries in all three cases. Accordingly, the second half of the handbook presents "how-to" chapters on these critical instruments.

Every effort is made in these "how-to" chapters to present available knowledge about these instruments and their use. Since operational research is so scanty in the developing-country context, the insights presented must necessarily be tentative. Since many handbook users will be working in an information-poor environment, all chapters supplement presented material with key operational references and, wherever possible, Internet links. The framework presented in the handbook is also used in the World Bank Web site on Public Policy and Private Participation in Health.[1] Handbook users are encouraged to check this site for newly completed research or other resources. Each chapter is intended to function as a stand-alone piece as well as an integral part of the handbook. Thus, some repetition is unavoidable.

Before reading and using the "how-to" chapters, handbook users are strongly urged to read chapter 1. This chapter sets the context for the handbook and presents the framework underlying its approach to public policy toward the private health sector. It also presents the strategic categories described above in more detail, as well as the full range of instruments commonly used in working with the private sector (such as training, franchising, information dissemination, or integration into referral networks). It is envisioned that subsequent work by the World Bank and its partners will develop additional tools for developing-country policymakers. New "how-to" chapters will then be added to this handbook, both on-line and through publication, to expand the knowledge base for choosing and using instruments to work with the private health sector.

In addition to stimulating new policy initiatives, the changed perspective on the private sector's role in delivering health services has triggered a rapprochement within the health and development field. It has created a common ground for analysts and policymakers, who up to now have perceived themselves as members of opposing camps—the "private sector is perfect" camp versus the "private sector is malign" camp. Most debates between these two camps in the 1980s and 1990s were grounded more in ideology than evidence, and centered on the advantages and disadvantages of privatization. Members of both camps now realize that this debate holds little relevance for developing countries, especially the poorest countries. It is in these countries that the state's capacities are most limited, and where the private sector already provides most services. Debates and, more important, policy research are now turning to a host of more pragmatic issues, such as how and when different strategies work to integrate the private sector into health sector policy. Mechanisms such as contracting, regulation, training, and franchising hold the promise of building on what is already there. To realize that promise is a huge challenge. We hope the handbook will help World Bank clients, partners, and staff to meet this challenge.

Note

1. http://www1.worldbank.org/hnp/pvtsector_index.asp

References

Gwatkin, D. R., S. Rustein, K. Johnson, R. P. Pande, and A. Wagstaff. 2000. "Socioeconomic Differences in Health, Nutrition, and Population in India." HNP/Poverty Thematic Group, World Bank, Washington, D.C. Available electronically at: http://www.worldbank.org/poverty/health/data/index.htm

Rosen, J. E. 2000. *Contracting for Reproductive Health Care: A Guide.* Health, Nutrition and Population Publications Series. World Bank (Health, Nutrition and Population), Washington, D.C.

Uplekar, Mukund, Vikram Pathenia, and Mario Raviglione. 2001. Involving Private Practitioners in Tuberculosis Control: Issues, Interventions, and Emerging Policy Framework. Geneva: World Health Organization.

Waters, H., L. Hatt, and H. Axelsson. 2002. *Working with the Private Sector for Child Health.* Prepared for the USAID-sponsored SARA Project (Academy for Education Development), the World Health Organization, and the World Bank. Washington, D.C.: World Bank, Health, Nutrition, and Population Network.

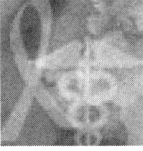

CHAPTER 1

Introduction to Private Participation in Health Services

April Harding

Attitudes toward private health care providers in developing countries are changing. More and more policymakers are attempting to incorporate private practitioners and facilities into overall sector policy, or are considering doing so. They are using, among other methods, contracting, regulation, training of private practitioners, franchising, and the integration of private practitioners into public referral networks. Developing-country experiences are rarely well documented, so policymakers and analysts are usually unable to learn from these initiatives. Rigorous evaluation of these efforts is even more rare, making it difficult, even perilous, to write policy guidelines based on those experiences. Mechanisms for working with the private sector in developed-country health systems are better understood, but the insights are not easily transferable. Nevertheless, options for enhancing health sector policies related to private delivery of health care can be reviewed, and this chapter will do so. The purpose of the review is to familiarize policymakers and sector experts with a wide range of strategies for enhancing the contributions of private health care providers—both for-profit and nonprofit—to sector objectives.[1] This introduction is intended to be comprehensive in nature, and is therefore, of necessity, somewhat superficial. Users seeking detailed information about specific strategies and instruments are referred to subsequent chapters in this handbook, to the World Bank Web site on public policy and the private health sector, and to the bibliography at the end of each chapter.

Following a brief overview this chapter reviews the basic prerequisites for effective interaction with private health care providers. In the third section three general strategies that have been used to improve interaction with private health care providers in developing countries are discussed. That section also outlines two important instruments—contracting and regulation—that are used to implement these three strategies.

The fourth section discusses applications of these strategies to improve health care access and outcomes for the poor, through work with the private sector. The fifth section examines the strategies' application to integrate the private sector into efforts to address public health issues. The sixth section discusses the challenges policymakers are likely to confront in making changes to improve public policy toward the private health sector. Finally, conclusions and lessons are drawn for policymaking in the private health sector in developing countries.

Overview

This chapter will address the formulation of public policy that affects private health service providers in developing countries. Experiences in both developed and developing countries will be discussed, but the developing-country experiences will be emphasized. A broad range of types of health service providers will be examined, including providers who are trained in biomedical medicine, traditional providers, and untrained practitioners, as well as pharmacists and drug sellers, who often deliver health services by advising on medicine selection (Hudelsohn 1998). Since the handbook's focus is on health-service delivery, the production and distribution of pharmaceuticals, medical equipment, consumables, and other inputs are not covered, and neither is private insurance considered. Although methods of contracting with or subsidizing private providers will be reviewed, other financing and insurance issues are not examined. The objective of the chapter is to identify available options and mechanisms for working more effectively with private health care providers. Considering the paucity of rigorous evaluation of these reforms, such guidance can be no more than tentative. The main contribution of this chapter is the comprehensiveness of its review of strategies and instruments for working with private health care providers and the explicit linkage to health systems development. In order to support policy discussion and formulation the review is pragmatic and avoids theoretical or ideological discussions of government failures versus market failures, and idealized versions of public or private operations. The interested reader or policy adviser would need to dig deeper into a specific topic to formulate sound policies. For more extensive review of some of these topics and guides to further resources, the reader is referred to the subsequent chapters of this handbook.

Background

Private health care providers play a large role in developing countries (table 1.1). Sometimes this prevalence is viewed as a sign of government and health system failures. Even where not seen as malign, however, it is often hoped that the operation of private health care providers is temporary, and that they will be displaced as soon as feasible by expanded and improved publicly provided services.

Recently, the viability and wisdom of this approach have been challenged. Examination of high-performing health systems has revealed mixed delivery systems—with private providers playing an integral and productive role, a role largely enabled by a strong direct or indirect government financing role. This perspective on the public-private mix in well-performing health services has generated additional scrutiny of private providers in developing countries, scrutiny that has served only to underscore the urgency of making public policy toward private health care providers more effective. Experience also shows, however, that to pursue equity and efficiency goals in mixed systems, governments must strengthen their role in

Table 1.1 Private Doctors in Developing Countries

COUNTRY	PRIVATE DOCTORS PER MILLION POPULATION	PRIVATE DOCTORS AS PERCENTAGE OF TOTAL
Morocco	78	41
Algeria	86	24
Pakistan	107	32
Tunisia	153	36
Oman	185	43
Turkey	254	42
Jordan	661	69
Middle East Crescent average	147	35
Indonesia	6	6
Papua New Guinea	16	25
Thailand	40	18
Malaysia	202	57
India	286	73
Republic of Korea	398	86
Asia average	232	60
Paraguay	28	5
Panama	112	10
Mexico	277	36
Jamaica	331	67
Chile	657	62
Latin America and the Caribbean average	332	46
Burundi	2	7
Malawi	4	25
Madagascar	4	N/A
Zambia	13	13
Kenya	30	40
Senegal	35	38
Liberia	35	41
Zimbabwe	86	67
South Africa	168	56
Africa average	92	46
All average	213	55

N/A – Not available.
Note: Averages are weighted by population.
Source: Hanson and Berman 1998.

financing providers, a topic addressed elsewhere (Musgrove 1996; World Bank 1993; World Bank 1997b; and Preker, Harding, and Girishankar 2000).

The private sector is typically involved in every aspect of health services delivery in developing countries. Private practitioners are most prominent in delivery of primary and curative care, largely due to relatively low capital requirements, high demand, and patients' willingness and ability to pay (Hanson and Berman 1998). This pattern involves them directly in core "public health" activities such as treating patients with malaria, tuberculosis (TB), and other communicable diseases, as well as treating sick children and pregnant women. In many of the poorer countries, as illustrated in table 1.1, the private sector is the main provider—with much of the health care delivered by unqualified or traditional practitioners, as well as pharmacists and drug sellers (Hanson and Berman 1998; and Bennett, McPake, and Mills 1997). Despite widespread concern about clinical quality, patients often bypass public facilities to utilize private providers—frequently citing reasons of convenience and responsiveness (World Bank 2001a). Many people in developing countries, including the poor, would have no access to health care without these privately provided services.

Rationale

The premise underlying this handbook is that developing-country policymakers should stop ignoring private health care providers. Indeed, they should look for ways of working with private providers as an integral means of achieving sector objectives. In many countries it is necessary to work with private providers to expand access and coverage to improve health outcomes for a large portion of the population. Such policies, when supported by financial resources, may provide much-needed financial protection against the cost of illness. In addition to improving the responsiveness or consumer quality of services, governments are increasingly resourceful in reaching out to private providers to improve the clinical quality of care (Waters, Hatt, and Axelsson 2002).

In most developing countries everyone goes to the private sector for at least some health services. The poor often go to the private sector; most of the poor often go to informal providers (Ronde and Viswanathan 1995). This pattern is widespread, but more prevalent in rural areas where the poor are often concentrated. Since nearly all payments are out-of-pocket these treatments are a serious burden and a source of risk for the poor, for whom a hospital stay or prolonged illness can lead to a slide into poverty, after they have depleted all their savings and assets. Box 1.1 presents evidence of this phenomenon in Vietnam.

This handbook takes, from the *World Health Report 2000* framework, the premise that arrangements for service delivery have a strong impact on health outcomes and responsiveness of health services, while risk protection issues are best addressed by means of financing arrangements (WHO 2000).[2] From this perspective the negative impact of private providers' fees on household incomes originates in the absence of effective financing mechanisms, and not in the absence of the public ownership of the service delivery system. Publicly provided services are often justified as a means of relieving the poor of the financial burden of illness. Most public services in developing countries are severely underresourced, however, leading to widespread formal and informal payments, which severely undermines this objective (Lewis 2002). Since public provision often does not achieve this goal of financial protection, and since the widescale utilization of private practitioners seems to be quite difficult to alter, policymakers in many countries will clearly have to work with private providers to affect the care that a large portion of the population is receiving, at least in the short to medium term.

Theoretical Underpinnings

The evidence is growing that working with private providers is better than ignoring them, and that cooperation can be an effective strategy for pursuing some important sector goals. What about the conceptual underpinnings for the public-private mix in health service delivery, however? Do they shed light on how and when to pursue such cooperation? Unfortunately, the relevant theoretical literature provides guidance only as to which activities the government should be involved in, but not on intervention methods or the appropriate ownership of various services. Contrary to common wisdom the theoretical literature does not support public provision for all services that merit government intervention. Rather, it leaves the

Box 1.1 Impoverishment from Health Payments in Vietnam

The graph illustrates the magnitude of impoverishment generated by health care payments in Vietnam. Households are arranged by consumption levels. Their consumption is plotted on the vertical axis and their rank in the consumption distribution on the horizontal axis. The households beneath the poverty line are classified as "poor." The "drips" show the out-of-pocket payments for each household. Some drips are large enough to take previously nonpoor households below the poverty line. Some previously poor households become even poorer. Comparing the headcount below the poverty line "before" and "after" out-of-pocket payments gives a crude idea of the impoverishment caused by out-of-pocket health care payments. In this case, the proportion of poor people increases from 34 to 38 percent.

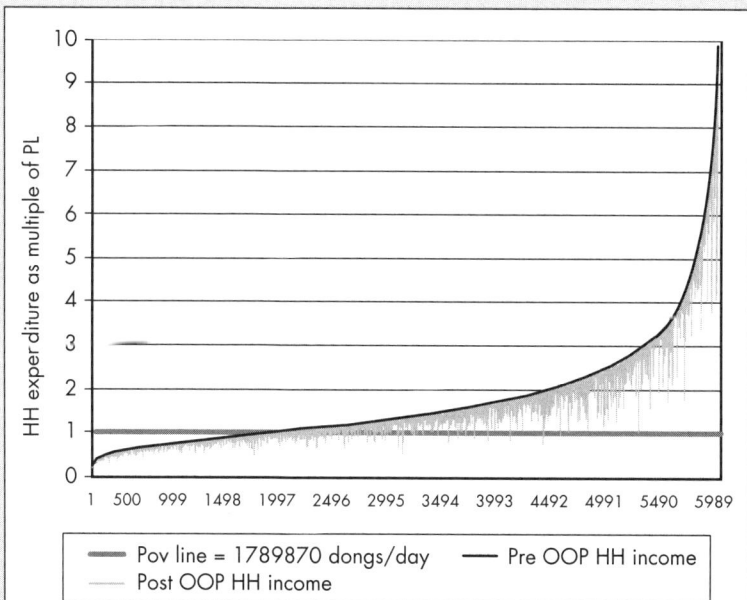

Legend:
— Pov line = 1789870 dongs/day   — Pre OOP HH income
— Post OOP HH income

Source: Wagstaff, Watanabe, and van Doorslaer 2001.

question unanswered, or, in some interpretations, supports a discriminating approach to structuring a government's engagement in health service delivery. Below we very briefly review this literature.

The traditional public goods criteria from neoclassical economics (nonexcludability, nonrivalry, and rejectability) justify government intervention for only a small set of health goods and services. A much broader range of justifications for public intervention in health activities has come to be accepted, including enhancement of equity in access and other social objectives. These criteria do not provide guidance on the appropriate mechanisms for government intervention, however. Musgrove, as well as other authors, has proposed that governments ought to use the least intrusive instrument that will achieve the desired objectives (see table 1.2). The institutional economics literature, which analyzes the impact of governance arrangements on organizational performance, similarly supports a discrimi-

Table 1.2 Government Tools for Influencing the Private Sector

LEVEL OF INTRUSIVENESS	TOOL OR METHOD	APPLICATION
Most intrusive	Direct provision	• Rural public hospitals and clinics • Preventive services • Sanitation
	Financing	• Budgetary support • Subsidies • Concessions • Contracting
	Regulation and mandates	• Taxation • Licensure • Accreditation • Employee health insurance • Required immunization of schoolchildren
Least intrusive	Information	• Research—product testing • Provider information—treatment protocols, recommended drugs • Consumer information—provider quality comparisons, consumers' rights, dangers of smoking, rehydration methods, birth spacing

Source: Musgrove 1996.

nating approach. The findings strongly discourage indiscriminate reliance on public ownership and production (Williamson 1991).

To provide guidance on the appropriate choice of government instrument to ensure supply of identified goods and services, Preker, Harding, and Girishankar (2000) proposed the criterion of "buyability." Using this criterion governments should contract for delivery of goods or services that a government can buy (as defined by the goods' or services' level of measurability and contestability). Public production is appropriate for goods and services that justify government intervention and are not "buyable" by this criterion.

Empirical Basis

Theory supports a discriminating approach to structuring the government's role with regard to health services. The empirical evidence on systems performance with mixed systems as opposed to public delivery systems yields no answers. Examination of health system performance among developed countries reveals no consistent differences between those with predominantly public delivery and those that rely on mixed delivery systems (table 1.3). A single-

Table 1.3 Performance Indicators, Industrial Country Health Systems

	PERFORMANCE INDICATORS			
TYPE OF HEALTH SERVICE DELIVERY SYSTEM	INFANT MORTALITY RATE (PER 1,000 LIVE BIRTHS, 1999)	UNDER FIVE[a] MORTALITY RATE (PER 1,000 LIVE BIRTHS, 1999)	LIFE EXPECTANCY AT BIRTH (YEARS, 1999)	HEALTH EXPENDITURE (U.S. DOLLARS PER CAPITA)
Mixed delivery				
Austria	4	5	78	2,162
Belgium	5	6	78	2,184
France	5	5	79	2,377
Germany	5	5	77	2,769
Netherlands	5	5	78	2,140
Predominantly public delivery				
Denmark	5	6	76	2,732
Finland	4	5	77	1,722
Norway	4	4	78	2,953
Sweden	4	4	79	2,146
United Kingdom	6	6	77	1,597

a. Under five years of age.
Source: World Bank 2001b.

minded focus on the public delivery system is not justified with reference to performance of the better health systems. More immediately, the prevalence and widespread use of private health care providers in developing countries are sufficient reasons to work with them to influence the care people receive. Such an approach is further supported by the often disappointing impact of public delivery–focused strategies to reach a range of sectoral objectives related to access and quality (Uplekar, Pathenia, and Raviglione 2001; and Waters, Hatt, and Axelsson 2002).

Ultimately, the decision of how to structure the government's role in the health sector depends on a society's values, inherited structures, and political processes. The foregoing discussion is presented only to illustrate that there are no technical grounds to rule out working with private providers or allowing private provision of public services.

In some instances a public delivery–focused strategy may be the best way to pursue certain objectives. This may be true, for instance, in sparsely populated areas. This may also be the best strategy where the needed service is monitoring or evaluation, or is related to establishing systems for dissemination of health information. In many instances, however, private health care providers' presence and capacities will necessitate working with and through them to pursue desired objectives. In other instances, the benefits of working with private providers come from their greater responsiveness to patients; flexibility; awareness of local circumstances; and their less-politicized operation (Filmer, Hammer, and Pritchett 1998; and Griffin 1989). This handbook, therefore, takes as a starting point the understanding that a health system with substantial private delivery can function well. The discussion that follows will focus on options for moving toward such a system.

Basic Prerequisites for Getting More from Private Health Care Providers

Examination of the public-private interface in well-performing health systems reveals several mechanisms for interaction that appear necessary in order for private providers to play an effective role in a health system. They include: knowledge (on the part of policymakers) about the private sector; ongoing dialogue between public and private stakeholders; and institutionalized policy instruments for interacting with the private sector (especially financing, regulation, and dissemination of information). Regardless of sector priorities or the modalities being considered for working with the private sector, all three factors are present in all the well-performing mixed delivery health systems.

Knowledge

The health systems mentioned above each have in place a system for collecting accurate information about the capabilities of private health care providers and their activities, which is used to assess and channel their contribution to national health priorities. This information may be collected and processed by outside organizations or by the government. In most cases, however, the government takes the lead in funding and coordinating such efforts.

The National Agency of Accreditation and Evaluation in Health is a quasi-independent public agency in France, created to collect information about the operation of health care facilities, both public and private.

The Joint Commission on Accreditation of Health Care Organizations is a nongovernmental organization in the United States that collects and assesses information about nearly 19,000 health care organizations and programs. It is the country's predominant standard-setting and accrediting body in health care. Since 1951 the Joint Commission has worked with professionals in the field to develop accepted standards; it has evaluated the compliance of health care organizations against these benchmarks.

Unlike the foregoing examples, in many developing countries, neither governmental nor nongovernmental agencies collect information on private providers or their patients. Under these circumstances policymakers have no opportunity to identify and use positive features or address problems associated with private provision.

Dialogue

In addition to a reasonable amount of information about the private sector, well-performing mixed delivery systems have ongoing, transparent communication between government officials involved in health policy and private health care providers. This communication leads to better policy design by taking into account private health care providers' perspectives and likely reactions to policy initiatives. Good regulation, in particular, relies on ongoing interaction between the regulators and the regulated (Better Regulation Taskforce 2000). Communication during policy formulation supports the implementation of policy changes, since affected providers will already be informed and likely will be prepared for changes. Since communication takes place in a transparent forum, it minimizes the opportunity for specific private entities to exercise inappropriate influence over government policy. Countries that have institutionalized such dialogue include Australia, Canada, Germany, the Netherlands, and the United States.

Due to historical segmentation, hostility toward the private sector, and weak institutional capacity, such dialogue between policymakers and the private sector is usually absent in developing countries. While in a few countries there is some interaction between private entities and health policymakers, it is most often ad hoc and based on personal or political ties. In a few extreme cases government policies appear subject to the influence of particular private sector interests.

Institutionalized Policy Instruments

A review of the well-performing health systems that have substantial private delivery consistently reveals a set of institutionalized policy instruments for dealing with the private sector, as well as capable government officials who are comfortable using these instruments. These institutions usually include: an insurance system; a framework for direct regulation (including licensing and certification of health personnel); and support for self-regulation. The most critical instrument is a universal provider-financing system that contributes to equity, sustainability, and financial protection.

In many developing countries the public sector is extensively involved in the production of health services, even where the financing of services or other critical stewardship activities are not being addressed. This structure of intervention in the health sector is often seen as contributing to access and quality problems in health care delivery.[3] In health, as in other sectors, an overextended role is frequently associated with poor performance of key government functions (World Bank 1997b; and Filmer, Hammer, and Pritchett 1998).

Strategies for Getting More from Private Health Care Providers

Over the longer term developing-country governments may strive to establish the capacities outlined above. The more immediate question, however, remains "What can be done in the short run to increase the contribution of the private sector to health objectives?" We outline below the range of strategies a policymaker has at hand to bring about such improvements. All of these strategies are sometimes referred to as "public-private partnerships," a term we will avoid using due to its ambiguity (box 1.2). Depending on the objectives identified and the current activities of private providers in the country, policymakers may consider three strategic approaches:[4]

1. Harnessing the existing private sector—to take advantage of the private providers that are already in place

2. Growing the private sector —to encourage private providers to expand their services offered, and patients or areas served, where this will contribute to sector or program objectives

3. Conversion—to shift publicly provided services to private hands when this is expected to improve access, efficiency, or quality.

Harnessing the Existing Private Sector

The private service delivery sector is large in many countries, including many low-income countries. Governments in some of these

Box 1.2 Public-Private Partnerships

In health, the term public-private partnership (PPP) is used to refer to virtually any ongoing relationship between the public and private sector. Three distinct forms of partnership are most relevant for the health sector:

• Global public-private partnerships
• Domestic public-private partnerships with commercial sector, both production and distribution
• Domestic public-private partnerships with health care providers.

Since this handbook deals with domestic policy toward private health services, it looks only at domestic public-private partnerships with providers of health care. Such partnerships provide a method of involving private health care providers in delivering public services. They also provide a vehicle for coordinating with nongovernmental actors to undertake integrated, comprehensive efforts to meet community needs.

Domestic public-private partnerships are distinct from global public-private partnerships among international organizations, corporations, and nongovernmental organizations (NGOs). This latter type of partnership is becoming increasingly common in the health field, but is not the object of one country's public policy decisions, and therefore is not within the remit of the handbook.

countries are taking steps to get more out of these providers; they recognize the importance of influencing these providers' interactions with the population, if critical goals related to public health and health systems performance are to be reached. These steps can lead to substantial improvements, especially in countries with a large private sector, and in countries where government is currently not interacting much with these providers. This segmented situation is fairly common among developing countries. The most frequently used instruments for influencing these providers are: contracting; regulatory reform; and a range of outreach mechanisms to providers and patients, including information dissemination, education, and persuasion.

Contracting. As noted above, awareness is growing about the effectiveness of various instruments for influencing private providers in the health sector. Contracting is emerging as a powerful tool for harnessing the resources of the private sector to help achieve sector goals. Contracting of health services is a process whereby the government or a government agency engages in an ongoing relationship with private providers to procure health services. Providers' interest in the funding associated with contracts empowers the government "buyer" to influence the behavior of the providers. The move to contract for social services is growing worldwide (Salamon and Anheier 1996).

To use contracting as a tool government must meet several basic requirements. First and foremost, contracting requires financial resources. For many developing countries all resources for health services are devoted to public production—which precludes governments from engaging private providers through contracting (DeRoeck 1998; and Jeon and others 1998).

Contracting for health services is also a complex process. It requires substantial government capacity to plan, negotiate, implement, and continuously monitor the services for which it contracts. Although it can be a very useful tool governments must approach contracting strategically—weighing costs and benefits of direct provision against contracting for each service considered. This decision is similar to the "make or buy" decisions faced by managers in most industries.

Contracting requires a drastic mind shift for public officials, from thinking of themselves as administrators and managers of public employees and other inputs, to thinking of themselves as contract managers with ultimate responsibility for delivering services. Although contracting does not involve public officials in the day-to-day business of delivering services, it expands their responsibilities in providing strategic direction. Contract management can reside in a subordinate organization—but senior policymakers must provide the strategic direction and framework within which contracting takes place. Contracting is the means by which private providers are involved in continental Europe's social health insurance systems, for example. In this case, quasi-independent state agencies contract with health care providers.

The prototypical example of contracted health services is clinical services, either at the primary or tertiary level. The range of services that may be contracted for in health is much broader, however—and often nonclinical services are easier to contract for than clinical. Examples of nonclinical services that are relatively easy to contract for include: educational services to teach health workers; public health outreach efforts (such as conducting an antismoking campaign); and auxiliary services in health facilities (such as cleaning or catering), and delivery of nutritional supplements. In addition, governments may contract for regional coverage of a range of services rather than specific services. Governments in both developed and developing countries are exploring these contracting options, as well as many more.

Thus, a wide range of services is supplied under contract, and there are also many contractual options for engaging the services. The most common mechanism is contracting out—where the government purchases a service from an outside source that provides the service using its own work force and resources. However, governments can also hire outside managers to come in and manage an internal work force or service—which is referred to as contracting in. Less formal subsidy arrangements may be established, often with nonprofit providers. In this case, the government gives financial support in exchange for the alteration or expansion of service provision in targeted areas. In some cases governments have developed a valuable "brand" for an important health good or service, and allocated a franchise to some service providers. The franchise contract includes the right to use the "brand" name or symbol (which increases demand for their services) in exchange for agreeing to operate in a prescribed manner, usually in terms of service quality, services offered, or patients served.

Contracting looks very different to the service provider than it does to the government. Contract management must take differences in those perspectives into account. In particular, the contract arrangements must be sufficiently attractive to appeal to competent health care providers. In addition, ongoing communication among all parties (contracting agency, service providers, community) is critical to establishing the level of trust that is required to make contracting successful. Absent such consideration, no contract or monitoring arrangements can ensure appropriate service delivery. Even nonprofit organizations must sustain their operations, and hence usually require contractual pricing to cover average costs.

Payment methods and price-setting mechanisms directly determine incentives for providers. Appropriate choices in this area are a key policy issue. The options and their advantages and disadvantages are discussed in chapter 3 of this handbook.

Setting up effective arrangements to monitor contracted services is as important as the payment and pricing mechanism. These two must also complement each other. Capitated payment arrangements, for instance, lead to cost savings but can motivate skimping on quality—which makes it doubly important to monitor quality under capitated contracts (Savedoff and Slack 2000). Fee-for-service arrangements, on the other hand, offer incentives for overservicing—enhancing the need to monitor volumes and appropriateness of services.

The length or term of the contract is very important. Policymakers must choose the contract's length, balancing their desire for predictability and constraint of expenditure against the disadvantage of inflexibility or "lock-in" that occurs with regard to service delivery over the term of the contract. Policymakers with longer term contracts may find themselves in the position of buying services they no longer want, or that are delivered in an outmoded fashion, due to contract terms being outstripped by innovation in service delivery.

Market structure must also be taken into account. In contracting, the impact on competition must be kept in mind. Enough providers should remain in the market to establish and maintain competitive pressures.

Regulatory reform. Another strategy for enhancing the contribution of existing private providers is to improve health services regulation. Regulation is often considered primarily a means of improving quality of care, but it is used to pursue a much broader set of objectives. For example, regulation is used to reduce inequality and disparities in quality or access (geographic or economic) to health care. Regulation is also used to improve technical and allocative efficiency and to reduce waste and corruption. Finally, regulations are often used to hold down costs, thus contributing to the financial sustainability of the health system.

The function of health services regulation is to protect the public by countering market failures, bringing efficiencies to areas in which the market has been impeded, or by correcting the market's emphasis on a single dimension, such as cost. Some regulations have an economic focus, aiming to address provider monopolies, combat scarcity of certain necessary services (such as primary care), or curb wasteful service utilization in insurance arrangements. Other, more socially oriented, regulations aim to improve equity and access through geographic redistribution and antidiscrimination statutes; or protect the public by controlling the quality of health services.

Because the objectives are varied, so too are the targets of regulation. Regulations may be established targeting various phases of the health care production process (input, process, output, and outcome). Traditionally, regulation focuses on the first two stages, the quality of input factors of production (human resources, consumables, pharmaceuticals, capital stock, and equipment) and the quality of the installed infrastructure or process for producing services. More sophisticated regulation targets the third stage, the production of actual services, and ultimately the impact on outcomes (outcome-targeted regulation). This complex form of regulation is not common in developing countries. Most health sector regulation is targeted at health service prices, quantity and distribution, and quality.[5]

A wide range of instruments is available for regulating health care services. The three general categories are (a) regulation through control, (b) incentives, and (c) market structuring. The most familiar type of regulation consists of legal restrictions or controls that require providers to conform to legislative requirements. If they do not abide by these laws they are liable to punishment. Types of regulation that are usually accomplished by means of control include:

- Price regulation;

- Capacity regulation (for example, volume and distribution of services);

- Regulation of market entry and levels of service;

- Regulation of entitlements;

- Regulation of antitrust and market structure;

- Regulation of quality of care;

- Health facility licensing;

- Heath facility accreditation;

- Health personnel credentialing;

- Utilization reviews and medical audits; and

- Outcomes research, practice guidelines, and clinical protocols.

A more complex form of regulation offers providers incentives—either financial or nonfinancial—to change their behavior, thereby leading to improvements in the target variable (such as price or quality). An even more sophisticated form of regulation implements changes to market structure that cause the market to generate pressures to encourage providers to undertake the desired behaviors.

Regulation is more than laws and directives. Effectiveness of health care regulation is directly related to the way the processes and institutions are structured. Therefore, any efforts to enhance the regulatory framework require analysis of existing regulatory arrangements and often require their alteration. Reviewing the structural options used in other countries can provide some guidance, although these insights must be tailored to the local context.

Government officials and agencies can undertake many regulatory actions. However, in developed-country systems many agents and organizations support and complement the governments' role. The most important regulatory agents outside government are self-regulatory organizations and professional associations. Increasingly, however, community and consumer organizations are playing a more influential role. A government seeking to enhance the effectiveness of the regulatory framework will need to ensure that the various organizations performing regulatory functions work in a coordinated manner.

Once it has been established that the government will perform a regulatory function, many important design issues still must be considered. These issues include:

- Scope of operations;
- Organizational form: regulatory agency versus a commission;
- Governance: intragovernmental versus a separate agency;
- Degree of regulatory discretion;
- Administrative procedures and judicial review;
- Accountability and regulatory oversight;
- Agency staffing;
- Terms of reference; and
- Agency funding.

If another body is to perform a regulatory function the government will likely need to coordinate, collaborate, delegate, or otherwise support their performance.

Moving toward an effective regulatory framework. To improve the functioning of health regulation a number of issues must be addressed. Policymakers need to select a balanced package of sticks (controls) and carrots (incentives). Identifying the policies to be implemented will need to take into account the government's limited capacity— and therefore to encourage and guide regulatory forces provided by professional organizations and other NGOs, as well as community and patients' organizations. In many areas these groups, sometimes with strategic support or review by government, have more motivation and capacity to regulate important health care activities and objectives. Throughout the process government must have an overview of all the influences on the behavior of health service providers, so that they can use their own resources efficiently, and also to ensure that their own efforts do not undermine systemic integration and cohesiveness.

Despite all the technical criteria outlined, regulation is an inherently political and cultural process. Efforts to improve regulation must necessarily build on knowledge related to stakeholders' perspectives, and acceptable and appropriate standards for the country context. Although many critical health service issues require regulation, regulation itself is a costly undertaking. In addition, regulation may bring about unintended and negative consequences (such as creating unnecessary barriers to entry, raising operating costs, or reducing competition). Design of regulatory reforms must therefore take into account both the benefits and costs of existing regulations and the impact of new ones under consideration. In some cases, removing ineffective or counterproductive regulations is an important part of regulatory reform.

Perhaps more than any other regulated sector, with the exception of telecommunications, health care is a fast-changing activity. Innovations in diagnostics and treatments are multiplying. It is therefore critical that regulation in general, and the government's regulatory role in particular, is an ongoing and adaptive process.

Outreach mechanisms to providers and patients. The third set of instruments for influencing the private providers' behavior consists of a wide range of outreach mechanisms that governments can use to indirectly influence providers and patients. These are discussed below in order of intensity of effort.

- *Information dissemination.* Making information available to patients and the population can be a powerful mechanism for empowering them to demand appropriate care. Both governmental organizations and NGOs can play such a role. In the Netherlands, for example, patients' organizations play a strong role in educating patients about specific diseases and treatment options. These organizations have increased patient participation in treatment decisions, have increased the prevalence of information on provider products (including quality and price), and have enhanced communication between patients and providers (Sommers 1999). The Uruguayan Cystic Fibrosis Foundation has been instrumental in improving the treatment of that disease. For nongovernmental patients' organizations to develop and flourish many of the issues related to the enabling environment for nonprofits come into play, just as it does with service delivery (box 1.3). Regardless of who initiates the information dissemination, various mechanisms have been successfully used, including community leaders, peers, user groups, public providers, and mass media (Smith, Brugha, and Zwi 2001). Information dissemination can be used for many different purposes, as outlined below.

  - *Expand demand among identified groups.* Behavioral change communication can be used to expand demand and hence utilization by target populations (the poor, sex workers, and mothers).

  - *Raise awareness of service quality and consumer rights.* This mechanism is commonly used in developed countries to pressure providers into increasing the quality of care they deliver. Such efforts include developing physician profiles to help patients select their practitioner, establishing and disseminating "patients' rights" charters, increasing patient representation on government oversight and regulatory bodies, and establishing relations with physician or hospital associations. Due to the complex nature of health care, even in developed countries, these efforts have a greater impact on consumer quality[6] (that is,

**Box 1.3 Public Policy and Health Service Delivery
by Nonprofit Organizations**

Throughout this chapter the discussion of public policy that is directed toward the private sector refers to both for-profit and nonprofit organizations involved in health service delivery. However, there are several policy issues unique to the involvement of nonprofit organizations in the delivery of health services. Nonprofit organizations that deliver social services are usually deemed to merit special assistance from the government, most frequently in terms of tax exemptions and tax deductions for donations to their operations. Furthermore, some countries exempt social service nonprofits from import tariffs for health-related equipment and medicines. While many countries strive to support the operation of socially beneficial nonprofit organizations, others, by omission or commission, have not created a supportive environment. Thus, in addition to being affected by the general state of the economy and enabling environment for businesses, nonprofit organizations are affected by both regulatory and fiscal aspects of the nonprofit enabling environment. The following factors are important for the operation of health service nonprofit organizations:

- *Legal environment.* The legal environment should be supportive, including being free of state intrusion and inappropriate interference. Clear criteria for qualification as a nonprofit organization, while not allowing abuse of the nonprofits, should be in place. Regulation must respect their autonomy as independent bodies.
- *Fiscal factors.* The tax framework should provide exemptions from income and profits taxes for nonprofit organizations, although this need not extend to business or economic activities. Other tax benefits may be appropriate—exemptions from customs duties, and value-added

(Box continues on the following page.)

Box 1.3 (continued)

taxes on imports; or individual tax deductions for donations of time or funds.
• *Other factors.* Access to government training schemes; or
provision of medical supplies at reduced or no cost may
be appropriate.

The legal and fiscal issues are beyond the scope of health
sector policy. However, if nonprofit providers are to play
a vital role in service delivery, health officials may need to
contribute to a process that improves their environment.

Why nonprofit health care providers are important. Nonprofit organizations often provide a means to reach the
poor and other target populations in order to provide services to them. This comparative advantage often comes from
nonprofits' historical patterns of development, their close-
ness to communities, and their ability to harness volunteer
activity.

Why problems may occur. NGOs are often politically contentious. They sometimes play a role in exposing the narrow
interests of particular ruling parties, or may be otherwise
aligned with opposition political interests. This political aspect of NGO activities may add to a negative stance on
the part of the government toward NGOs (and hence constraining policies), including NGOs that provide valuable
social services.

However, the interests of nonprofit organizations whose
main activity is service delivery most often align closely
with those of the government in the health sector.

All too often, even when governments are actively developing policy toward the private sector, they leave out consideration of issues specific to nonprofit organizations.

Source: World Bank 1997a.

the now medical aspects of quality) than on clinical quality. Patients' organizations usually play a substantial role in directly raising such awareness, while government efforts are frequently channeled through mass media. A few developing-country governments (such as India) have initiated efforts in this area recently. Patients' organizations have begun to be active in a number of developing countries (including Argentina, Bangladesh, Brazil, Bulgaria, Chile, Croatia, the Czech Republic, Ecuador, El Salvador, Estonia, Hungary, India, Indonesia, Lithuania, Mexico, Nigeria, Poland, Romania, the Russian Federation, the Slovak Republic, Slovenia, South Africa, Tunisia, Uruguay, and Zimbabwe). The majority of these organizations focus their advocacy on a single, usually chronic, disease, such as multiple sclerosis, cystic fibrosis, or diabetes. An increasing number, however, have a broader mandate, aspiring to improve access to health care, or pharmaceuticals, and to improve treatment, often through formal "patient's rights" charters.[7]

- *Publish information for users on maximum permitted prices.* Information publishing is most often used with regard to pharmaceuticals. Governments require prices to be listed in pharmacies, published in pricing guides and in the media, and printed on the packaging. There is some evidence that widespread price publication does lead users to put pressure on providers and retailers to contain prices.[8] Cambodia, the Philippines, and Colombia have successful consumer information strategies on maximum permitted prices (Smith, Brugha, and Zwi 2001, p. 56).

- *Education.* Instead of, or in addition to, disseminating information, more intense educative efforts may be necessary in order to alter the practices of private health care providers and the demand for their services.

  - *Expand or alter demand by educating users.* For priority services or population groups, focused education campaigns can be instrumental in expanding or altering their demand for goods and services. Examples include education efforts targeted to sex workers in order to encourage them to demand treatment of sexually transmitted diseases (STDs); or to mothers in slum areas, to expand their demand for appropriate treatment for key childhood illnesses.

- *Increase demand for services through community education.* Another way of increasing the use of priority services is by implementing community education efforts, structured to enhance demand for identified goods or services. Such programs have been successfully used to expand demand for vaccination, malaria treatment, nutrition supplements, and treatment for key childhood illnesses.

- *Training support to providers.* Such training may take the form of regular programs such as continuing medical education for allopathic providers, or may focus on providers who are not trained in biomedical medicine—depending on where the targeted diseases or populations are treated and which providers are "reachable" (Marsh 1999, p. 42; and Hudelsohn 1998). In Kenya, for example, shopkeepers were trained in the proper use of drugs to treat childhood fevers. A study showed a substantial improvement in the behavior of the use of these drugs, because of shopkeepers' oral advice and printed information distributed in the shops.[9]

- *Persuasion.* Evidence indicates that it is often necessary for knowledge to be reinforced, since knowledge alone is frequently not sufficient to change provider or prescriber behavior (Soumerai, McLaughlin, and Avorn 1989). A number of the more successful training efforts include interventions to motivate the providers to "stay on track."

  - *"Detailing."* Detailing consists of face-to-face interaction and guidance through personal encounters with practitioners. Pharmaceutical companies use this method very effectively to influence prescription practices throughout the world. More recently, governments have utilized this method to improve physician behavior in targeted areas. Such efforts have proven effective in changing physician behavior in treating common childhood illnesses in Kenya and Indonesia (Tawfik forthcoming).

- *Negotiation.* Negotiation may be viewed as an intensive form of persuasion. An example of this method is Private Practitioner Treatment Improvement Intervention (PRACTION). PRACTION is a systematic initiative that starts with assessing current private practitioner behavior. Subsequently an agreement or informal contract for modified behaviors is negotiated with the practitioner. Such efforts have been implemented successfully in India, Indonesia, and Pakistan (Northrup 1997).

- *Public financing.* Besides paying for goods or services directly and through contracting arrangements, governments can use public funds in other ways to influence the behavior of private health care providers. This form of interaction with private providers is most common with regard to nonprofit organizations.

  - *Financial subsidies.* One means of influencing behavior is to provide financial subsidies to certain organizations that perform activities or deliver products important for achieving social objectives. The earmarked grant is the most common form of financial support for private providers, especially with regard to preventative services. The state government of Tamil Nadu (India) pays part of the cost of family planning services provided by private hospitals (DeRoeck 1998).

  - *Bed grants.* Another common mechanism for providing financial support to private providers that are serving public objectives is bed grants, a government payment based on the number of beds allotted to serving indigent patients. For example, the government of Tanzania provides a payment per approved bed to NGO hospitals designated as district hospitals (Gilson, Dave, and Mohammed 1994). Governments also occasionally opt to provide financial subsidies to private facilities in exchange for establishing an exemption mechanism for poor patients (McPake and Banda 1994).

- *Seed funding.* Another type of financial support used is seed funding for the start-up of services or activities. Support from the government of India to Parivar Seva Sanstha, an NGO specializing in reproductive health care, for example, covered 75 percent of the costs of opening a new clinic.

- *Tax subsidies or exemptions.* In some cases, financial subsidies are provided indirectly through tax subsidies or exemptions. For example, in Nepal nonprofit organizations receive tax exemptions for health commodities and services on the recommendation of a national NGO umbrella group (DeRoeck 1998). Church NGOs in Malawi that buy drugs from the government's central medical store at preferential prices receive an indirect subsidy (Gilson, Dave, and Mohammed 1994).

- *In-kind support.* Alternatively, in-kind support may be supplied to the providers. Many NGOs and an occasional for-profit practitioner receive this type of support. In several African countries governments either second staff to mission facilities, as in Uganda, or pay the mission facility's staff salaries, as in Ghana and Malawi (Gilson, Dave, and Mohammed 1994). The ministry of public health in Bolivia subsidizes staff salaries in PROSALUD clinics located in rural areas (DeRoeck 1998). In-kind support may also include other inputs such as medical supplies, or even facilities: the government of Guatemala provides Rxiin Tnamet (a local NGO) with medical supplies for its preventive health outreach services (DeRoeck 1998). In Ghana the government provides buildings, equipment, and drugs for NGO hospitals (Gilson, Dave, and Mohammed 1994).

- *Critical supplies free or at a discount.* Some governments use these same methods to influence private practitioners (for-profit entities) by supplying critical supplies free or at a discount (including vaccines or nutritional supplements), while allowing the practitioner to charge a fee and make a profit to expand delivery of important goods and services. This type of intervention has been successfully used in Malaysia.

- *Vouchers.* The government may, alternatively, expand demand
  for priority services by subsidizing their purchase through
  means of vouchers. In this case vouchers may be given to a targeted population to expand their utilization of a priority service. In Nicaragua, for instance, vouchers for STD treatment
  were distributed to sex workers who were able to redeem them
  at a range of public and private providers. The scheme was successful in reaching poorer groups, and the overall incidence of
  gonorrhea has declined (Sandiford, Gorter, and Salvetto 2002).

Growing the Private Sector

Although working better with existing private providers is often useful for improving system and service performance, certain situations
call for another strategy. Many programs requiring new or expanded
health care provision can be implemented by working with private
providers. In some instances these providers are particularly well
placed to undertake such activities—they may already be present in
a targeted district, or may be heavily utilized by a targeted population. When this is the case governments can use a number of tools
to encourage or "incentivize" the appropriate providers to undertake
the delivery of additional services. We refer to these efforts as strategically "growing" the private sector. The tools governments may use
to promote such activities overlap considerably with those they can
use to influence the private sector in their current activities described in the preceding section. Hence, the difference is in what the
programs are aiming to get private providers to do, not in the tools
they use to influence them.

Contracting and subsidies. The most direct means of supporting the
expansion of private provision in identified activities or regions is
through ongoing purchasing of (or contracting for) their goods or
services. For example, the Guatemalan government contracted with
existing NGO service providers in order to expand services in areas
inhabited by indigenous peoples, following a long civil war, during
which time public facilities had ceased to operate in these areas.

Alternatively, services or goods may be financed on the demand side, through endowing users with a reimbursable claim to targeted services by means of vouchers. Governments use a range of additional financial mechanisms to encourage the expansion of the private sector—mechanisms such as tax exemptions, or subsidized or targeted credit. In Pakistan, for example, the government offers tax exemptions to practitioners setting up in rural areas. In some countries the government will allocate land to encourage the construction of a health care facility in an underserved area.

Regulatory reform. Governments may also use indirect means to encourage targeted expansion of private provision. For example, they may take steps to reduce unnecessary constraints that increase the cost of operation by reducing or abolishing import restrictions. "Sometimes governments create monopolies unnecessarily and deny entrepreneurs (and other providers) the opportunity to compete fairly with established service providers by erecting entry barriers, blocking credit and access to foreign exchange, taxing dividends and profits inequitably, imposing unfair import duties, and establishing bureaucratic hurdles" (Kessides 1993). Although this quote refers mainly to utilities, it is equally valid for health infrastructure and services. Hence, removal of such barriers can be an important tool that can be used to "grow" the private sector.

Enabling environment. Regulation is undoubtedly necessary to prevent opportunism and protect patients. However, often there are unnecessary constraints on providers—some of which are specific to the health sector, while others are present in the overall enabling environment. In developing countries there are often burdensome and unnecessary costs to register an organization as well as problems obtaining access to critical inputs, including human resources, pharmaceuticals, other consumables, and essential public services (such as a predictable supply of electricity and access to clean water). These issues can deter private operators from expanding their health care services.

Nonprofit organizations face yet another set of issues related to the enabling environment. In many developing countries the legal framework supporting nonprofit operation is weak, unfavorable, or nonexistent. Often there is no support for contributions or other forms of philanthropy. In particular, many developing countries lack a clear and supportive regulatory framework regarding the tax-exempt status of nonprofit organizations or donations to them (Simon 1995; and box 1.3).

Some governments impose needlessly cumbersome and time-consuming demands on NGOs by demanding detailed financial accounting and planning of activities (De Jong 1991). Removing these requirements can promote the expansion of privately delivered services.

Governments can also encourage expansion of private health care delivery through behavioral change communication programs that expand demand for key goods and services the private sector delivers. The range of goods and services for which this approach is being utilized has expanded from population and reproductive health goods and services to include bednets, oral rehydration salts, fortified foods, and the like.

Conversion

Throughout the world a trend has emerged of turning over operation of public services to private hands—momentum has gained as experience has built up, and positive results have been achieved (Savas 2000; Domberger 1999; and Donahue 1989). Based on the consistently positive results from conversion of other social and public services, governments are expanding such efforts to publicly run health services (GAO 1998; Melia 1997; Zuckerman and de Kadt 1997; and Lyon 2000). Various reasons are put forth for this move toward conversion. If a government appears to be overextended, conversion can be part of a strategy aimed at focusing on its "core competencies." Alternatively, or in addition, governments may feel that the private sector will run the service or services more efficiently, or improve quality in the service, or both.[10] Governments have also recently become interested in developing "public-private partnerships" to attract private funds for expanding facilities and services—which may entail the transfer to private hands of some services, of the operation as a whole, or even of the facilities (boxes 1.4 and 1.5). These types of reforms have been taking place in Australia, Chile, Germany, Sweden, Thailand, the United Kingdom, as well as in South Africa. From the fiscal perspective many governments are motivated to consider conversion to better manage the risk associated with different health-related expenditure streams (Blair 1998).

Conversion in the health sector is much more complex than conversion of other public services, because government must establish an ongoing relationship with the provider to ensure services are delivered appropriately. In addition, monopoly power can emerge in some health care markets, especially in acute care services. These conditions make it necessary to address several issues simultaneously when conversion of health care services is undertaken.

If the provider is to continue to deliver public services the transaction itself will have to be directly tied to ensuing service contracts. These transactions, along with the service contracts, must be viewed together to ensure adequate performance by the provider. Sensible service contracts entail sophisticated funding arrangements for the service providers. If funding of public delivery is currently based on inputs, or even on blocks of services, substantial changes will have to be implemented to enable the conversion to proceed. Whether or not it is applied systemwide, contracting with private health care providers requires "active purchasing" (Preker, Jakab, Baeza, and Langenbrunner 2000). The case of Port Macquarie Base Hospital illustrates the difficulties of undertaking hospital conversion when the funding arrangements do not support sensible service contracts (box 1.5).

When public providers deliver services critical issues such as quality, cost containment, and efficiency can be addressed administratively. When services are turned over to private operators, however, in addition to tightening the service contracts, the regulatory

Box 1.4 Port Macquarie Base Hospital Conversion: Obtaining and Demonstrating Gains Is Critical

In Australia in the late 1980s the New South Wales Department of Health (DOH) needed to expand the range and quantity of hospital services in the Macleay-Hastings District. After extensive review the DOH decided to proceed with a build-own-operate arrangement with the private sector. The tender was completed in 1991, and the contract signed with the Hospital Corporation of Australia in 1992. The hospital began operations in November 1994. It is widely accepted that the quality of and access to hospital services in the region have improved since privatization, yet many people still take a dim view of the project. The biggest problems can be traced to the service contracts, specifically to the hospital's funding arrangements. The funding system did not generate enough information about the cost of services to allow the DOH to set sensible prices for the new hospital's services. The service agreements therefore ended up reimbursing the hospital at a high rate, in addition to a lump sum availability charge. After a number of reviews, conclusions as to how "bad" a deal the DOH is getting are still wide-ranging, but the conversion, on the whole, is not judged a success. The funding and fee-setting arrangements are neither sufficient to ensure good value for the DOH, nor sufficient to verify the gains of private participation.

Source: New South Wales Auditor-General 1996.

framework for service delivery will likely need to be enhanced, to ensure that social objectives continue to be met. Thus, conversion often requires strengthening of the regulatory framework and implementing bodies, to complement the changes in the service delivery arrangements.

Box 1.5 Conversion of Public Hospitals in South Africa

South Africa has extensive experience of funding hospital services delivered by both for-profit and nonprofit facilities. In 1995 17 percent of all hospital beds were operated by private organizations. Broomberg, Masobe, Mills (1997) evaluated three conversions. Two were build-own-operate transactions—privately constructed and operated district hospitals, supplying acute, district-level hospital services under 10-year service contracts. In a third hospital the government contracted for private management for what was still a publicly owned facility. The authors matched these hospitals against similar public facilities and compared their performance. The privately operated (or managed) hospitals demonstrated higher productive efficiency, largely tied to lower staff costs and more efficient deployment of staff resources. The authors conclude that conversion "appears to hold the potential to generate substantial efficiency gains, both through the securing of services of comparable or higher quality at lower cost, and through the ability of the contractors to fill temporary or permanent gaps in government capacity." Weak contract implementation and management appear to have deprived the government of gains. For more on this topic, see chapter 3 of this handbook.

Source: Broomberg, Masobe, and Mills 1997.

The market environment in which the converted providers will operate must also be taken into account. As noted above, hospital markets are often subject to geographic monopolies, which must be taken into account in both the transaction and service contracts. To obtain the full benefit of conversion concerted efforts are frequently needed to promote competition in this market.[11]

Any needed changes in the regulatory and purchasing framework as well as the market environment must be considered, planned, and simultaneously implemented with the transaction to ensure that conversion brings about desired results. See appendix 1.A for further discussion of health services conversion reforms. This complexity makes health service conversion a complex and challenging reform.

Private Health Care Providers and the Poor

Despite the financial burden numerous recent surveys reveal that the poor in many countries receive many of their health services from the private sector (figure 1.1). Private health care providers are now seen as central to strategies to improve the health of the poor because of this recognition. Figure 1.1 presents the proportion of the poorest 20 percent of the population, in a number of developing countries, that sought treatment for recent illness in the private sector.

Improving Service Quality for the Poor

Not only are the poor using private providers, they most often utilize informal, unqualified, and poorly skilled practitioners or pharmacists. Since most attempts to alter these utilization patterns have failed, in some countries policymakers are exploring methods to improve the quality of care these providers offer as the most direct instrument to improve health care for the poor (Chakraborty, D'Souza, and Northrup 2000).

A major challenge to this approach is that private providers in general are harder to influence than providers in public clinics. In addition, the providers used by the poor are often even more difficult to reach, because they tend to be in the informal sector, and less well-organized than formal, registered doctors. Perhaps the principal obstacle to working with these providers to improve the care the poor are receiving is the unwillingness on the part of government

Figure 1.1 Percentage of People Treated Outside the Public Sector for Their Most Recent Illness (poorest 20 percent of population)

Percent

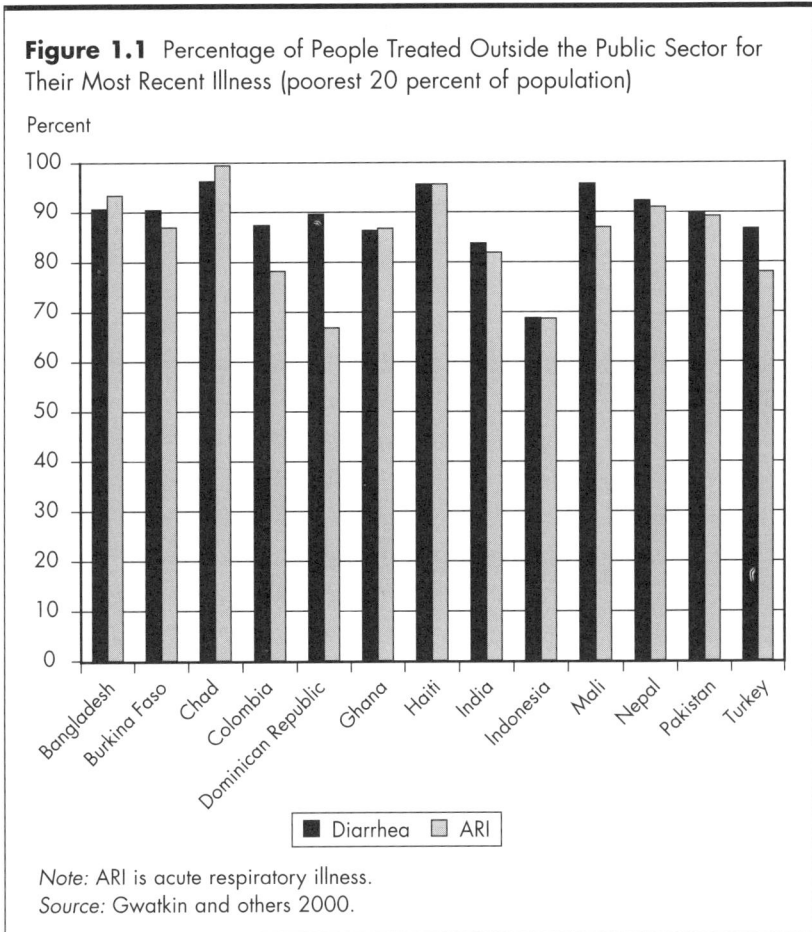

Note: ARI is acute respiratory illness.
Source: Gwatkin and others 2000.

officials to engage them. Professional associations are also often strongly opposed to engaging these providers. Nevertheless, a few governments are undertaking to engage the providers used by the poor. The instruments they use are discussed below.

Purchasing. In order to improve the quality of services poor patients receive, governments can contract, or otherwise finance, key services, using their financial leverage to enhance quality standards. Services might be purchased directly for identified, poor patients. Otherwise, governments may focus their contracting and funds on diseases that disproportionately affect the poor, or on services of critical importance to the poor, such as maternal and child health services. Another alternative, utilized by the Guatemalan government among others, is to contract for services in regions where poor inhabitants are concentrated (Nieves, La Forgia, and Ribera 2000).

Regulation. To improve the services received by poor patients governments may work to extend and enhance quality regulations to providers used by the poor (informal providers or providers located in rural areas or slums). Alternatively, they may create or enhance enforcement of regulations targeted at services that are particularly important to the poor.

Information, education, and persuasion. Outreach efforts to enhance the services provided by private health care providers are becoming increasingly common. Such efforts can be targeted to services that the poor use frequently; providers they frequent; regions they inhabit; or they can target poor patients directly (where feasible and cost effective).

Mandates. Mandates are effective only when there is either enforcement capability or provider compliance incentives. Enforcement requires a relatively high level of monitoring capacity, which is rare in developing-country governments, especially for informal and traditional practitioners. Incentives are most often provided through financing mechanisms, as discussed above.

Expanding Services to the Poor

Dissatisfaction with the extent of outreach to poor clients through publicly run services has led some governments to experiment with methods to expand services, by enabling poor patients to expand utilization of private providers. Governments wishing to expand services in this way must first identify the providers that serve the poor, or that could do so due to location, orientation, or service profile. The instruments most commonly used to encourage providers to expand services rendered to the poor include the following.

Purchasing. The most powerful instrument for expanding privately delivered services to poor patients is payment for these services with public funds. These funds may be allocated to providers or to users. Providers can be funded for services to the poor by means of contracting or other less specific subsidies (such as input or in-kind subsidies). Service delivery to poor users can also be generated through vouchers issued to patients for use at private clinics, with government or other payers reimbursing providers for these claims.

As with all forms of transfers to the needy, effective targeting is an issue. As a means of targeting some governments have focused on contracting with NGOs whose patients were already drawn mainly from poor populations (Nieves, La Forgia, and Ribera 2000). This is especially useful where individual targeting is not possible or is not cost-effective. An alternative form of targeting is for the government to contract for services that are especially important to the poor (such as maternal and child health services[12]) or for treatment of diseases particularly prevalent among the poor (such as TB and malaria). The Reproductive and Child Health program in India uses three methods to expand access to the poor: contracting with NGOs located in poor areas, who were better at reaching the poor; setting targets related to reaching poor populations; and focusing on services of particular importance to poor populations (Rosen 2000).

To expand services governments may give direct subsidies to providers (especially NGOs) that predominantly serve the poor, or operate in areas inhabited by the poor. Vouchers have also been used to reduce the cost of a good or service at the point of service—with subsequent redemptions using public funds. They are most commonly used to reduce the price for poor people of targeted goods, such as bednets. Occasionally vouchers are used to reduce or eliminate a fee for services, however. An example is the voucher program for STD treatment established for poor sex workers in Nicaragua (Sandiford, Gorter, Salvetto 2002).

Regulation. A commonly used regulation intended to enhance access to services for the poor is to make registration as a nonprofit, with attendant benefits, contingent on an organization's devoting a proportion of its services to poor populations.

Expanding community financing. To increase access for the poor to insurance, or reduce the payment at point of service, governments can pay part or all of the contribution for poor members in community financing schemes. Alternatively, they can subsidize the scheme directly following set criteria regarding socioeconomic status of membership. For schemes whose members are predominantly poor, governments are exploring options to ensure the availability of reinsurance—to enhance these schemes' sustainability.

Mandates. Another method for expanding services available to the poor is through promulgation and enforcement of mandates; an example might be, for instance, requiring doctors or other medical staff to serve in poor areas as a prerequisite to receiving their license. Another example, for hospitals, might be for the government to require a certain number or proportion of beds to be used to serve the poor. Caution must be used in this regard, because these efforts often lead to monitoring problems and hence empty "poor" beds.

Private Health Care Provision and Public Health

Public health services are oriented to directly benefit the public, either as individuals, communities, or larger populations. These services are often public goods, as is the case for most oversight functions, or they may have significant positive externalities.[13] Examples include:

- Population or community-based services, such as water chlorination and salt iodization

- Individual preventive health services, such as immunizations

- Individual or community health promotion activities, including nutrition education (such as messages on breast-feeding and weaning practices); hygiene education; education to foster awareness of symptoms and treatments for better home management (such as oral rehydration therapy for family members with diarrhea); and education about safe sexual behavior, or against smoking or tobacco, drug, and alcohol abuse

- Special campaigns of public priority, using multiple approaches against specific diseases or risk factors with high externalities, such as acquired immune deficiency syndrome (AIDS), TB, malaria, or substance abuse.

The private sector is commonly excluded from national public health programs—sometimes simply from habit, occasionally from fear that involving private providers, some of whom are unqualified, could be seen as formal recognition and encouragement for those who are unqualified to continue their substandard practices. Nevertheless, in many instances, these private providers are integral to addressing public health concerns (Pathenia 1998; Tawfik forthcoming; and Uplekar, Pathenia, and Raviglione 2001). For instance, private practitioners are now acknowledged to be an important source of treatment for diarrhea, acute respiratory illness (ARI), and malaria—which together account for over one-half of childhood mortality in developing countries (Waters, Hatt, and Axelsson 2002). In many countries private providers treat a large proportion of TB symptomatics, especially in Southeast Asia and the Western Pacific where the disease burden is highest (Uplekar, Pathenia, and Raviglione 2001). Private drug retailers are usually the first and often the only point of contact with the health system for a wide variety of conditions of public health concern, including maternal and child health (Kafle and others 1996). Private provision essentially raises two major issues with regard to public health: insufficient attention to and delivery of promotive and preventive services; and poor quality of diagnostic and curative services.

Expanding Provision of Preventive Health Care Services

Many people in developing countries visit private health care providers for their everyday health needs. Unfortunately, these interactions often omit critical promotive and preventive care. Individuals undervalue these activities (such as vaccinations and health education) relative to curative care—with the result that providers, too, underemphasize them. Private providers are usually excluded from public health programs, exacerbating this tendency to underemphasize critical promotive and preventive care. Recently some governments have been taking steps to include private providers in implementation of public health efforts to expand utilization of preventive health care services (World Bank 2001a). This undertaking is challenging. However, private providers are often interested in participating in these efforts, feeling that it may enhance their attractiveness to patients (such as for immunizations or nutrition supplements). Care must be taken, however, to match the task with the providers. Hudelsohn proposes several criteria:

- The provider must be well placed to undertake the task.

- The provider must be capable.

- The provider must be willing.

- It must be feasible to train the provider to undertake the task.

- It must be acceptable to users that the provider performs the task.

- Government and government officials must be willing to work with the private sector and adequate resources must be devoted to the tasks (Hudelsohn 1998).

As is clear from this list of criteria, a thorough knowledge of the local health system and private providers' tasks within it is critical to the success of such efforts. This kind of understanding hinges on effective communication with private providers, which is rare in developing countries.

Once the prevention-related tasks that are the focus of an initiative, and the providers with which the government will work, are identified, instruments for working with private providers take several forms.

Outreach to providers. Some private practitioners can be motivated to expand delivery of promotive or preventive care by simply providing them with relevant information (such as information on the importance of hand washing, and other hygienic practices). Some practitioners can be influenced by their inclusion in government-sponsored training programs. In many cases, however, information dissemination and education are not enough. Often, increases in knowledge do not translate into improvements in practice (Soumerai, McLaughlin, and Avorn 1989). Efforts to change the incentives of providers are therefore extremely important. Examples of such efforts are described below.

- *Outreach to patients.* Behavioral change communication can be used to increase demand for products and services with a public health benefit (such as vaccinations and nutrition supplements). Patient-education materials can be made available for distribution in private clinics. Social marketing–type methods have been used in many cases to make participation in public health programs profitable for private providers.

- *Direct payment or reduced prices for public health goods and services.* Many providers are willing to change their behavior in minor, although possibly significant ways. If the added service activity is too costly or time consuming to deliver, however, the governments will need to allocate funds to cover the additional costs to the provider, if the changes are to be sustained. Governments can pay for, or otherwise subsidize the delivery of, promotive-preventive services (contracting). In a recent review of developing-country programs seeking to involve the private sector in achieving child health objectives, approximately 63 percent utilized contracting, while 51 percent used grants (Axelsson 2002). Again, the ability to contract depends on the measurability of the good or service delivered. Nutrition counseling and supplements, for example, have proven relatively easy to deliver through contracting, as has STD treatment (Marek, Diallo, Ndiaye, and Rakostosalama 1999).

- *Indirect subsidies and supply of critical inputs.* Government can supply priority inputs to practitioners to encourage them to deliver related services (such as free or discounted vaccines, or STD treatment packs).

- *Subsidizing inclusion in insurance packages.* Governments can subsidize the inclusion in insurance packages of goods and services deemed to address high public health priorities (such as population and reproductive health–related goods and services, or vaccines).

- *Mandating inclusion in insurance packages.* Governments can require inclusion of certain goods and services in insurance packages in order for an insurer to be licensed, or to provide insurance to publicly insured patients. Examples include reproductive health–related goods and services.

Improving the Quality of Curative Treatments

Private providers and their patients focus heavily on delivery of curative care. Care is frequently of low quality, however, an issue that concerns not just individuals but society at large. Effective curative treatments are critical to the achievement of many public health priorities, including effective diagnosis and treatment of childhood illness, malaria diagnosis and treatment, TB diagnosis and treatment, population and reproductive health, and maternal health interventions. Mechanisms for guiding these interventions include the following.

Direct subsidies and contracting. Because some services are more easily measured, and thus more amenable to contracting, than others, governments will more easily be able to contract for and monitor their delivery (box 1.6). TB treatment, for example, has proven "contractable," because the impact of treatment can be readily verified (Pathenia 1998).

Outreach to providers. Several outreach methods to improve providers' treatment in critical areas have been tried, with varying de-

Box 1.6 Public-Private Cooperation to Effective Treatment for Tuberculosis

Private doctors in Hyderabad, India, were given access to a respected local health institution (Mahavir Hospital) that treats TB patients, and were allowed to supervise their patients' treatment. In the hospital their patients received effective and affordable treatment for TB. This expanded the access to effective TB treatment for poor people in slum areas. It also reduced the development of drug-resistant strains of TB and reduced the number of infections.

grees of success.[14] While the circulation of information is a low-cost outreach method, it is also less intensive. These less-intensive outreach efforts seem to have less impact on treatment than direct contact with providers. With increasing frequency, more-intensive methods are being tried in developing countries. In the area of child health the World Health Organization has developed a guide for investigating retail practice and for designing interventions to improve retail dispensing of pharmaceuticals by discouraging the sale of antidiarrheal drugs and antimicrobials, and by encouraging the use of oral rehydration salts in the treatment of diarrhea (WHO 1993). Trials of this guide in Kenya and Indonesia have demonstrated the positive impact of this approach (Ross-Degnan and others 1993). In Nepal a course was developed to improve the practices of unlicensed drug sellers, where successful completion endowed participants with certification and registration as drug "professionalists." Improvements in prescribing practices were identified (Kafle and others 1992). In Uganda prepackaged drugs to treat STDs were provided to doctors (box 1.7). A more intensive outreach method involving negotiation has been developed under the title PRACTION (see above p. 33). PRACTION is a program that starts by assessing current private practitioner practices, and then negotiates with them an informal

---

Box 1.7 Providing Drugs to the Private Sector: Enhancing STD Treatment

Under the "Clear 7" program in Uganda private practitioners, clinics, and pharmacists were provided with prepackaged, subsidized drugs for distribution to men with urethral discharge. Drug shops enhanced their reputation by selling effective and affordable treatment. The packaging expanded access to a complete and effective course of treatment for men with STDs, and reduced development of drug-resistant strains of the disease.

Source: Ochwo 2000.

---

contract in order to modify behaviors. It has been implemented successfully in India, Kenya, and Pakistan with respect to treatment of childhood illnesses (Northrup 1997).

Outreach to patients. Behavioral change communication had been used successfully to improve patient receptivity to appropriate treatment (such as oral rehydration therapy as a substitute for antibiotics to treat diarrhea), or to encourage appropriate health-seeking behavior (such as for TB or malaria treatment).

Access to public referral network. Private doctors usually do not have access to public or NGO treatment centers. One way of improving the quality of public health–related curative care is to give private doctors access to these centers. In some countries identification and treatment of communicable diseases have been improved through such efforts. Referral rights must be combined with education related to appropriate referral.

Indirect subsidies and supply of critical inputs. In some instances governments have been successful in improving service quality by supplying related inputs. Treatment of diarrheal disease in children has been improved by providing oral rehydration salts. STD treatment has been improved by providing appropriately "bundled" pharmaceuticals.

Implementation of Public Policies toward Private Providers

Implementation of health sector reforms is extremely challenging, and more often than not goes awry. Useful analysis for developing an implementation plan for general health reforms can be structured in several ways (Reich 1996; and Walt 1998). Here we will talk about the unique set of challenges likely to come up when a government attempts to improve and increase its interaction with private health care providers. These issues are likely to arise regardless of strategy or instruments.

Lack of familiarity with private sector. A historical pattern of segmentation between the public and private sectors is common, and therefore actors on both sides usually lack knowledge of and familiarity with one another. While most governments can call upon basic data regarding the capacities and activities of public facilities and practitioners, similar data regarding private health care providers are rarely available to policymakers.

Lack of forum for dialogue and collaboration. The existence and functioning of an ongoing consultative mechanism between the private and public sector have proven crucial for successful implementation of efforts to work with the private sector (Stone 1998). In developing countries' health sectors, however, there is often no forum for dialogue between the public sector (especially policymakers) and private providers. In many countries the private sector is not well organized, so only a small number of representative organizations are able to serve as a counterpart in consultations with the government. This lack of organization is even more problematic with informal and unqualified practitioners—who are especially important to the poorer segments of the population.

Ideology and mindset. Efforts to establish policies and mechanisms to work with private health care providers often encounter significant challenges associated with government officials' and health sector staff's deeply engrained mindset of mistrust toward the private sector. Because of obvious problems with clinical quality and other associated market failures, negative attitudes toward the private sector, particularly the for-profit sector, must be dealt with if policies to constructively engage the private sector are to move ahead.

Special problems often arise when actions are being contemplated to increase interaction with practitioners who are not trained in biomedical medicine, or who are unqualified—because this will often be seen as a threat to the interests of the staff trained in biomedical medicine that dominate publicly operated health care operations.

Public employees. In addition to problems associated with ideology or mindset of public officials and health staff the members of the operations staff will usually feel threatened when private sector collaboration or conversion is being contemplated. Their concern is often well founded in the sense that, at least in part, these reforms are often directed toward enhancing productivity or flexibility in public sector operations, and may even constitute a threat to the staff's continued employment. Any efforts to enhance collaboration with the private sector must explicitly address these stakeholders' views and political strengths.[15] As with all health reforms, these reforms will often be threatened if they are opposed by medical professionals, who have a great deal of credibility and access to the public, and who are adept at portraying any reform that they oppose as undermining the "public interest."

Private sector skepticism. Due to a historical pattern of segmentation between the public and private sectors in health, private providers may not initially respond to government initiatives.

Lack of capacity for public officials to take on new roles. Both in terms of the new structure envisioned and in terms of managing the reforms, government officials will find it extremely challenging to operate in new ways and to take on new roles. Hence, any reform to increase interaction with the private sector must include efforts to develop the capacity of government officials to take on new roles.

Government staff members are usually accustomed to dealing with organizations and staff in a subordinate relationship, and therefore have a tendency to approach policymaking in centralized and top-down fashion—that is, they tend to be "heavy handed." They may miss out in collecting key information about the private sector and its strengths and weaknesses, and may add to suspicions about the government's intentions (Green and Matthias 1997).

Impact on public sector. Any initiative to work with the private sector must take into account the likely impact on the public sector. Utilization may go down at public facilities. Expanding private sector activity may encourage staff to move out of public sector work. Governments will need to deal proactively with such possibilities, in order to ensure that they do not further reduce public sector capacity.

Outreach methods. A review of efforts to improve the operation of private providers indicates a tendency to overreach, trying to bring practitioner behavior up to standard on a number of fronts. These unfocused efforts tend to be relatively ineffective. Efforts are more successful when focused on a narrow range of activities (Chakraborty, D'Souza, and Northrup 2000). Evidence to date also underscores that successful outreach efforts should not be too time-consuming—since private practitioners value their time highly and will not be willing to incur the income loss associated with long training programs. This observation highlights a more general point—that all efforts to work with private providers must take into account their constraints and incentives, and their need to earn their keep and their interest in making a profit.

Conclusions and Using the Handbook

Working with private providers costs money, both in terms of direct payments and in terms of ensuring adequate staffing resources to manage relations with them. Many governments undertake work with private providers only under conditions of extreme fiscal pressure, thereby undermining the impact of these efforts. While working with private providers may result in some efficiency gains and cost savings, sometimes it may be more costly to work with heterogeneous, disintegrated, private practitioners. If people go to private practitioners for treatment, it may be necessary for the government to work with them in order to achieve certain objectives.

In developing countries it may be easier to work with private providers on public health–related activities (such as vaccination, treatment of STDs, or delivery of nutrition supplements) than on clinical activities—since both the service and the outcome can be more readily observed and measured in the former case.

Efforts to work with private practitioners are best thought of as systemic reforms—rather than "stand alone" reforms. These changes must be based on a clear strategy for what the private and public sectors will be doing in the medium term, in order to ensure any needed complementary reforms are forthcoming.

Undertaking improvements in public policy toward private health care providers in developing countries requires new and expanded analysis—to assess the private sector's current role and to evaluate the effectiveness of instruments for working with them. Dialogue with the private sector is critical, both to identify opportunities and to implement new policies.

Comparing strategies. Attempting to harness the private sector or to grow the private sector in a targeted way are relatively low-risk strategies. Both strategies require reallocating resources toward new efforts (such as contracting, regulation, information dissemination, or tax breaks). In both cases structural changes are incremental—leaving in place most arrangements for service delivery and seeking only to change private providers' behavior on the margin. The potential downside from failed efforts, therefore, consists mainly in not achieving such changes—leaving the status quo in force.

Conversion is a riskier strategy, since existing service-delivery arrangements are interrupted as operations are transferred to private hands. If efforts go awry quality and even access to certain services may suffer. Such efforts are most risky when key elements of the enabling framework are missing (such as public funding and contracting, or health service regulation).

The way forward. The evidence on the effectiveness of instruments for working with the private sector is relatively sparse, but the evidence on the folly of ignoring private health care providers is not. It is clear that the way forward in virtually all developing countries must include enhanced interaction with private providers. Although recognition of this fact is widespread, most attempts to operationalize such interaction are random and ad hoc—an occasional contract for cleaning a public hospital, the odd delivery of vaccines to a private clinic. These efforts are often undermined by the lack of information about the private sector, and hence are undertaken in a relative vacuum.

Development of public policy toward private health care providers, just like sector policy in general, should be done comprehensively and strategically. This will require government policymakers to greatly increase their knowledge of and interaction with the private sector. The private sector is, after all, their partner in protecting the health of the population.

Although it is wise to move forward cautiously in implementing new strategies, in terms of enhancing information gathering and interaction with the private sector, the approach should be anything but cautious. In most developing countries such an information-gathering exercise will reveal the extent to which the private sector is central to many critical health sector objectives.

The subsequent chapters of this handbook can help policymakers move forward from this point. Chapter 2 provides guidance on how to assess the private health sector in a developing-country context. Chapters 3 and 4 review the basic principles and processes on contracting for and regulation of health services, respectively. Several other instruments for working with the private sector are discussed in chapter 4 (such as training and franchising). It is anticipated that the World Bank will publish stand-alone pieces on several of the more important instruments at a later date.

Appendix 1.A Health Services Conversion

Transactions. The transaction is the mechanism used to turn over publicly operated services, facilities, or public employees to private employment, management, or ownership. In health services common transactions can be categorized as follows.

• *Transaction categories*

  • *Conversion of existing facility or operations.* When a government decides to turn over public facilities or activities to private operators it may use a range of options (Table 1.4). It may sell outright, or lease the facility to an investor or nonprofit organization. Alternatively, more incremental methods may bring in a private party to operate the facility under a management contract, which allows the government closer control over the operations and can be structured to offer stronger or weaker incentives for profitability. Facility staff may remain in public employment (box 1.5). Another alternative to bring efficiency gains while maintaining public sector management is to compel facility managers to contract out (and establish competition) for auxiliary services (such as laundry, food, or billing services).

    Sometimes primary care operations are transferred to private hands by converting publicly employed doctors to self-employed status, under contract to the government payer or social insurance organization. This form of conversion is common in Central Europe, where many countries have moved from a vertically integrated Semashko (Soviet) model to a social insurance system with mixed delivery (box 1.8).

  • *Existing facility that requires capital investment for expansion or rehabilitation.* If the government is to attract private funds to support significant expansion or rehabilitation of health facilities, investors need a reasonable amount of control over the facility and predictable access to revenue streams for a defined period. Commonly, the government payer defines the bulk of the market—and hence, this type of transaction hinges

Table 1.4 Transaction Methods for Conversion of Health Facilities or Operations

TYPE OF TRANSACTION		DEFINITION	EXAMPLES (COUNTRIES, STATES)
Conversion of existing facility/operations	Sale	Private firm buys facility, operates under a service contract.	Australia, Germany, Sweden (Stockholm)
	Lease	Government leases a facility to a private organization, which operates it under a service contract.	Australian states
	Management contract	Private firm is contracted to maintain and operate a government-owned facility; government pays firm a management fee.	S. Africa, Malawi, Kenya, many countries in Latin America and the Caribbean, Saudi Arabia, Australia, Mongolia, United States
	Outsourcing of auxiliary services	Publicly owned facilities establish contract with private service providers to deliver auxiliary services (such as laundry, food services, billing, collection).	Everywhere
	Service/operation Conversion-individual contracting-primary care	Publicly employed primary care doctors are converted to self-employment and contracted by state/insurance organization for services.	Croatia, Macedonia, Slovenia, Poland, Hungary, Estonia, Brazil, Czech Republic, Slovakia, Sweden
	Service/operation conversion-individual contracting-surgeons	District government contracts with district surgeons.	S. Africa

58

	Service/operation conversion-integrated care		
Existing facility-requiring capital investment for expansion or rehabilitation	Lease-build-operate	Private firm leases facility from government, operates it under a concession, expands and/or rehabilitates it.	São Paulo
	Wrap-around addition	Private firm expands a government-owned facility, owns only the expansion, operates entire facility.	
Construction of new facility or capacity	Build-transfer-operate	Private firm finances and builds new facility, transfers to public ownership, then operates (20–40 yrs).	Australia, United Kingdom
	Build-operate-transfer	Same as above (build-transfer-operate), but facility is transferred after 20 to 40 yrs.	Australia, United Kingdom
	Co-location	Private firm develops an additional unit adjacent to or within a government facility, owns only the expansion.	Australia, United States

(Table continues on the following page.)

59

Table 1.4 (continued)

TYPE OF TRANSACTION	DEFINITION	EXAMPLES (COUNTRIES, STATES)
New operations to be undertaken		
Contracting for services in new areas	Government initiates contracting for health services in areas not initially served by public facilities.	Guatemala, Cambodia, Haiti
Conversion to nonprofit status		
Conversion to new nonprofit	Creation of and transfer of facility to nonprofit organization	
Sale or transfer to nonprofit organization	Transfer to existing nonprofit organization	U.S., Venezuela
Facility ceases public services		
Sale to private service provider	Facility is sold to be operated in delivering privately funded services (acute, long-term care, specialty care).	Georgia (Former Soviet Republic), Czech Republic
Sale-nonhealth facility	Facility is sold to be used for non-health-related activities.	

Box 1.8 Primary Care Conversion in Central Europe

Most Central European countries have abandoned their centrally planned "Semashko" type health systems and started to develop the institutional arrangements of a "social insurance" or "Bismarckian" system (Preker, Jakab, and Schneider 2002). The newly created social insurance agencies are increasingly tying reimbursement to outputs. This change has made it possible to establish contracts with private providers.

Hence, in several countries—including Croatia, Estonia, Poland, Germany (eastern part), Hungary, and Slovenia—social insurance contracting has allowed primary care conversion to proceed without threatening people's access to medical care.

Source: Wasem 1997; Kruuda 2001.

on the service contracting arrangements (box 1.9). Examples of such transactions include lease-build-operate and wrap-around arrangements.[16]

- *Construction of new facility or capacity.* To benefit from private sector advantages in building a new facility or adding capacity in an existing one, governments use a range of transactions.

    1. Under a build-transfer-operate contract the facility is privately built and the public sector takes ownership upon completion. In other cases, the private sector builds, and then operates, the facility for a period of time—then at the end of the period the facility is transferred to public ownership, a build-operate-transfer contract.

    2. To complement existing publicly run health services, some health policymakers have undertaken co-location arrange-

Box 1.9 Ensuring Access to Privatized "Safety-Net" Hospitals: Nonprofit Conversion in the United States

Many U.S. community hospitals have been privatized in the past 15 years. Conversion of these facilities has been especially complicated due to some unique aspects of the U.S. system. Unlike other developed countries, the United States lacks universal health insurance coverage, and an estimated 40 million Americans are uninsured. The large network of community-owned hospitals has traditionally functioned as a safety net for uninsured individuals. Therefore, it was believed that access for these people was threatened by conversion of these facilities, assuming they would begin to concentrate on the "bottom line." Communities sought to deal with the issue through different mechanisms. Some set up or expanded funding channels to reimburse providers for uncompensated care. Others sought to maintain access via channeling patients to other facilities. Some communities chose to restrict the pool of potential operators to nonprofit organizations—believing that their commitment to serving underprivileged patients would alleviate any access problems. Evaluation has led to a generally positive conclusion about the impact of these reforms—with no clear distinctions according to the method of ensuring access.

Source: ESRI 1999.

ments (Bloom 2000). This transaction entails the establishment of a privately owned health operation on or near the campus of a public facility (usually a hospital). The co-located facility may be held by an investor-owned (for-profit) or nonprofit entity. It may provide comprehensive or selected services. It may be physically located on premises leased from the public hospital, or it may occupy a floor, or a separate pavilion, in the public facility. Co-location refers strictly to the physical proximity of the two facilities, not to any particular form of ownership or contractual relationship. In Australia, where wide coverage of private insurance expands the demand for private hospital services, this type of arrangement is becoming common.

• *New operations to be undertaken.* In some situations health policymakers may decide to expand operation of publicly funded services into new areas or product lines by contracting for these services with private providers. While some conversion may be involved, this strategy is essentially the same as "growing" the private sector, as discussed above (p. 35).

• *Conversion to nonprofit status.* Occasionally, policymakers will determine a preference for service delivery by nonprofit organizations—and hence will transfer public facilities or services to either existing or a new nonprofit provider organization.

• *Facility ceases public services.* When a government identifies excess capacity in the public system it may decide to undertake true divestiture, putting into private hands not just ownership but also responsibilities for providing and funding services. Such a transfer can be done with or without conditions on the subsequent use of the facility—or that it continues as a health facility or not.

Such conversion is undertaken in accordance with health service planning analysis—to ensure that there is, in fact, excess capacity, and to identify where publicly supported services may cease without harm to the nearby population. This type of divestiture is sometimes used inappropriately to reduce government responsibilities for critical services, in essence constituting budget-driven downsizing rather than changes to improve the health system's functioning.

Technically, this type of transaction is much simpler—since the conversion is in essence a straightforward transaction—with none of the complications related to ensuring the continued delivery of important services. One aspect of these conversions can be much more difficult—labor relations. In all the transactions discussed above, the government's purchasing plans give it a great deal of leverage to smooth any labor adjustments the conversion may entail. If the government is no longer buying services from the facility, treatment of the converted facility's staff will be left completely to the new operator's discretion.

The conversion method selected will depend on the objectives sought, the level of profitability of the existing facility or operations, availability of interested providers or management companies, specificity or "buyability" of services, infrastructure and up-front capital requirements, and the risk each party can and will take on.

Transaction issues. In addition to determining what the objective is for the conversion and which type of transaction is appropriate, there are additional transaction-related issues that must be dealt with.

- *Permissible buyers and investors.* Government must decide who is permitted to participate in conversion of health care services. It must develop criteria to ensure that capable, financially sound operators of health services are involved. It must also decide whether to permit all participants, regardless of their legal form, or to restrict participation to certain categories (nonprofit only versus open, domestic bidders only versus open).

- *Unbundling of "nonbuyable" services.* Services for which the government will remain responsible may have to be separated from those the converted organization will deliver. For instance, it may make more sense to separate medical education and research from health care delivery services, as these are significantly more difficult to contract for.

Contracting-financing arrangements. Just as governments can use contracting to involve existing private providers in ensuring service delivery objectives are met, they can also use contracting to ensure a converted provider continues to deliver services to publicly funded patients. Since most conversions take place to improve quality and availability of public services, rather than to end those services, changes in the mechanisms to allocate funds to the providers are an integral part of conversion reforms.

Reforms that convert health care facilities are unique, to the degree that the transaction must be directly linked to the new contracting arrangements. This is true because the new operator will inevitably rely on the government payer for a substantial portion of revenue—so that the provisions for determining the volume of services to be purchased as well as the price-setting mechanism will directly influence the operation's profitability and sustainability. The service contract is thus as important as the structure of the transaction for the prospective private operator.

In designing the service contract government must seek to "get a good deal," but also must take into account the sustainability of the operation. For the operations of the converted facility to be sustainable the funding arrangements must ensure that everything is paid for or otherwise provided for in the transaction contract or regulatory framework. For example, if certain services are currently being cross-subsidized, incremental funding will likely be required to ensure their continued availability—since facilities operating in a competitive market usually cannot sustain cross-subsidization (patients who are net subsidizers will shift to using facilities where they can avoid such subsidization and pay lower prices). Payments must at least cover costs. (NGOs may be able to deliver certain services at a discount, but eventually they, too, must ensure operational viability; at most, contributions to nonprofits will support capital costs, not operating costs.)

To attract responsible operators to participate in the conversion the funding arrangements must be understood and believable. That means the government's service and expenditure commitments must be sustainable in its current fiscal environment. Otherwise, a responsible operator will not be interested, fearing unpredictable revenue shortfalls. If the government or relevant agency is known to be an unreliable payer, as is often the case in developing countries, conversion will require some sort of guarantee for the revenues associated with the service contract.

Regulation. When conversion takes place regulation of health services and facilities must often be expanded. After conversion the government will likely purchase many services, which will give them influence by means of their contracting and monitoring processes. However, some critical services may not be contracted for, and so their availability may have to be otherwise ensured (such as through requirements to continue to operate money-losing core services such as emergency services and trauma units, burn units, or neonatal intensive care units). In countries where the private sector does not operate these services, this may entail substantial enhancement of regulations and enforcement capacity, especially with regard to service quality, access, and cost containment.

Market structure. Many government-run facilities are geographic monopolies. While under direct government control exploitative monopoly behavior is constrained. After conversion, monopoly power could well be used to the detriment of the patients and the government payers. Therefore, in selecting and designing transactions, government must plan to reduce highly concentrated market power, where possible. In many cases, however, prospective investors have demanded long "exclusive" service contract agreements (up to 20 years), often endowing the operator with a geographic monopoly. More recent conversions have sought to reduce the length of this commitment. Where monopoly power is created, or maintained, governments have had to take steps to create at least competition "for the market," or contestability.[17]

Notes

1. Throughout this paper we use the term nonprofit organization and nongovernmental organization (NGO) interchangeably to refer to formal

organizations that have corporate objectives concerned with health service aims concerning groups outside the organization, and that do not make a profit and are outside the direct control of government.

2. Equity in access problems are better addressed through financing mechanisms such as subsidies, or insurance coverage for the poor, than through construction and operation of public clinics. For more detail see chapter 5, "Who Pays for Health Systems," in WHO 2000.

3. WHO 2000, chapter 4.

4. All three of these strategies are sometimes referred to as "public-private partnerships." As a result, this term is too vague to be useful in discussing policy options. See box 1.2, page 20, for further discussion.

5. Much regulation of health services is done indirectly via regulation of health insurance. However, this paper covers only direct regulation of health services.

6. Consumer quality refers to meeting patients' expectations and wishes about how they are treated.

7. The International Alliance of Patients' Organizations is a good resource for information on these initiatives (http://www.iapo-pts.org.uk/).

8. Janani, personal communication from K. Gopalakrishnan 2000, quoted in Smith and others 2001, p. 56.

9. Marsh, quoted in Smith and others 2001.

10. These results are more directly tied to competition than conversion—although conversion may be instrumental in establishing competition.

11. There are, however, many instances of service delivery conversion, even in the presence of monopoly power. In these cases, alternative mechanisms are used to ensure efficient operation (such as benchmarking or other performance assessment, or concessions).

12. Poor people often experience high under-five mortality partly due to poor access to health services (Gwatkin and others 2000).

13. An externality exists when the use of a good or service by one actor affects other actors. An example of a positive externality is immunization, whereas an example of a negative externality is pollution.

14. See Hudelsohn 1998 for a concise review of nine experiences with governments using outreach to private practitioners to improve maternal and child health services.

15. A political mapping exercise should be considered to design a strategy to manage implementation that will address potential opposition (Reich 1996).

16. A wrap-around transaction takes place when a private firm expands a government-owned facility, owning only the expansion but operating the entire facility.

17. Contestability may be established by tendering the right to be the service provider every 10 years, for example, or via management contracts.

Bibliography

Axelsson, H. 2002. "Private Sector Participation in Child Health: Learning from World Bank projects, 1993–2002." Unpublished manuscript.

Bennett, S., B. McPake, and A. Mills. 1997. *Private Health Providers in Developing Countries: Serving the Public Interest?* Zed Books: London.

Better Regulation Taskforce. 2000. U.K. Cabinet Office. http//www.cabinet-office.gov.uk/regulationtaskforce.htm

Blair, S. 1998. Presentation on *Private Participation in Hospitals*, made at the World Bank Private Sector Development Forum, May 1998, Baltimore, Md.

Bloom, A. 2000. "Case Study: Planning a Public-Private Hospital Co-location in Queensland." Unpublished manuscript.

Broomberg, J., P. Masobe, and A. Mills. 1997. "To Purchase or Provide? The Relative Efficiency of Contracting Out versus Direct Public Provision of Hospital Services in South Africa." In S. Bennett, B. McPake, and A. Mills, eds., *Private Health Providers in Developing Countries*, chapter 13. London: Zed Books.

Chakraborty, S., A. D'Souza, and R. Northrup. 2000. "Improving Private Practitioner Care of Sick Children: Testing New Approaches in Rural Bihar." *Health Policy and Planning* 15 (4): 400–07.

De Jong, J. 1991. "Nongovernmental Organizations and Health Delivery in Sub-Saharan Africa." Population and Human Resources Department, World Bank, Washington, D.C.

DeRoeck, D. 1998. *Making Health-Sector Nongovernmental Organizations More Sustainable: A Review of NGO and Donor Efforts.* Special Initiatives Report 14. Bethesda, Md.: Abt Associates, Inc., Partnerships for Health Reform Project. http://www.phrproject.com/publicat/si/sir14ab.htm

Domberger, S. 1999. *The Contracting Organization: A Strategic Guide to Outsourcing.* New York: Oxford University Press.

Donahue, J. D. 1989. The Privatization Decision: Public Ends, Private Means. New York: Basic Books.

ESRI (Economic and Social Research Institute). 1999. *Privatization of Public Hospitals.* Prepared for the Henry J. Kaiser Family Foundation. Published on-line at: http://www.kff.org/content/archive/1450/private_r.pdf

Filmer, D., J. Hammer, and L. Pritchett. 1998. *Health Policy in Poor Countries: Weak Links.* Policy Research Working Paper #1874. Washington, D.C.: World Bank.

GAO (General Accounting Office). 1998. *Social Services Privatization.* Report GAO/HEHS-98-6. Washington, D.C.

Gilson, L., P. Dave, and S. Mohammed. 1994. "The Potential of Health Sector Nongovernmental Organizations: Policy Options." *Health Policy and Planning* 9 (1): 14–24.

Green, A., and A. Matthias. 1997. *Nongovernmental Organizations and Health in Developing Countries.* London: Macmillan Press UK.

Griffin, C. C. 1989. *Strengthening Health Services in Developing Countries through the Private Sector.* Discussion Paper Number 4. International Finance Corporation, Washington, D.C.

Gwatkin, D. R., S. Rustein, K. Johnson, R. P. Pande, and A. Wagstaff. 2000. "Socioeconomic Differences in Health, Nutrition, and Population in India." HNP/Poverty Thematic Group, World Bank, Washington, D.C. Available electronically at: http://www.worldbank.org/poverty/health/data/index.htm

Hanson, K., and P. Berman. 1998. "Private Health Care Provision in Developing Countries: A Preliminary Analysis of Levels and Compositions." *Health Policy and Planning* 13 (3): 195–211.

Hudelsohn, P. 1998. *Possible Roles for Nongovernmental Health Providers in IMCI.* Prepared for the World Health Organization, Department of Child and Adolescent Health, Geneva. Unpublished.

Jeon, A., S. Kleefield, W. Leonardson, J. Norris, and C. Brintnall. 1998. "Health Reform in the Municipality of São Paulo, Brazil: Public Finance and Private Provision." Harvard Medical International. Unpublished.

Kafle K. K., R. P. Gartoulla, Y. M. Pradhan, A. D. Shresta, S. B. Karkee, and J. B. Quick. 1992. "Drug Retailer Training: Experiences from Nepal." *Social Science and Medicine* 35 (8): 1015–25.

Kafle, K. K., J. Madden, A. Shrestha, S. Karkee, P. L. Das, Y. Pradhan, and J. Quick. 1996. "Can Licensed Drug Sellers Contribute to Safe Motherhood? A Survey of the Treatment of Pregnancy-Related Anemia in Nepal." *Social Science and Medicine* 42 (11): 1577–88.

Kessides, C. 1993. "Institutional Options for the Provision of Infrastructure." Discussion Paper 212. World Bank, Washington, D.C.

Kruuda, R. 2001. "An Analysis of the Privatization of Primary Care Services in Estonia and Croatia." Unpublished Masters Thesis, MPH, Boston University.

Lewis, M. 2002. "Informal Health Payments in Eastern Europe and Central Asia." In E. Mossalios and A. Maresso, eds., *Funding Health Care: Options in Europe.* Buckingham, U.K: Open University Press.

Lyon, K. 2000. "And They Said It Couldn't Be Done." In Bloom, A., ed., 2000, *Health Reform in Australia and New Zealand.* South Australia: Oxford University Press, Chapter 15.

Marek, T., I. Diallo, B. Ndiaye, and J. Rakostosalama. 1999. "Successful Contracting of Prevention Services: Fighting Malnutrition in Senegal and Madagascar." *Health Policy and Planning* Dec. 14 (4): 382–9.

Marsh, V. 1999. Quoted in Smith, E., R. Brugha, and A. Zwi. 2001. *Working with Private Sector Providers for Better Health Care: An Introductory Guide.* London: Department for International Development (United Kingdom). Page 42.

McPake, B., and E. Banda. 1994. "Contracting Out of Health Services in Developing Countries." *Health Policy and Planning* 9 (1): 25–30.

Melia, R. 1997. "Public Profits from Private Contracts: A Case Study in Human Services. Pioneer Institute White Paper. Boston: Pioneer Institute.

Musgrove, P. 1996. "Public and Private Roles in Health: Theory and Financing Patterns." Human Development Department, World Bank, Washington, D.C.

New South Wales Auditor-General. 1996. NSW *Auditor-General's Report for 1996*. Vol. 1, Appendix 4 (Infrastructure Projects-Port Macquarie Base Hospital). Sydney: NSW Government.

Nieves, I., G. La Forgia, and J. Ribera. 2000. "Guatemala: Large-Scale Government Contracting of NGO's to Extend Basic Health Services to Poor Populations in Guatemala." LCSHD Department, World Bank, Washington, D.C. Unpublished manuscript.

Northrup, R. S. 1997. "The Private Sector: Critical Partners in Improving Child Health and Survival." BASICS. BASICS Quarterly Technical Newsletter 4: 1–9.

Ochwo, M. 2000. *Clear-7: Prepackaged Treatment Kit for Urethritis* Presentation at "Making the Most of the Private Sector." A Workshop Organized on behalf of the Department for International Development (United Kingdom), May 11–12, London.

Pathenia, V. 1998. "The Role of the Private Health Sector in Tuberculosis Control and Feasible Intervention Options." Health, Nutrition and Population Unit; and East Asia and Pacific Region, World Bank, Washington, D.C.

Preker, A. S., A. Harding, and N. Girishankar. 2000. "The Economics of Private Participation in Health Care: New Insights from Institutional Economics." In A. Ron and X. Scheil-Adlung, eds., *Recent Health Policy Innovations in Social Security*. Geneva: International Social Security Association.

Preker, A. S., M. Jakab, and M. Schneider. Forthcoming. "Health Financing Reform in Central and Eastern Europe and the Former Soviet Union." In E. Mossalios and A. Maresso, eds., *Funding Health Care: Options in Europe*. Buckingham, U.K.: Open University Press.

Preker, A. S., M. Jakab, C. Baeza, and J. Langenbrunner. 2000. "RAP Concept Note: Resource Allocation and Purchasing Arrangements that Benefit the Poor and Excluded Groups." World Bank, Washington, D.C. Available on-line at: http://wbln0018.worldbank.org/HDNet/HDdocs.nsf

Reich, M. R. 1996. "Applied Political Analysis for Health Policy Reform." *Current Issues in Public Health* 2: 186–91.

———. 2000. "Commentary: Public-Private Partnerships for Public Health." *Nature Medicine* 6 (6): 617–20.

Ronde, J. E., and H. Viswanathan. 1995. *The Rural Private Practitioner.* New Delhi: Oxford University Press.

Rosen, J. E. 2000. *Contracting for Reproductive Health Care: A Guide.* Health, Nutrition and Population Publications Series. World Bank, Washington, D.C.

Ross-Degnan, D., S. Soumerai, J. Bates, P. Goel, J. Makhulo, and J. Sutoto. 1993. "Improving Diarrhea Treatment Practices in Kenya and Indonesia." Presented at the Asian Conference on Clinical Pharmacology and Therapeutics, Yogyakarta, October 31–November 4. Unpublished. Quoted in Kafle, K. K., J. Madden, A. Shrestha, S. Karkee, P. L. Das, Y. Pradhan, and J. Quick. 1996. "Can Licensed Drug Sellers Contribute to Safe Motherhood? A Survey of the Treatment of Pregnancy-Related Anemia in Nepal." *Social Science and Medicine* 42 (11): 1577–88.

Salamon, L. M., and H. K. Anheier. 1996. *The Emerging Nonprofit Sector.* Manchester: Manchester University Press.

Sandiford, P., A. Gorter, and M. Salvetto. 2002. *Vouchers for Health: Public Policy for the Private Sector.* World Bank, Washington, D.C. Available online at http://rru.worldbank.org/viewpoint/HTMLNOTES/243/243summary.html.

Savas, E. S. 2000. *Privatization and Public-Private Partnerships.* New York: Chatham House.

Savedoff, W., and K. Slack. 2000. *Public Purchaser–Private Provider Contracting for Health Services: Examples for Latin America and the Caribbean.* Sustainable Development Department Publication. Washington, D.C.:

Inter-American Development Bank. URL: http://www.iadb.org/sds/doc/slack.pdf.

Simon, K. 1995. "Privatization of Social and Cultural Services in Central and Eastern Europe: Comparative Experiences." Paper presented at A Recipe for Effecting Institutional Changes to Achieve Privatization, Conference at Boston University, April 26.

Smith, E., R. Brugha, and A. Zwi. 2001. *Working with Private Sector Providers for Better Health Care: An Introductory Guide*. London: Department for International Development (United Kingdom).

Sommers, A. S. 1999. "The Structure and Function of Patient Organizations in the Netherlands: Lessons for the American Health Care System." AHSR Abstract. www.ahsr.org.1999/abstracts/sommers2/htm

Soumerai, S. B., T. J. McLaughlin, and J. Avorn. 1989. "Improving Drug Prescribing in Primary Care: A Critical Analysis of the Experimental Literature." *Millbank Quarterly* 67: 268-317.

Stone, A. H. 1998. "Private Sector Assessments Best Practice Note." Online Intranet Text. World Bank, Washington, D.C. URL: http://afr.worldbank.org/aft2/pvtsect/psa.htm.

Tawfik, Y. Forthcoming. "Utilizing the Potential of Formal and Informal Private Practitioners in Child Survival: Situation Analysis and Summary of Promising Interventions." Support for Analysis and Research in Africa Project and World Bank HNP Series. World Bank, Washington, D.C.

Uplekar, M., V. Pathenia, and M. Raviglione. 2001. Involving Private Practitioners in Tuberculosis Control: Issues, Interventions, and Emerging Policy Framework. Geneva: World Health Organization. URL: http://www.who.int/gtb/publications/privatepractitioners/index.htm.

Wagstaff, A., N. Watanabe, and E. van Doorslaer. 2001. *Impoverishment, Insurance, and Health Care Payments*. World Bank, Health, Nutrition, and Population Network, Washington, D.C.

Walt, G. 1998."Implementing Health Care Reform: A Framework for Discussion." In R. Saltman, J. Figueras, and C. Satellarides, eds., *Critical Challenges for Health Care Reform in Europe*. Buckingham, U.K.: Open University Press.

Wasem, J. 1997. "Health Care Reform in the Federal Republic of Germany: The New and Old Lander." In *Health Care Reform in Germany*.

Waters, H., L. Hatt, and H. Axelsson. 2002. *Working with the Private Sector for Child Health*. Prepared for the USAID-sponsored SARA Project (Academy for Education Development), the World Health Organization, and the World Bank. Washington, D.C.: World Bank, Health, Nutrition, and Population Network. URL: http://www1.worldbank. org/hnp/pub_discussion.asp.

WHO (World Health Organization). 1993. *Guide for Improving Diarrhea Treatment Practices of Pharmacists and Licensed Sellers*. Geneva.

———. 2000. *World Health Report 2000. Health Systems: Improving Performance*. Geneva. URL: http://www.who.int/health-systems-performance/whr2000.htm.

Williamson, O. 1991. "Comparative Economic Organization: The Analysis of Discrete Structural Alternatives." *Administrative Science Quarterly* 36 (June): 269–96.

World Bank. 1993. *World Development Report 1993*. Washington, D.C.

———. 1997a. handbook *on Good Practices for Laws Relating to Non-Governmental Organizations*. Prepared for the World Bank by the International Center for Non-Profit Law. World Bank. Available on-line at: http://www.icnl.org/handbook/

———. 1997b. *World Development Report 1997: The State in a Changing World*. Washington, D.C./New York: World Bank/Oxford University Press.

———. 2001a. *India, Raising the Sights: Better Health Systems for India's Poor*. Health, Nutrition, Population Sector Unit, India, South Asia Region.

———. 2001b. *World Development Indicators 2001* (print edition). Washington, D.C.: World Bank.

Zuckerman, E., and E. de Kadt. 1997. *The Public-Private Mix in Social Services: Health Care and Education in Chile, Costa Rica and Venezuela*. Washington, D.C.: Inter-American Development Bank; and Social Agenda Policy Group.

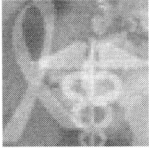

CHAPTER 2

Conducting a Private Health Sector Assessment

Sarbani Chakraborty and April Harding

This handbook is intended to support developing-country policymakers seeking to make changes in health policies and administration that will enhance the contribution of private providers to sectoral objectives. Among the largest barriers to formulating such policies is the dearth of relevant information available to these policymakers. Therefore, this chapter provides general guidelines for collecting and evaluating information about the private health sector or a segment of it (also called the private health sector assessment, or PHSA). These guidelines are intended to help health policymakers, in collaboration with other key stakeholders, to understand the existing configuration of the private health sector in their countries, and to identify policies that will improve interactions between the public and private sectors in order to enhance sector performance generally or in specific areas.[1] In conjunction with chapters 3 and 4 on contracting and regulation, guidance is also provided on which instruments to use to engage which private entities and toward which aims. Additional instrument chapters will subsequently be developed covering additional strategies. Interested readers are encouraged to consult the World Bank's Web site for health, nutrition, and population for new materials in these areas.

Since selecting and implementing strategies to work with the private health sector sometimes implies a reconfiguration of public and private roles, this chapter begins with a brief review of the main conceptual foundations regarding the role of the state in the health sector. First it describes perspectives from public finance and institutional economics that are often applied to determine or rationalize the structure of a government's activities in the health sector. Next, the broader literature and the empirical evidence are reviewed, to identify areas in which the private sector's contribution to health sector objectives can be increased. Third, applying this framework, the chapter guides users in conducting the following components of an assessment:

- Collecting information for a PHSA based on primary and secondary data sources

- Using the framework to analyze the data to understand the structure and function of private health care markets and to evaluate the current interaction between the public and private sectors

- Using this analysis to develop effective strategies for increasing the private sector's contribution to health objectives

- Working with key stakeholders to promote communication between public and private stakeholders, and to generate needed "buy-in" on policy recommendations.

These guidelines may be used to put together a comprehensive report on the private health sector. However, just like any sector report the assessment can be structured to target a specific issue (child mortality) or a specific subsector (hospitals).

Conceptual Framework for the Public-Private Mix in Health Services

A quick scan of the world's health systems reveals a huge amount of variation in the role of government compared with markets. This balance is not static, but rather evolves over time in response to directed policies as well as to underlying, spontaneous forces. In a similar way, health systems vary widely in the balance of public versus private health service provision. It is widely agreed, and supported by the principles of public economics, that government should fund or ensure funding for a wide range of services. Public or collective expenditure is merited based on the existence of market failures, or more simply, based on the belief that certain goods and services should not be allocated based on the ability to pay.[2] There is no such prevailing wisdom on the right "mix" of service providers, however.

Absent a "technical" answer to this question, governments throughout the world have developed their own health service delivery arrangements, reflecting their history, their cultural and social values, and the distribution of influence emerging from their political systems. Some governments rely heavily on public provision as the "instrument of choice" to address market failures and preferences related to distribution. In these integrated systems, private provision of goods and services plays a marginal role. On the other hand, some governments rely on financing arrangements, regulation, and other such instruments to create a framework within which public and private providers operate to achieve critical sector goals.

Among developed countries there are highly performing health systems of both types. Among developing countries, unfortunately, we often observe a dysfunctional amalgamation: a government heavily focused on public provision and extensive private delivery and out-of-pocket (nonpublic, nonpooled) expenditure on health goods and services. Absent both an adequate public delivery system and the complementary instruments of financing arrangements, regulation, and the like, these countries' health systems simply do not generate the quality, efficiency, or distribution sought by patients or policymakers.

Using Financing Arrangements to Guide Provision

As noted above, financing is one of the instruments that governments may use to correct market failures in the health sector. A range of criteria has been developed, based on public finance and cost-effectiveness, to aid in prioritizing items for public expenditure

(Musgrove 1999). Economic factors are combined with other criteria to determine how public funds should be allocated for health. The following is a summary of resource-allocation criteria that are based on generally accepted principles for allocation of public resources in health:

- Public money should favor the poor and the sick (that is, should have vertical and horizontal equity).

- Public money is the principal financing source for public goods and interventions, which private markets will not offer because of low private demand.

- Public money is also the principal source of financing for partly public goods with large externalities (that is, there is spillover of benefits to nonusers) since private demand is inadequate for these goods and services.

- The above objectives should be achieved before consideration is given to financing other goods and services, regardless of the providers or producers of those goods and services.

Public expenditure is only one instrument for addressing market failures in the health sector. Virtually all countries have regulations and regulatory processes to address problems related to quality, efficiency, cost containment, and so on. Many governments also support dissemination of information to help patients and private payers make better choices. Such practices can address market failures directly, through improving the health-seeking behavior of patients, or indirectly, through guiding demand to higher quality or more efficient providers. Hence, the criteria listed above apply to allocating scarce administrative capacity as well as to allocating public funds.

Altering the Status Quo

Governments have a range of alternative instruments to ensure provision of priority goods and services, including information disclosure, regulation, and contracting.[3] Selecting which instrument to use is complex, and is burdened by connections to social values; altering these arrangements is politically and administratively costly. As a result such calculations are often not made, engendering ad hoc arrangements for fulfilling governments' responsibilities in the health sector. While policy recommendations should never be developed without reference to existing institutions and political constraints, the instruments to be used to pursue health sector objectives can and should be considered in a rational and strategic way. Such analysis is at the heart of efforts to improve the interaction with the private health sector.

While public economics refers only to allocation of public funds, institutional economics provides some guidance on the choice of instrument to reduce market failures. Synthesizing principles and evidence from this field, Preker, Harding, and Girishankar (1999) suggest that the poor incentives and information problems that are frequently associated with public provision justify a thorough consideration of alternative instruments for pursuing policy objectives and addressing market failures. This reasoning underlies pursuit of alternative strategies, such as public funding for purchasing of privately produced health goods and services, while public production remains concentrated on health goods and services that are difficult to buy. Following this approach the choice of policy instrument is determined on a case-by-case basis, grounded in the extent to which the goods and services are "buyable."[4] The characteristics of goods and services that determine their buyability are their intrinsic levels of contestability, information asymmetry, and measurability, as defined below.

- Contestability exists when firms can enter the market freely, without any resistance from other firms, and exit without losing any of their investments. Low barriers to market entry and exit generally characterize contestable goods. In contrast, noncontestable goods have high barriers to entry such as sunk costs, monopoly market power, geographic advantages, and asset specificity. Generally, primary care—including the delivery of priority services related to effective treatment of communicable diseases and childhood illnesses—has high contestability. In contrast, the provision of sophisticated hospital services is less contestable, since entry and exit from the market can be cumbersome.

- Information asymmetry is the degree to which users, beneficiaries, or contracting agencies are unable to assess the quality of a good or service. Information asymmetry is a particularly difficult problem in the health sector, and is applicable to varying degrees for most health goods and services.

- Measurability is the precision with which inputs, processes, outputs, and outcomes of given goods and services can be measured. In general, the outputs and outcomes of health goods and services are hard to measure, although goods are usually more measurable than services.

Health goods and services can be categorized according to their combined levels of contestability and measurability (table 2.1).[5] This table plots a wide range of goods and services in the health sector.

Table 2.1 The Nature of Health Care Goods Based on Institutional Economics

	HIGH CONTESTABILITY	MEDIUM CONTESTABILITY	LOW CONTESTABILITY

High measurability	Type I
	• Retail of
	  • Drugs
	  • Medical supplies
	  • Other goods
		Type II
		• Wholesale
		  • Drugs
		  • Medical supplies
		  • Other goods
			Type III
			• Production
			  • Pharmaceuticals
			  • High technology

Medium measurability	Type IV • Routine diagnostics • Hospital support services	Type V • Management services • Training	Type VI • High-tech diagnostics • Research

Low measurability	Type VII
	• Ambulatory clinical care
	  • Medical
	  • Nursing
	  • Dental
		Type VIII
		• General hospitals
		• Public health services
		• Health insurance
			Type IX
			• Policymaking
			• Monitoring and evaluation

A number of goods and services, such as retail medical supplies and pharmaceuticals, are relatively contestable and measurable, enabling governments to purchase needed items. Not surprisingly, in the vast majority of countries these goods and services are sold by private vendors.

Opposite these easy-to-buy goods and services in our table we find a few health goods and services with both low measurability and low contestability, such as policymaking; and core tasks related to monitoring and evaluation. The inherent difficulty associated with buying such services justifies reliance on direct public provision, which (again) is widely observed in reality. Unfortunately, in the health sector most goods and services fall somewhere in between in terms of "buyability." Goods such as wholesale pharmaceuticals and medical equipment, and support services such as catering, cleaning, and facilities maintenance, are relatively straightforward to buy. Again, this buyability ranking is borne out by widespread private production and delivery. Even less buyable goods and services, such as pharmaceutical production and ambulatory care, are, as a rule, privately delivered, again with suitable contracts and regulation playing an important role. Without getting bogged down in discussions of the more contentious goods and services, it is clear that the majority is buyable, at least in certain contexts.[6] That is, most goods and services can be adequately produced and delivered through the private sector, provided that the public sector undertakes financing (where appropriate), undertakes essential regulatory functions, promotes dissemination of critical information, and creates enabling conditions for private sector participation, where appropriate. In performing these functions the public sector has to provide the leadership, but it can work with a range of governmental and nongovernmental organizations (NGOs) in fulfilling the various functions.

To summarize, the public and private sectors can and do play a range of roles in the organization, financing, and management of health services. The role of the public sector in the health system can be encapsulated in its overarching responsibility for stewardship of the sector. At a minimum, this responsibility entails financing a wide range of services for the vulnerable, and those critical goods and services that will not be readily financed through private means. It also entails creating a policy environment in which private providers and producers deliver needed goods and services, under the influence of the range of instruments at the government's disposal.

Conducting the Private Health Sector Assessment—Steps

A PHSA is designed to collect information on the role of the private health sector and the strengths and weaknesses of these markets (including the regulatory environment and the role of the public sector in fulfilling its stewardship function), and the general economic and policy environment for private sector development in the health sector. This information is necessary to identify instruments that will harness existing private providers and producers, and to develop policies that will support strategic growth of the private sector in health.

PHSA activities can be divided into three parts:

1. *Part 1:* The first task is to assemble enough general, easily available information to identify the most important health- (or health system–) related problems, in which the private sector plays, or could play, a role. The following are the areas in which information is needed: information on the organization, management, and financing of health services, including basic information on the private provision of health services; basic country information, with a focus on the economy and socioeconomic conditions; and information on the general environment for private sector activities.

2. *Part 2:* The second task is to identify the most pressing or promising public-private policy issues, as well as potential strategies to address them. This is accomplished through analysis of the information gathered and consultation with informed stakeholders. Potential strategies to be explored in more depth should be within the remit of the ministry of health or other primary counterpart, since it is desirable that the recommendations be "actionable."

3. *Part 3:* The third task is to undertake in-depth studies on one or more of these issues. The studies should have an operational focus, informing decisions regarding possible strategies to address problems or to take advantage of opportunities identified.

Examples of PHSAs include:

- An inquiry into the capacity of NGOs to meet a particular need, such as primary care, ambulatory care, acute care services, or the needs of a particular population

- A disease- or program-focused study to assess the private sector's ability to contribute to tuberculosis, sexually transmitted diseases (STDs), or human immune deficiency virus/acquired immune deficiency syndrome (HIV/AIDS) detection and treatment

- An investigation into the specific issues related to regulating the private sector and into the strengths and weaknesses of existing arrangements

- Determination of the potential and prerequisites for the private sector to contribute to expanding capacity in long-term care, to enable hospital rationalization

- An evaluation of successful public-private partnerships with the objective of expansion.

This chapter cannot provide detailed guidelines for all possible focused studies. Instead, the reference section lists a range of available materials that will support the development of necessary terms of reference (appendix 2.A).

The time needed for a PHSA will depend on the size of the country; the strength and size of the private sector providing health services; the amount of information available on the health system and private provision of health services; the scope of the study (described in box 2.1); and the resources available. For example, a PHSA in India was undertaken in the context of a larger World Bank study on public-private partnerships. The PHSA, consisting of desk reviews and primary data collection in two states of India, took approximately 12 months from start to finish (box 2.1). In contrast, a PHSA conducted in the West Bank and Gaza over 4 months included a focused study on government contracting with NGOs for the delivery of health services. However, unlike the PHSA in India, the West Bank and Gaza PHSA depended primarily on a literature review and key informant interviews.

Box 2.1 Private Health Sector Assessment Examples

India—Private Health Sector Assessment (Peters 1999). The objective of this PHSA was to determine how India could take advantage of the private sector to meet social goals. Specifically, the study sought to improve understanding of constraints, incentives, subsidies, and the ways current functioning of the private sector should influence policy formulation and project design; to identify possibilities for new partnerships in delivering and financing health services; to identify new approaches to regulation and quality assurance; and to promote new public accountabilities and benchmarking of standards for health services delivery. The studies contained an extensive literature review and primary data collection in one northern state (Uttar Pradesh) and one southern state (Andhra Pradesh).

Ecuador—National survey of private health facilities. This survey of 300 public and private health facilities in Quito and Guayaquil examined interaction between the public and private sectors and each sector's providers and clients. It looked at general characteristics of the providers and clients, physical structure, equipment, and stores of drugs and other medical supplies. In addition, financing, management, and operational aspects of each facility were explored. The samples of facilities were drawn from the four distinct domains: (a) large, complex, inpatient, public hospitals; (b) private hospitals and clinics providing inpatient services; (c) public, outpatient facilities (such as ministry of health; and municipal and social security health centers and dispensaries); and (d) small, private, outpatient facilities. A local Ecuadorean research firm, Centro de Estudios de Paternidad Responsible, was contracted to conduct fieldwork and data entry. The survey instrument was developed by the

Initiatives and adapted by the local researchers to capture issues specific to Ecuador. This survey can be accessed through http://www.jsi.com (go to "Initiatives Project").

Ghana—Private health care provision in the Greater Accra region. This study uses Ghana's Greater Accra region as a case study to explore the contribution of private health care providers to health care delivery in Ghana, and to recommend policy instruments for enhancing the role of private health care providers. The study methodology entails the use of primary and secondary data sources, including a series of questionnaires distributed to private practitioners, pharmacists, traditional health providers, and midwives. Key findings of the study include that all socioeconomic groups patronize private health care services and that clients' perception of services provided by the private practitioners was generally more favorable than their perception of services provided by public facilities. In light of these findings the study recommends policy development that supports and regulates the private sector and that responds to the different types of private health care in the region. This study, including survey instruments, can be accessed through http://www.phrproject.com (go to "Publications" and then to "Small Applied Research").

PHSA Part 1: Collecting and Organizing Information

The purpose of Part 1 of the PHSA is to collect and organize information on the following:

• Basic macroeconomic and social indicators, such as gross domestic product (GDP) per capita, population growth rates, dependency ratio, urban-rural ratio, and percentage of the population living in poverty

• The organization, financing, and management of the health sector, critical problems, and health sector goals, including policies and plans in the medium and long terms

• The general environment for private sector activity in the country, irrespective of the particular sector within the private sector

• Private sector participation in health, focusing on the demand and supply and price characteristics of private health care markets (structure), and the way these characteristics interact to produce specific behavioral responses (function).

The following steps are necessary to complete Part 1 of a PHSA.

• Collect information on the country, the health system, and private sector participation (general and health).

• Identify gaps in the available data on private provision of health services and undertake primary data collection (qualitative and quantitative).

• Analyze the information and identify key points about the role of the private sector in the provision of health services, and the main strengths, weaknesses, and opportunities for supporting an effective public-private mix in achieving health sector goals.

• Develop a policy note describing the main points about public-private mix.

Background Information

The background information needed includes:

• Basic country information such as GDP per capita, population growth, urban population (percent of total), urban population growth, and percent of population below the poverty line

- Data on major causes of morbidity and mortality in the country (burden of disease information)

- Health financing system data, including total health expenditures (public and private), the purposes for which public and private funds are used, the type of financing system, the existence or nonexistence of public and private insurance systems, use of funds for specific types of services (hospital, ambulatory drugs, or vertical programs), and the extent of out-of-pocket payments,[7] risk pooling, and purchasing arrangements

- Information on the service delivery system, including the number and configuration of public and private hospitals, primary health care centers, physicians (including specialists), nurses, pharmacies, diagnostic clinics, and laboratories

- Information on any critical problems facing the health sector in terms of health outcomes, and demand and supply of health services and the factors influencing these patterns

- Description of government policies, plans, and priorities for the medium and long term.

General socioeconomic and health sector information can usually be obtained from any of the following sources:

- Ministry of health documents, especially five-year plans.

- Donor and multilateral reports, particularly sector reviews such as those conducted by the World Bank, or health system reports undertaken by the World Health Organization (WHO) and public expenditure reviews conducted by the World Bank (http://www1.worldbank.org/publicsector/pe/p1pers.htm), including benefit-incidence studies, poverty assessments, and health care demand studies.

- International databases, which provide comparative information on the economy, health, sector outcomes, financing, and delivery system.

- World Bank's Statistical Information Management Analysis system: http://sima.worldbank.org/ (internal Web site); and http://www.worldbank.org/data/ (external Web site).

- World Development Indicators: http://www.worldbank.org/data/wdi/home.html.

- WHO databases: http://www.who.int/whosis/; regional offices of the WHO, such as the Pan-American Health Organization, http://www.paho.org/, and the Regional Office for Europe, http://www.who.dk/, often have useful data and country studies with qualitative information about the private health sector.

- World Bank Health, Nutrition, and Population statistics, http://ddg-as4/hnpstats/.

- The U.S. Agency for International Development (USAID)–funded Partnerships for Health Reform maintains a database with a number of useful publications reviewing the status of the private health sector in specific developing countries. This database can be searched at http://www.dcdata.com/abt/abt.htm. Materials can be downloaded or requested, free of charge.

Though there are currently no standardized instruments in use in developing countries that are structured specifically to render information on private delivery of health services, the following surveys and databases do provide some useful information.

- Measure DHS + is a USAID-funded organization that supports Demographic and Health Surveys (DHSs). DHS is a household survey with an optional service provision module that renders useful information on the service delivery arrangements. This optional module has been implemented in more than 35 countries. Information can be found at http://www.measuredhs.com.

- The Living Standards Measurement Survey (LSMS) is a household survey supported by the World Bank's Research Department that renders some useful data regarding private delivery and uti-

lization of services. The World Bank's Web site, http://www.
worldbank.org/lsms/, is externally accessible and provides access
to all the survey data obtained to date, as well as links to research
papers based on the data.

• Service Delivery Surveys, the World Bank's Research Department, has recently launched an initiative to support development
and widespread utilization of Quantitative Service Delivery Surveys. These surveys will provide a good source of information on
private providers. As this information comes in it will be posted at
http://www.worldbank.org/research/projects/publicspending/
tools/.

In most countries basic economic and social indicators and information on health financing and delivery will be available from various government ministries. These documents and any sector assessments conducted by the World Bank, WHO, or other international
organizations, supplemented with data from international databases,
should be enough to provide the basic information on the health system. If a health sector review has not been undertaken the necessary
information will have to be gathered to produce a health sector note
that broadly sketches the health system. Without this contextual information it is not possible to conduct the necessary analysis to develop policies to support enhanced contributions from the private
sector-to-policy objectives.

Private Sector Environment

The general environment for private sector development can provide valuable information for evaluating the potential for enhanced
public-private interaction in health. A sound business climate for
private sector development would mean that, if the government implemented health sector policies to enhance the contribution of certain private subsector activities, the private sector would be able to
respond. Alternatively, the presence of serious constraints in the
macroeconomic and business environment, such as exchange rate

and tax policy problems, will render the private sector less responsive to government efforts to harness or grow the private sector toward health objectives. Health policymakers must therefore be aware of such constraints and their potential to undermine their own efforts. In this regard, information on the role of the private sector in the economy (Stone 1999), and on constraints to private sector growth and competitiveness, can be useful.

The private sector's role in the economy may be synthetically characterized by:

- The scope of government activity, as measured by government expenditures as a proportion of GDP
- The extent of public ownership of economic assets
- The extent of private participation in infrastructure and public services.

Constraints to private sector growth and competitiveness can be characterized by:

- The effectiveness of the functioning of the judicial and legal system as measured by backlogs and delays
- The security of private property provided by the legal framework, and norms
- Corruption
- The financial system's level of development
- The existence and effectiveness of competition regulation
- The extent of the country's integration with the global economy, trade barriers
- Tax rates.

Information on these topics can be obtained from:

- Private sector assessments completed either by the government or by donors. For example, the World Bank has completed private sector assessments in 39 countries that present an analysis of the general environment for private sector activity. Policy briefs on the private sector assessments conducted by the World Bank can be obtained through http://www.worldbank.org/html/extdr/topic-psd.htm.[8]

- General economic development reports completed by the government or donors (such as World Bank Economic and Sector Work, government five-year plans)

- Surveys conducted by business groups within the country or international business groups, for example, the Global Business Environment Surveys, http://www1.worldbank.org/beext/resources/assess-wbessurvey.htm, or the World Economic Forum's *Global Competitiveness Report* and the *World Competitiveness Yearbook* published by the International Institute for Management Development (World Bank 2000b).

- The World Bank maintains an annotated list, with hyperlinks, of all country surveys of business environment, and general government effectiveness related to institutional quality. This can be found at: http://www1.worldbank.org/publicsector/indicators.htm.

Nonprofit organizations—a special case. Nonprofit organizations play an important role in delivering health services in many countries, and the preconditions for supporting their participation are slightly different from those for the for-profit sectors. For example, the legal and regulatory environment must be conducive to nonprofits' formation and sustainable operation.[9] Therefore, in addition to the general business environment, information on legal and regulatory issues specific to nonprofits is useful. This kind of information concerns (Simon 1995):

- Laws and regulations that allow the formation of nonprofit organizations, societies (both religious and lay), and foundations

- Financial incentives to nonprofits (for example, tax breaks for participating in activities that are beneficial to society (providing so-

cial services for underserved groups); and the right to receive donations, especially from foreign sources)

• Transparent and uncomplicated procedures for obtaining licenses
to establish nonprofits and reporting requirements.

The International Center for Non-Profit Law has developed a
database of assessments of the environment for nonprofits in a large
number of developing countries. This database can be searched at:
http://www.icnl.org/databasesearch.asp.

Professional associations, consumers, or patient's rights groups are
also likely to be organized as nonprofits. The review must collect information on these entities as well, since they can contribute substan-
tially to the assessment, as well as to subsequent policy actions. Their
participation is also likely to be central to implementing some policies
arising from the assessment. The International Alliance of Patients'
Organizations maintains a database of patients' groups throughout
the world, which can be a useful starting point for identifying local
organizations: http://iapo.surfnet-is.com/cgi-bin/directory.cgi.

Obtaining Information on the Role of the Private Sector and Health

The activities outlined above focus on obtaining broad information
on the country's health sector and the general environment for private sector, including nonprofit, participation. The search for general health sector information will undoubtedly render some information pertaining to the private sector. This section outlines the
collection and organization of information on the private sector's
role in health, and the factors that are responsible for demand and
supply of private health care services. For example:

• Private expenditures as a percentage of total health expenditures

• Private expenditures on hospital care, outpatient visits, and drugs

• The number of private hospitals, physicians, and retail pharmacies

• Utilization of private services

This information provides important insights into the demand and supply of private sector health services. In many countries there is a positive correlation between private expenditures on health and the extent of private sector participation. Good examples are India and Lebanon; in both of these countries private expenditures make up about 70 percent of total health expenditures, and the private sector provides most health services. The information obtained through the health sector review will be at the aggregate level, however, and will need to be complemented with additional information. The purpose of collecting this information would be to obtain answers to the following questions:

- Is private sector participation in health prevalent across socioeconomic groups, or is it restricted to higher income groups? Where are the focal points of demand for, and utilization of, private health care services?

- In which activities is the private sector involved (for example, are they hospital-based services; ambulatory care; diagnostic centers and laboratories; retail pharmacies; or ancillary services)?

- Who are the private providers? Are they in the formal or informal sector? Do they practice in both the public and private sectors? What is known about the ownership of private facilities (are they for-profit, not-for-profit, foundations, or associations)?

- What is known about the technical quality of care among private health providers? Is there any information on perceived quality and client satisfaction?

- Do parallel public and private providers deliver a similar package of health services? Do public and private providers compete?

- Do the existing public financing mechanisms support private sector participation?

- How and to what extent does the public sector fulfill its stewardship function? In which areas of the health system does it fulfill that function (for instance, in financing, service delivery, resource mix, or in overall coordination)?

Since the goal of Part 1 of a PHSA is to draw upon available information, this section should depend largely on the following sources of information:

- A literature review

- Household surveys (for example, DHS or LSMS)

- Facility surveys

- National health accounts (NHAs)

Household surveys. Analysis of data from household surveys, especially when disaggregated according to income quintiles, can provide important clues about various socioeconomic groups' private expenditures on health care and their use of the private sector. Obtaining information on current utilization and expenditure patterns can be an important breakthrough in addressing private sector participation in health. In addition, data from household surveys can be used to conduct regression analysis for understanding why people seek health care in the private sector. Many countries regularly undertake household expenditure surveys, which include health as one of the determinants. Several countries also undertake health care utilization and expenditure surveys. These are an excellent source of information on demand for health care (in addition, the LSMS has been conducted for more than 30 countries (http://www.worldbank.org/lsms). Information from household surveys for most countries can be accessed at the following Web site: http://www.worldbank.org/poverty/data/povmon.htm).

DHSs are available for 66 countries and contain information on utilization of reproductive and child health services. Most of these data sets are in the public domain and can be downloaded through http://www.measuredhs.com. The World Bank has used DHS data to obtain information on maternal and child health indicators by asset quintile (proxy for socioeconomic status). Although these data do not demonstrate the extent of use of the private sector, they do have information on percentage of population seeking care for common childhood illnesses such as acute respiratory illnesses (ARI) and diarrhea and the percentage seen in a public facility. This provides some clues regarding use of the private sector among specific income quintiles. These data can be accessed through: http://www. worldbank.org/poverty/health/index.htm.

Another study has analyzed DHS data from 11 developing countries to understand health-seeking behavior for maternal and child health services in the public and private sectors (Berman and Rose 1994). It can be accessed at the following web address: http://www. hsph.harvard.edu/ihsg/publications/pdf/No-18.PDF.

Health facility surveys. Health facility surveys that include the public and private sectors are becoming more common. These surveys—which capture information on the types of providers, services, quality of care, and information on clients—could provide important information on the private sector. For example, the DHSs increasingly include Service Provision Assessments (SPAs), which survey the types of reproductive and child-health facilities available in the country. Though restricted to certain aspects of health care, these surveys can be an important complement to other available information on private providers. The SPAs can be accessed through the same Web site as for the DHS (http://measuredhs.com).

National health accounts. Typically, NHAs disaggregate health expenditures by type of service. For example, a country's NHAs can reveal where most public and private funds go. A recently completed NHA in a middle-income country found that most public funds pay for private hospital services and private expenditures, which are mostly out-of-pocket, for drugs and ambulatory care visits. Tracking where the money goes is an excellent way to determine the extent of private sector participation in a country. In addition, NHAs typically include a description of public and private providers. NHAs are now available for many countries in Africa, Asia, the Middle East and North Africa, and Latin America and the Caribbean. Information about NHAs can be accessed through http://www:who.org and http://www. phrproject.com.

If a country has developed NHAs, useful information on demand for health services and health expenditures (public and private) can be obtained. Through a collaborative effort, a "Global NHA Database" is under development, containing NHA time-series data for 1972–98 for 193 countries.

At this point in the PHSA the information gathered from the literature review and analysis of existing data should be reviewed to see what is disclosed about private delivery of health services and to determine the scope of primary data collection that will be necessary during Part 2 of the PHSA. As mentioned earlier, most countries do not have comprehensive data on the private sector, and in most cases, the PHSA will require collection of information from primary sources.

Tools and Techniques for Primary Data Collection

In most countries primary data collection on the private sector and public-private mix issues will be needed to supplement the information obtained from the literature review and secondary data analysis. Depending on the resources available data collection can be primarily qualitative or a combination of quantitative and qualitative. In addition, it is useful to identify the areas in which additional information must be collected. Areas might be, for example:

• The particular sector—hospitals; ambulatory care including preventive and primary health care services; diagnostic facilities and laboratories; and retail pharmacies

• The topics on which to focus—the private sector's demand and supply characteristics; the factors responsible for the particular demand and supply characteristics; and the behavior of private providers and the factors underlying these behavioral responses

• The area or areas to be covered in the survey—urban, rural, or both.

Various qualitative and quantitative techniques can be used to collect primary data on private providers. Generally, quantitative techniques are better suited for rigorous analysis but require more time and resources. Qualitative techniques, especially rapid assessment techniques, can be used to get a quick overview of critical issues in private provision but may not allow much flexibility for analysis. The most complete approach is to use a combination of quantitative and qualitative techniques, such as household and provider surveys (quantitative) and key informant and focus group interviews (qualitative). Often, the development of quantitative surveys will require the use of qualitative methods to fully identify the issues that should be included (triangulation).

Qualitative methods. Interviews and focus group discussions with providers. Private providers are an important source of data on private providers. This section provides a step-by-step approach for using qualitative techniques, such as interviews and focus group discussions, to obtain information from private providers. A qualitative private provider survey can be used to obtain information on:

- Characteristics of private providers, including their background, qualifications, type of services offered, schedule of fees, organizational characteristics, payment methods, types of patients seen, hours of work, and organization of services, including for-profit and not-for-profit services

- Key problems in private provision (poor quality of care, supplier-induced demand, cost escalation, or monopoly)

- Key constraints experienced by providers in the delivery of health services (competition with the public sector; lack of access to capital, skilled workers, and technology; high cost of providing health services, such as in rural areas)

- Environment, including the political economy environment, for private provision of health services; insights into the changes that are needed to make the environment conducive to private sector participation.

Key informant interviews with private providers—methodology and design. The scope of primary data collection will be a critical factor in deciding which type of private providers or facilities to interview and visit and where the provider survey will be carried out.

Deciding whom to interview. Qualitative techniques typically do not use formal sampling. However, it is important to make sure that no single group of providers or type of facility is over- or underrepresented in the data collection. For example, if there were a mix of large, medium, and small hospitals in a locality, if the survey were to include only large hospitals it would bias the survey. In determining the types and numbers of facilities to sample, it would be useful to include some information about the private providers' characteristics in the survey—at least enough information to ensure representation of the various types. For example, if large private hospitals provide a similar range of services, it is not necessary to oversample from that group. However, if size, type of facility, and services offered among small hospitals are quite dissimilar this group should be oversampled.

In terms of formulating the list of providers to be interviewed, the best place to start is with provider associations (such as hospitals, physicians, nurses, or pharmacists). Provider associations can be an important source of information regarding the configuration (for example, the types of practices) of their members, and can provide easy access to a vast network of providers. Since private providers, who are generally pressed for time, are often reluctant to participate in interviews and are suspicious about the way the information will be used, approaching them through these associations can greatly enhance access to them. If there are no private provider associations (which is unlikely in any country with an active private sector), the next-best sources are ministries of commerce or business development, who are responsible for licensing health facilities. It is best to develop a list based on facility or provider type (for example, commercial orientation, organizational form, or type of service, if available) and then select a few from each category. No fixed numbers of interviews need be completed. However, sampling at least 30 will allow some quantitative analysis, such as cross-tabulations.

In many developing countries, although the informal sector generally makes up a large part of the economy, especially in remote rural areas, information on this group is usually sparse. Studies in several countries, however, have shown that the poor are more likely to use informal sector providers (Chakraborty, D'Souza, and Northrup 2000). Since an important policy goal in many countries is improving the poor's access to quality health services, collecting data on informal sector health care providers is important. Box 2.2 describes techniques that have been used to identify and obtain information from informal sector providers who serve the poor.

Developing a questionnaire. Examples of the types of questions that can be used to obtain information are included in appendix 2.B. The sample questionnaire was developed for ambulatory care facilities. This sample questionnaire should be adapted by whoever conducts the provider surveys to fit the country context and the types of facilities to be covered. In addition, since qualitative interviews are essentially unstructured, the interviewers should merely use these questions as a guide, to increase the likelihood of discovering some unanticipated comments or insights.

Training the interviewers. The effectiveness of qualitative interviews is enhanced if the interviewer is well informed about the topics to be covered and can probe as needed. This means that the interviewer must have some health sector expertise, be fully acquainted with the questionnaire, understand the rationale for asking certain questions, and take different approaches to get answers to the questions. To ensure that all the interviewers are on the same wavelength, an orientation session is useful. Orientation may be necessary even if a market research firm is hired to conduct the survey, because it might not have previous experience conducting provider surveys.

Conducting the interviews. Once the names of providers or facilities included in the survey are available, the questionnaires have been pretested, and the orientation session is finished, the interviewers are ready to conduct the survey. Interviewers need to remember some simple tips during the survey.

- They must fully document the conversation with the provider as soon as the interview is over and complete as much of the ques-

Box 2.2 Obtaining Information on Informal Sector Private Providers

Informal private providers such as drug vendors in Africa and unqualified medical practitioners in South Asia are important sources of health care for poor households in developing countries. It is often difficult to obtain information from these providers, especially in Africa where they are frequently itinerant. Several studies have used innovative techniques to reach these informal providers.

Drug vendors in Africa. A study in Abidjan (Côte d'Ivoire) interviewed 60 female drug vendors who sold drugs for the treatment of STDs. The study obtained basic information on the characteristics of the drug vendors, the magnitude and types of drugs sold, the type of clients, and the quality of care. Another study used a simulated client technique, where trained interviewers pretend to be clients, to interview drug vendors in rural Eritrea (http://www.basics.org) (go to "Publications—General Child Survival"). As in the case of the Côte d'Ivoire study, this second study obtained information on the characteristics of drug vendors, the types of drugs normally prescribed for common childhood illnesses (such as diarrhea and ARI) and the drug vendors' knowledge and training to dispense medications for these diseases.

Unqualified medical practitioners in South Asia. In South Asia, particularly in Bangladesh, India, and Pakistan, unqualified private providers in urban and rural areas are the most important source of health care for poor households. At least six separate studies in India have documented that these providers treat 95 percent of all major diseases among the poor, including childhood diarrhea, childhood ARI, tuberculosis, malaria, and STDs. Several of the studies have used interviews with randomly selected mothers in the study areas to identify the providers and seek them out for interviews. These studies have collected detailed information about the characteristics, magnitude, and types of services; demand and supply issues; and quality of care among these providers.

tionnaire as possible as soon as possible. At the beginning of the interview, the interviewer must ask the provider for his or her permission to take notes or not. If the provider does not mind, the interviewer should take notes.

- They should share information with other interviewers to determine if the interviews are going as planned and if there are some experiences that each can draw upon to improve the interviews.

Analyzing the results. Since the sample size for these provider surveys is small, not much quantitative analysis will be possible. However, if at least 30 general practitioners are interviewed, it will be possible to do some tabulations (number and percentages, and cross-tabulations) regarding their characteristics. Information on structural inputs such as training, availability of basic medical equipment, and cleanliness can also be used to reach some judgments about quality of care. However, most of the analysis will be qualitative. To reiterate, the purpose of the analysis is to determine what the survey reveals about:

- Characteristics of private providers, including type and magnitude of health services provided, and the providers' incentives and motivations
- The key factors affecting supply of private services
- The key problems with the technical quality of services
- The environment for private provision of health services, including insights into changes needed to make the environment conducive to private sector participation.

This information has to be integrated into the information obtained from the literature review and secondary data analysis. For example, if there were large gaps in the section on provider characteristics, these gaps should now be filled with information obtained in the survey.

Focus group discussions with private providers. Focus group discussions are a cost-effective qualitative technique for obtaining information; the technique has its own set of strengths and weaknesses. Cost-effectiveness is one strength, as mentioned. If the group consists of outgoing persons who enjoy discussion and debate, focus groups can contribute to a rich understanding of selected topics. The weakness of focus groups is that some participants may be shy and unwilling to speak in front of others. In this situation one or two individuals sometimes dominate the discussion, thereby biasing the information. This happens most often when the group consists of both men and women, in which case women tend to speak less. Conducting a focus group discussion, unlike conducting an in-depth interview in a hospital or a doctor's clinic, does not allow the collection of information on the environment in which the provider conducts his or her business. However, this methodology is well suited for gathering information on the business environment and private providers' supply constraints.

Conducting focus group discussions. Focus group discussions require trained facilitators who can use a list of questions to guide the discussion and keep the discussion on track. Too large a group can reduce a focus group's effectiveness. It is best to limit the number of participants to no more than 10 at a time. Typically, participants should be a homogenous group. For example, mixing government officials and private providers in the same group would be ineffective, because then discussion can easily turn into a dialog of the deaf, with a limited disclosure of information.

Interviews and focus group discussions with government officials. Interviews and discussions with key public sector officials will be an important complement to the information obtained from private providers (see appendix 2.C). Changes are needed in government policies and programs directed toward the private sector in order to truly harness the private sector to advance health services. Private providers will be an important source of information on government policies that inhibit private sector delivery of health services. In addition, private providers will be able to provide information on government programs that regulate and contract with the private sector, since many providers may already participate in these programs. However, public sector officials will provide additional information on topics related to public-private interactions, use of government instruments, and opportunities for and constraints on involving the private sector. It is also important to remember that the lack of information and resultant misguided perceptions are often as important a barrier to private sector participation as tangible policy barriers, and that public sector officials are often suspicious of the private sector. Finally, supporting private sector development often implies to the government a reduction in its power and functions if it has been the main provider of health services. All these factors strongly reinforce the need to interview public sector officials.

Deciding which public officials to interview. Ministry of health employees will be an important group to identifying which officials to interview—in particular, this group comprises employees who are in charge of government programs such as contracting, registration, licensing, and supervision of private providers and health facilities, quality-of-care regulation, and other functions related to private sector programs. This group will help provide additional information about the programs and identify possible constraints on improving and expanding the programs. The director of health services should also be interviewed, as should other individuals who are responsible for delivering public sector services (such as primary care or hospital care services). These officials are critical for understanding how public and private facilities compete or interact in the health system and how interactions between the public and private sectors could be enhanced.

Questionnaires. Detailed information will have to be collected in order to understand government contracting arrangements, regulatory structures, and standards.

Interviews and focus group discussions with consumers. Speaking with consumers can provide important perspectives on factors influencing demand for private and public providers, consumer perceptions of the strengths and weaknesses of the private sector, the role of the government in health care, and consumer responsiveness to an enhanced role for the private sector in health.

Deciding whom to interview. The easiest and most cost-effective way of determining whom to interview is to target consumers connected in some way to the facilities or providers included in the survey. For example, interviews could be conducted with patients waiting to be seen or those who have just completed treatment (exit interviews). The only problem with exit interviews is that the consumers may be reluctant to say anything negative about the encounter just completed. Therefore, it is important to keep the questions general and to focus on the public and private sectors and their role in health care delivery. Alternatively, a neighborhood group discussion on a particular day could be announced through the providers or facilities, and a focus group discussion could be conducted with the people who attend.

Consumer questionnaire. The following types of topics and questions should be included in discussion with consumers:

- Health-seeking behavior for various family members, particularly the interactions between the public and private sectors, and consumer perceptions about the public and private sector, especially with regard to quality of care and satisfaction

- Consumer perceptions regarding the constraints on using the public and private sectors, and "activities where the private sector could make a greater contribution" options on an enhanced role for the private sector in health care delivery.

Consumers in many developing countries use a combination of public and private facilities during a single illness. For example, in countries where out-of-pocket spending is the main form of private expenditures, consumers, especially the poor, use private ambulatory care but seek hospital care from the public sector, since hospital care is expensive. Understanding the interactions between the public and private sectors from the demand side is useful in developing private sector policies and addressing important issues such as continuity of care; these issues influence the efficiency and quality of health care delivery.

Quantitative methods. In order to understand private markets for health goods and services information on both the demand and supply side is required. Household surveys that focus on health, or that include a detailed section on health, are typically the main source of quantitative information on the demand side.[10] The use of quantitative techniques for obtaining information on the supply side (private providers) is limited in most developing countries, and the key features of quantitative provider surveys are worth highlighting.

Increasingly, provider surveys are being recommended as a part of a basic package of data collection for decisionmaking in developing countries. For example, provider surveys have been carried out in several countries, including the Arab Republic of Egypt and Poland (box 2.3) under a USAID-financed health project focusing on improving the analytical base for health sector reform. Similar provider surveys focusing on the private sector were carried out under the World Bank–supported PHSA in India (Peters 1999). Structured interviews with a randomly selected sample of private providers are a major part of these surveys. Sample sizes for these types of surveys vary.

Developing a questionnaire for a structured survey. An example of a structured provider survey questionnaire is included in appendix 2.B. These questionnaires should be pretested and adapted, as needed, to fit the country context.

Analyzing data from a structured survey. A larger sample size provides greater opportunities for data analysis. At a basic level, providers' characteristics will have to be tabulated. Next, providers could be classified according to the type of services offered and any available data on structural inputs. Information on providers' knowledge and process of care for specific diseases could also be collected. The information obtained can be tabulated to enable comparisons across different groups of providers.

Box 2.3 Poland: A Provider Survey

A provider survey was conducted in Krakow, Poland. It is one of the sources of data used for a provider market analysis (PMA), a tool developed by the Data for Decision Making Project for understanding the organization of health care delivery. Additional sources of data for a PMA include household surveys and other sources of secondary data.

In the Krakow analysis provider surveys were the main source of information for the private sector. The study focused on ambulatory care. The study included 154 private health care facilities, 160 private pharmacies, and about 100 dental practices. The surveys were designed to collect information on supply-related topics such as hours of work, number and specialization of medical personnel employed, number of patients examined, types of services provided, schedules of fees, statement of costs, and type of contracts with various financing agents.

The provider survey was combined with data from public health facilities to develop a typology of public and private providers such as the number of providers and the volume of services provided, the content of the services provided (type of human resources, scope of ambulatory services, and patient perceptions of quality), the governance of health facilities (public, quasi-public, private, for-profit, or not-for-profit), providers' motivations and incentives to maximize the supply of health services and deliver high-quality health services to their clients, and the principal types of payment methods. Based on this information, the study identified the implications for changes in the financing and organization of health services in Poland.

Source: Chawla and others 1999.

Analyzing the data. The purpose of collecting information on the health sector (public and private) and on the general business environment is to understand the structure and function of existing health markets. The objective is to determine the types of policy interventions needed to improve their functioning, especially as regards the interface between the public and private sectors. Where private markets are dysfunctional the analysis should focus on identifying the source of these problems and possible government policies to alleviate them. This requires using the available information in the context of the conceptual framework described earlier. This section of the chapter will help people who conduct the assessment to use the conceptual framework in order to identify appropriate policy interventions and to develop a policy note on public-private mix. Some of the core topics that should be included in the policy note are: (a) structure and functions of the private health care markets; (b) problems in private delivery of health care; (c) constraints on private participation; and (d) absence of private health care markets.

Private Health Care Markets

The structure and functions of the private health care markets. This section describes the main demand and supply characteristics of the private health care market.

The following information should be included under demand characteristics: What is the extent of consumer demand for private health care goods and services, among which groups, and for which products and services? How much do consumers pay for particular health goods and services? In what form are these payments made?

The following information should be included under supply characteristics: the organizational typology for providers (such as solo practice, dispensary, hospital-based, or group practice); the type of therapeutic system; whether the providers are in the formal or informal sector; the volume and types of services provided; the types of clients; and provider characteristics such as age, gender, background, and training (box 2.4). It is also useful to map the participation of the private sector in various areas of the health system, using the conceptual or analytical framework.

Box 2.4 Constructing a Typology of Private Providers

Private providers in most countries are extremely diverse; in order to identify the private sector, its contributions to the health sector, and possible public actions for improving private participation in health, it is important to classify the private providers. One useful way to organize them is according to the following criteria: organizational form, commercial orientation, and therapeutic system. Using these criteria, private providers can be classified on a continuum of high to low complexity.

1. *Organizational form.* Organizational form refers to characteristics such as formal and informal sector; the types, levels, and diversity of health services provided (such as ambulatory, inpatient care, preventive or promotive, general medical, or specialized medical care); type of ancillary services provided; and whether at a fixed or mobile location.
2. *Commercial orientation.* The for-profit and not-for-profit nature of health provision is a key distinction influencing provider motivations and incentives. Organizations such as nongovernmental organizations (NGOs) will typically fall under the rubric of nonprofit.
3. *Therapeutic system.* This characteristic helps classify providers according to different medical paradigms. Since many providers of alternative medical paradigms treat diseases that are important to public health, it is useful to link the types of services provided to the types of medicine practiced, in order to identify appropriate interventions. In addition, providers who practice alternative medicine often combine their practice with modern medicine (such as giving injections).

Source: Adapted from Hanson and Berman 1994.

The objective in this section is to understand how a market is be-having and to relate this behavior to its structural characteristics. For example, does the market operate in an acceptable manner, or are there significant problems or missed opportunities, and, if so, where? Are any of these problems related or susceptible to government poli-cies, such as lack of regulation or enforcement, poorly targeted fund-ing, or information provision?

Improving the functioning of markets for health goods and services. Many developing countries already have a large private sector in health, but limited stewardship. While providing access to much-needed goods and services, under these conditions the private sector is prob-ably not contributing much to other sector objectives, such as equity, efficiency, and quality. This section briefly describes the key weak-nesses of private sector delivery of health care goods and services and demonstrates ways of using available information to identify prob-lems, their determinants, and opportunities. These weaknesses re-late to cost escalation, quality of care, poor allocative and technical efficiency, and the types of services provided by the private sector.

Cost escalation. Rapid cost escalation is often a problem in health systems where there is wide-scale private delivery of health services and few mechanisms for modifying consumer and provider incen-tives and motivations to consume or provide costly and often un-necessary care. The type of provider payment systems used play a key role in controlling or exacerbating the cost of health services. For example, under third-party fee-for-service systems, costs esca-late rapidly because consumers and providers have no incentive to control costs. Under such a plan, the price the patient pays at the point of service is considerably lowered, creating incentives for pa-tients to seek unnecessary care. Providers, under such a system, also have incentives to deliver excessive and unnecessary care, contribut-ing to problems such as supplier-induced demand. The tendency among private providers to increase prices, which in turn contributes to cost escalation, may also be related to other types of problems such as the lack of laws supporting competition. In these situations, private providers may collude to raise the prices of health goods and services to the detriment of consumers. Rapid cost escalation and excessive utilization of health services are, in the long run, detrimental to overall health system performance, leading to problems of inefficiency, poor quality, and unsustainability.

Quality of care. The private sector is usually highly responsive to clients and creates an environment that generates highly satisfied consumers. Since the nature of health services is complex and highly technical, however, consumers cannot easily evaluate the technical quality of care. This can lead to a situation where private providers can skimp on certain aspects of quality, depending on their motivations and incentives. Policy actions to address quality problems are quite challenging, because they require information on structure, process, and outcomes of care. Health care quality can be assessed from the following perspectives.

- Structure refers to the key ingredients or inputs that providers must have in order to deliver high-quality care. Good examples include appropriate training, support staff such as nurses, and correct diagnostic tools. This is the most common mechanism to address quality concerns in developing countries.

- Measuring the process of care can be complex and requires evaluating provider performance against accepted standards of care. While evaluating the quality of health care processes is challenging, some useful analyses have been performed in Bangladesh, India, Indonesia, Pakistan, and Tanzania.

- Finally, outcomes are even more difficult to measure since the data needs are high in order to allow corrections for other factors that may influence health outcomes. Mechanisms to assess the impact on health of health care provision are fairly rare in developing countries.

Poor allocative and technical efficiency. A third possible problem that is commonly experienced in private provision of health services is the excessive use of health services that may not be valuable or cost-effective in terms of their health impact. This problem is also related to cost escalation and quality of care. An information gap between providers and consumers is partly responsible for this problem. For example, patients often equate good treatment with the number of medications and, in some cases, injections prescribed. They might even decide to choose one provider over another because of a reputation of a "quick cure." This puts pressure on providers to compete with each other by providing health services that are not necessarily beneficial, with subsequent implications for allocative efficiency. In addition, since preventive health services are not very popular among patients, responsive providers may underprovide cost-effective preventive health care.

Types of services provided by the private sector. The private sector is interested mainly in health services that are in high demand by consumers who are willing to pay for them. This often means that the private sector is not motivated to provide sufficient levels of preventive health services for which consumer demand is low. The private sector also may not adequately serve poor or rural people, since their willingness or ability to pay may be low, and the cost of providing quality health services in rural areas is high. Experience in several Asian, African, and Latin American countries has shown that, in these situations, distorted markets emerge, often consisting of unqualified providers. This has implications for the health and well being of poor populations in urban as well as rural areas.

Analyzing Problems with Private Sector Delivery of Health Care Goods and Services

As noted above, the key weaknesses of private sector delivery of health care goods and services include cost escalation, quality of care, poor allocative and technical efficiency, and the types of services provided by the private sector. Identifying the presence and prevalence of such problems in developing countries is often challenging.

Cost escalation. To see whether cost escalation is a problem in the health sector, time series data are needed that would cover public and private health expenditure data (as a percentage of GDP, or per capita health expenditure). This information will have to be combined with other information, such as an increase in the use of medical technology and expensive surgical procedures. All this information then must be analyzed within the country's demographic and epidemiological context.

Quality of care. The literature review and interviews with providers, key officials in the public sector, and consumers will provide information on quality of care. The PHSA team's job is to highlight the nature of the quality-of-care problem with private providers. Evaluation of the satisfactory or deficient care quality requires standards or benchmarks. The following should be taken into consideration when drawing any conclusions about quality of care:

• Do private physicians, nurses, pharmacists, and other medical personnel have the appropriate educational qualifications? National qualification requirements for each category of medical personnel could be used as a benchmark. General (global) standards can be used in the absence of national requirements (if these general standards are used this should be noted).

• Are medical personnel licensed to practice the type of medicine that they are practicing? As in the case of educational qualifications, national standards could be used as benchmarks. It is important to note whether there is an absence of national licensing standards. In analyzing the information, any examples of dual roles among medical personnel should also be noted. For example, do pharmacists give injections? Do nurses prescribe medicines? Do general physicians conduct minor surgery?

• Is there any information about other structural inputs regarding provision of health care? For example, do hospitals have the appropriate medical equipment for the types of services they provide? Do general practitioners have basic medical equipment (for example, a stethoscope and a blood pressure machine)?

- Obtaining information on process and outcome dimensions of quality of care is difficult and time-consuming. Therefore, the PHSA may well have to depend on structural dimensions to infer quality of care. In several countries, however, information is available on private providers' performance on disease management (process). For example, studies focusing on specific groups of providers have been conducted in many countries, using WHO guidelines for treating infectious diseases. A complete list of these studies is included in appendix 2.A. If the literature review yields any information, this should be included in the analysis.

- Finally, public and private providers' ratings on various measures of care quality can usefully be compared.

Equity. The equity dimensions address any evidence of adverse selection or access, or lack of services for certain groups in society (such as the poor, the elderly, or women). Equity should be analyzed from the broader perspective of the health sector as well as in relation to particular issues connected with private sector provision. The following areas should be explored:

- Who are the private sector's patients? If the private sector serves mainly the upper- and middle-income groups, the links between groups served and payment mechanisms should be analyzed. For example, upper- to middle-income groups may have private health insurance, social insurance, or an employer-based program. If the private sector does not provide services to the poor, why is that the case?

- Where are services delivered? If private services are concentrated in urban areas the reasons for that should be evaluated. For example, the most common reason for the private sector's concentration in urban areas is easy access to markets, including the market for inputs. This translates into lower cost of setting up a practice, higher demand for medical care (since education and income levels are higher in urban areas, and those are indicators for

health-seeking behaviors), access to medical insurance among patients, and access to capital. What would it take to encourage the
private sector to provide services in rural areas?

- What types of services does the private sector deliver? For example, the private sector may be involved only in ambulatory care
and not in acute or preventive health care services. In many countries the lack of health insurance means that private sector participation is low for the hospital sector but high for ambulatory care,
where many people pay out-of-pocket for services.

Efficiency. Efficiency relates to both public and private spending and
its impact on private provision of health services. For example, if public spending is targeted to government clinics and hospitals where
utilization is low, while private expenditures are used to run a parallel, private, health sector, the effects on the total health system are
likely to be highly distortionary. When consumers pay out-of-pocket
for health services they often get poor value for their money. This is
because of the peculiar nature of health care, where there is quite a
bit of disconnect between consumer and provider information (such
as information asymmetries, or the principal-agent problem).

Absence of Private Health Care Markets: Understanding the Problem

Private markets for health care goods and services in many countries
are either extremely small or are concentrated in certain service
areas. For example, in many of the Gulf countries where the governments provide good-quality free health care to all their citizens,
private markets for health care are almost nonexistent. In other
countries private markets are concentrated in the provision of medicines (in private pharmacies) and in ambulatory care. The emergence of private health care markets is heavily determined by a combination of the socioeconomic conditions in the country (such as
economic conditions and the levels of urbanization) and the types of
policies adopted by governments. Governments can play a key role

in supporting policies that create appropriate demand and supply conditions to improve the functioning of private health care markets. This section describes the characteristics of demand and supply that influence private provision of health care.

Demand. Box 2.5 describes factors likely to influence demand for private health care. These include: price (monetary and nonmonetary), quality of care (especially perceived quality of care), health insurance prevalence, and health-seeking behavior habits. If data from household surveys are available and time and resources permit, multivariate analysis could be undertaken to understand factors influencing demand for private health care. For example, a study in Egypt used the Egypt Household and Health Expenditure Survey to analyze the influence of price and quality on consumer choice of providers (http://www.hsph.harvard.edu/ihsg/topic.html#13). If quantitative analysis is not possible, qualitative information from discussions with consumer groups could be used to highlight the factors that are likely to influence demand for private health care.

Supply. Box 2.6 describes the factors influencing the supply of health services. As in the previous section, if quantitative data are available on the various factors, quantitative analysis will be possible. In the absence of this information, information from the interviews and focus group discussions can be used to identify the factors that influence the supply of health services.

Table 2.2 applies the list of demand and supply factors for private health care provision to a specific country context. A matrix can be a very useful way to organize and present information, because it conveys the information in an understandable format and is useful for presentation and dissemination during stakeholder workshops and business consultations. If the private sector is being analyzed across a number of health care goods and services, separate matrices could be developed for each activity. This would make the next stage of developing recommendations easier.

Box 2.5 Demand-Side Influences on Private Health Care Delivery

Price. The choice of a public or private health provider is influenced by the difference in prices between available comparable alternatives. Cross-price elasticities measure the change in demand for one type of provider with a change in another provider's price. An increase in the price of public providers will result in lower utilization of public providers, or increased self-care or substitution of private for public providers, if all other factors influencing health care demand remain constant. The price of health care includes both monetary and nonmonetary costs (such as the opportunity costs of traveling and waiting). Where the money price is low or zero (as is the case with free public services), non-monetary public and private prices become important.

Quality. Demand is influenced by consumer perceptions of quality. Consumer perceptions of quality are typically related to nonclinical aspects of care, such as proximity of facilities, ability to schedule appointments, waiting time, cleanliness of health facilities, and the interpersonal skills of the staff.

Health insurance. The presence of risk-sharing payment mechanisms (such as health insurance) gives major impetus to private demand for health care. On the demand side, health insurance and other risk-sharing mechanisms effectively reduce the price that consumers pay for health care at the point of service. Since the direct cost of health care is no longer the most important factor under health insurance, other nonprice factors such as expected benefit, convenience, and perceived quality become important indicators.

Public program reimbursement of private providers. In most countries public financing is the single largest source of expenditures for health services. In most industrial countries (with the exception of the United States) private health insurance provides supplementary benefits, and direct out-of-pocket payments are for cost sharing and the few uncovered services. In most developing countries the public sector is the largest single payer, followed by direct out-of-pocket-payments, and then private health insurance. Since hospital services are inherently expensive for patients who pay directly, and private health insurance is minimal, public funding is the main potential source of financing to support private hospitals. Governments in most developing countries use their funding almost exclusively to support public facilities, however. Thus, development of a private hospital sector is usually constrained by the lack of risk pooling and hence effective demand.

Structure of the medical referral system. The structure of the medical referral system also indirectly influences demand for health services, including private health services.

Source: Berman and Rannan-Eliya 1993; and Griffin 1989.

Key Constraints to Private Sector Participation in Health Services Delivery

A number of factors commonly block private participation in health services delivery in developing countries.

Barriers to entry and competition. A level playing field is critical to the creation of an environment within which competitive forces can emerge. In many cases however, governments, often in collaboration with donors, provide health product or service at such low prices that the private sector can't compete with the public sector. This is

Box 2.6 Supply-Side Influences on Private Health Care Delivery

The supply of private health care services depends not only on demand but also on the availability and prices of the main inputs for health services delivery (such as skilled and unskilled staff, equipment, medical supplies, pharmaceuticals). The availability of these inputs is strongly influenced by government action on a number of fronts. A good supply-side analysis will include evaluation of the impact of these policies on the supply of targeted goods or services.

Government regulations. Government regulations such as immigration laws and import regulations for medications and medical technology can significantly influence private sector participation in health care services delivery. There may be various barriers to market entry for the private sector such as costly and cumbersome licensing procedures for new businesses, restrictions on marketing products and services, restrictions on foreign ownership, and high taxes.

Public sector employment. Two factors related to public sector employment are likely to influence private delivery of health care: (a) a large public sector that employs the majority of the country's health personnel, and (b) adequate staff salaries, wages, and benefits in the public sector. If these two factors are in place personnel have little incentive to leave the public sector for private employment or to start a private practice. Public sector employment, combined with restrictions on immigration, can be a serious bottleneck in the supply of labor needed to privately delivered health care.

Capital. The supply of complex private services such as hospitals and diagnostic centers is often contingent on the availability of capital to fund start-up costs. Lack of long term financing is a barrier to development of such activities in many developing countries.

Labor. The supply of private health services is also contingent on the availability of trained medical personnel. Without enough trained personnel and under tight labor market conditions for medical personnel, the private sector will have to depend on labor from other countries. Importing trained medical personnel from other countries can considerably add to the start-up costs.

Source: Adapted from Berman and Rannan-Eliya 1993; and Griffin 1989.

often the case in delivery of contraceptives, where low-cost contraceptives are available in urban areas to a population whose willingness and ability to pay is higher than the price of the publicly provided contraceptives. In a situation such as this the private sector must work harder and spend more on marketing in order to promote its products and services, thereby making the prices of the product for those lacking access to the subsidized public supplies even higher. Other issues related to the business environment, highlighted earlier, also pose barriers to competition by making it unnecessarily difficult to start up production or service delivery.

• *No government contracting of health services.* Government contracting of outsourcing of health service delivery, either entirely or in part, can give a huge impetus to private sector participation. Many countries use public funds exclusively to finance public services, even in the face of consistent failure to achieve the objectives related to access, distribution, or quality, which was the initial justification for the use of public funds. It is critical, in these situations, to help governments take a more strategic or performance-oriented approach to ensuring service delivery. Analysis must therefore be done to support the government in reaching decisions about whether to continue to provide services themselves or

Table 2.2 Sample Analysis Matrix of Key Demand and Supply Factors Influencing Private Sector Participation in Health Services

CRITERIA	CURRENT SITUATION IN COUNTRY	IMPLICATIONS FOR PRIVATE SECTOR DEVELOPMENT
Price of health care	Extensive network of publicly owned and run health facilities has made access easy, and opportunity cost of seeking health care is low. Government provides extensive package of health benefits virtually free of charge to population and expatriates in public sector and at highly subsidized prices to expatriates working in private sector. Direct cost of seeking care is low.	Consumers have little incentive to seek care from private sector. Private sector has no incentive to enter market. Even in market niche, private sector cannot compete with government since the point-of-service price is very low and demand is limited in relation to country's size and geography.
Quality	Information on perceived quality is limited. There is some evidence that waiting time in public clinics may be a problem.	Some people in capital city seek care from private clinics because of convenient clinic hours and short waiting times. This demand creates very small market niche for private sector in areas where its prices are low (such as ambulatory care).
Public reimbursement	Public resources for health are directly used to fund public facilities.	The impact is negative on demand for private hospital and other high-cost health services; retards development of more sophisticated purchasing and related performance pressures for private sector.
Health insurance	Limited health insurance because of market size and risk exposure of private sector expatriates. Entire population and public sector expatriates are insured by government, largely financed by budget.	Has a negative impact both on demand for and supply of private health services and on private health insurance.

120

Health-seeking behavior and historical experience	Health-seeking behavior is adequate and high compared with that in other countries in region.	If people can pay for care, demand for private health care would be adequate to create a supply response, but given high costs of quality hospital care, such responses are likely to be limited to ambulatory care.
Government regulations	Licensing and regulation system for private clinics seems to work. Private sector is allowed to employ health personnel from neighboring countries.	Current system will have to be streamlined and refined if it has to address needs of a growing private sector.
Availability of capital and other resources	Government has program of land subsidies. Country's economic development is adequate.	Capital is potentially not the major problem; rather, it is lack of effective demand (such as public or private insurance-based reimbursement of private facilities).
Labor supply and policies including public sector employment	Doctors and nurses are mostly in public employment and are not allowed to have private practice. Most health personnel are expatriates with fixed contracts. Working conditions are good.	Health personnel have limited incentives to establish private practice.

121

to contract with the private sector (this is thus a make or buy decision). When conducting assessments to support such "make or buy" decisions the reader is referred to chapter 3 ("Contracting for Health Services") of this handbook.

- *Other barriers.* Cumbersome licensing procedures, high taxes for private entities, corruption, an inability to access capital for start-up costs, bottlenecks in the health care labor market, and restrictions on migration of skilled personnel and on medical technology and equipment can create huge barriers for private and NGO entry into the health market of many countries.

If one or more of these conditions is present, then initiatives to expand the supply of services will need to address these problems.

Public spending. The government can support private sector participation by shifting from the direct provision of health services to contracting with the private sector to provide these services. In some countries selective contracting with the private sector is common, especially for inputs into the health provision process. This does not really encourage private sector participation in the provision of health services, however, since it is a piecemeal approach; neither does it help the government reap any of the benefits of targeted purchasing of health services such as influencing the type and quality of services provided by the private sector. In the United States, for example, the government has considerable leverage on private health markets because of its direct financial support for health insurance programs for the elderly (such as Medicare). The PHSA can usefully identify ways that public spending could be used more effectively to support efficient and cost-effective private sector provision.

Regulation. Regulation of the private sector is an important function of the state. In many countries, though, the regulatory framework creates unnecessary barriers to private sector entry and fails to provide for sufficient monitoring of service quality and provider compliance with health sector standards. In some countries, although the regulatory framework is appropriate, laws and regulations have not been updated, nor are they enforced. For the purposes of a PHSA it is adequate to collect and evaluate information on the country's regulatory instruments and mechanisms and determine where the problems might lie for each. For example, in many developing countries with a vibrant private sector, self-regulation by providers is the most common form of regulation. However, in the absence of governmental and NGO (consumer organizations) activities that counterbalance the powers of the provider organizations, the effectiveness of regulation in addressing the problems in the private market for health services is much less. Reviews of the regulatory framework must also address the laws and regulations that either support or constrain private participation in the provision of health services. For example, if the government has cumbersome licensing procedures, this not only acts as a barrier to easy entry but also creates opportunities for corruption. The lack of national quality standards and the absence of mechanisms to ensure compliance with the standards usually translate to inadequate quality of care.

Information dissemination. Another very important function of the state is to serve as a vehicle for public information. Information empowers consumers of health care to take charge of their health through appropriate behavior modifications and to successfully navigate the public and private health systems. When consumers pay out-of-pocket for health care, the negative effects of being misinformed are extremely high, and the consumer is liable to receive health services that are poor value for money. A PHSA should collect and analyze information on this topic to determine if the state is performing this function and, if it is, to identify the strengths and weaknesses of the particular program with regard to private health care provision.

Identifying Policy Options

Following analysis along the lines discussed above, the next step is to identify goals and objectives for private sector participation in the provision of health services. The goals and objectives can be broadly classified into (a) improving the operation of the existing private health sector in the areas of equity, quality, and cost-effectiveness; and (b) supporting expansion of private sector health care delivery to address issues such as coverage and access. In some countries a blend of both goals and objectives might be selected. In others, depending on the extent of private health markets, the goal might be defined as the creation of a policy environment conducive to effective private sector participation. Based on these goals and objectives the next steps are to use the information from the PHSA to identify the priority problems in each area, to identify their determinants, and to make policy recommendations that will address the problems. Besides identifying the various policy options, it is also important to specify the actors, groups, or level at which the policies are targeted (for example, these might be third-party payers, providers, or consumers).

In developing policies, reference to the conceptual and analytical framework described in chapter 1 is necessary, regarding the appropriate domains of action for the public and private sectors. To recapitulate:

• There are key market failures in private health markets that are related to public goods, externalities, competition failures, asymmetric information, and missing markets.

• The public sector has a range of instruments for correcting these failures, including financing, information provision, and regulation. These are core activities for governments in the health sector, falling in the domain of its stewardship responsibilities.

• The government must take responsibility for the health care goods and services used by the population, and not just their own publicly operated facilities.

• The particular nature of a health good or service, as determined by contestability, measurability, and information asymmetry, provides guidance as to which private activities are more amenable to policy influence.

Key Policy Areas to Consider in Formulating Policy Recommendations

In most developing countries, five policy issues will be of concern.

Enhanced targeting of public expenditures. Usually, the most powerful instrument at the government's disposal for influencing the private sector is the use of public funds. Therefore, in order to improve their interaction with the private providers, policymakers must be willing and able to calculate and identify the most important uses for public funds—and must evaluate the potential impact of funding public and private provision. Absent such comparison, public funds are likely to flow exclusively to public facilities, and opportunities to achieve sector objectives through working with private providers will be missed. For example, the data may show that, although public expenditures are allocated for government provision of primary health care, the majority of the poor pay local providers out-of-pocket for inadequate or low-quality care. In that case, the recommendations should explore whether primary health care allocations can be better used by buying services directly from the private sector, and should consider the leverage that might give government in regulating the private sector. In addition, the fact that the government decides to contract or outsource primary health care services could encourage the entry of new private providers, thereby improving provider choice for patients. The right kind of contracting could prove a win-win situation for the public and private sectors (see chapter 3, "Contracting for Health Services").

Improving the effectiveness of contracting arrangements. In many cases the government may already be contracting with the private sector for specific inputs or health services, but the contracting process may not be efficient or transparent. This information should become known in the course of interviews and focus group discussions with the private sector and key public sector officials, and should be presented in the PHSA analysis. This section of the PHSA should highlight some key weaknesses in current government contracting arrangements and outline approaches for improving the system. Depending on the availability of the information the recommendation could highlight the need for additional analysis, which can be addressed through a PHSA Part 3. If adequate information is available the policy recommendations could suggest ways to improve the current system. The recommendations should include ways to make the government a more informed and more efficient purchaser of services from the private sector. It should also present ways of improving government business practices to make it a better business partner for the private sector.

Improving the effectiveness and implementation of regulations. The improvement of the regulatory framework and the implementation of these frameworks in the context of private provision are major concerns in many developing countries. Essentially, governments can use a combination of legal restrictions and incentives to regulate and encourage the private sector by, for example:

- Designing regulations in areas such as quality of care, standard setting, and others if these do not already exist. If such regulations do exist recommendations should focus on ways of improving them, such as by strategic updating.

- Getting rid of regulations that create barriers to private sector entry.

- Improving the implementation of regulations by developing incentives and censures through direct and indirect mechanisms, and by increasing the resources and attention devoted to regulation.

The formulation of policy recommendations is context specific. For example, in many countries a regulatory framework for the private sector may not exist or may be outdated and ineffective. In these cases, the regulatory framework will have to be strengthened. Other countries may have an adequate regulatory framework but implement it poorly. Another group of countries may have to strengthen both the regulatory framework and its implementation.

Developing a workable plan for improving regulations, in light of a country's types and forms of institutions and organizations, may require additional data collection and analysis of different options from those in use. For example, in a country that has a rich tradition of NGOs working in the health sector, some regulatory functions could be contracted out to these NGOs. (For details on regulatory strategies and institutional arrangements adopted by different countries, see chapter 4 ["Regulation of Health Services"] of this handbook.)

Improving competitiveness. Government policies play a critical role in making the business environment more competitive and reducing the opportunities for the growth of monopolistic cartels that tend to control prices. In Australia and the United States antitrust laws and regulations prevent private organizations, including health care organizations, from forming monopolies and colluding to control prices.

Mitigating the adverse selection problem. One source of problems in the private (for-profit) sector is the profit motive, which offers every incentive to maximize the difference between revenues and expenditures. This may lead providers to *cream-skim*, choosing to serve only young and healthy patients, particularly if the payment mechanisms are not risk adjusted. Government's policy role here is important in order to prevent adverse selection issues—that is, those issues that are related to private health insurance and private delivery of health services. For example, by adopting the correct provider-payment mechanisms for contracting the government can mitigate private providers' opportunities for adverse selection. The government also plays a role in ensuring that poor and vulnerable groups are not excluded from health care in the private market context, particularly through mandating community ratings and risk pooling.

Information resources at completion of PHSA, Part 1. Upon completion of PHSA Part 1, information about the following should be available:

- Structure and function of the private health care market and its place within the overall health sector

- Main demand and supply factors influencing private sector provision

- Main weaknesses with regard to private provision (for example, quality of care and equity); recommendations on actions to mitigate the problems; and relation of these problems to failures of government's stewardship function

- Main constraints on private sector development, in either a particular sector, area, or type of service, and recommendation for public policies that can be adopted to reduce these constraints.

PHSA Part 2: Organizing a Business Consultation or Stakeholder Meeting

Once the information from PHSA Part 1 is available in the form of a policy brief, the next step is to organize a stakeholder consultation. The development and implementation of policies to support private sector participation in health care requires consultation and collaboration between the government and key stakeholders (defined as private for-profit and NGO providers, and consumers). In most countries the channels of communication between the government and these stakeholders are limited or even nonexistent. Therefore, the earlier the consultation and participation process is started the easier it will be to get key stakeholders on board for implementation of selected policies to engage the private sector. The PHSA, Parts 1 and 2, is a good starting point for the consultation process, since the information from Part 1 can be extremely informative and provide grounds for discussion about Part 3. Participation can be solicited in various ways, such as by:

- Involving stakeholders (defined as private for-profit and NGO providers, and consumers) in the coordinating group for the private sector and health strategy that is likely to emerge from Parts 1 and 2 of the PHSA.

- Consulting with stakeholders throughout the Parts 1 and 2 process and while formulating the strategy.

- Ensuring stakeholder representation in particular thematic areas and groups that will feed into the overall strategy development. For example, consumer groups may play an important role in regulation, and may be the direct beneficiaries of government programs for empowering consumers through information. Therefore, it makes sense to involve consumer groups in assessing this thematic area. For the thematic groups on "making the business environment conducive to private sector participation" and "contracting as a mechanisms for harnessing the private sector," it makes sense to involve private providers, who are the key stakeholders in the process.

Throughout the PHSA process it is important to remember that the stakeholders in private sector participation are often unaccustomed to being consulted by the government. Private providers who have little interaction with government may feel threatened by the idea of participating. Therefore, it is important for the government and those organizing the stakeholder workshops to be extremely open and transparent about the goals and objectives of the consultation process, and to ensure that the time stakeholders spend at the workshops is well used and that their thoughts and comments are taken seriously. In addition, it is important to maintain continuity in the process, and to organize at least several meetings with the stakeholders and to report to them if specific recommendations have been followed up.

PHSA Part 3: Developing Workable Strategies and a Policy Brief

Part 3 of the PHSA is designed to collect and analyze information on the private sector with the objective of developing specific, workable strategies. This work could include:

- An inquiry into private sector capacity to meet specific needs, such as primary or ambulatory care and acute-care services, or the needs of a target population in a particular region. For example, the World Bank's Latin America and Caribbean Region has developed survey instruments for evaluating the capacity of NGOs based in rural areas to provide primary care services under contract.

• A disease- or program-focused study to strengthen the private sector's ability to contribute to child health services, tuberculosis (TB), STDs, or HIV/AIDS detection and treatment. Box 2.7 describes several studies that have focused on these areas.

• Strategies for improving the regulation of private health services.

Regardless of the focus or the findings, the results should be presented in a policy brief. This brief should be user-friendly and jargon-free, and the recommendations should be "actionable." User-friendliness can be enhanced greatly by selecting the story or story line of the brief, to enhance the structure and narrative flow.

The purpose of Parts 1 and 2 of the PHSA is to raise decisionmakers' awareness of the current role and status of private sector participation in health and to help identify policy actions toward the private sector. At the completion of Part 3 decisionmakers and other stakeholders should be able to identify a few areas within private sector participation in health that are important in the context of the country's priorities in the health sector. For example, decisionmakers may support the idea of encouraging private sector participation in the hospital sector in certain urban centers. In these cases a more in-depth study, focusing on the strategies needed to mobilize private sector participation in this area, will be necessary. Several examples of such studies are listed in appendix 2.A.

In order to conduct a detailed study of this nature and identify strategies, it is necessary to be clear about:

• The segment of the private sector that is targeted (for example, whether hospitals, primary care providers, or retail pharmacies)

• The type of services targeted (whether encouraging the private sector to provide preventive and promotive health services, contracting out surgical procedures to private hospitals by the government, improving drug prescription practices among retail pharmacies)

Box 2.7 Studies Exploring Strategies for Enhancing the Private Sector Contribution to Public Health Objectives

NGOs and women's health services in Haiti. This study examines the work of three NGOs in Haiti in the delivery of women's health services. The study uses several conceptual frameworks to evaluate NGO performance—to compare NGO development strategies; to describe health services; to document innovative strategies; and to summarize lessons learned. According to the study the NGOs provided approximately 70 to 88 percent of essential women's health services, and are working to eliminate the three delays that most influence maternal mortality. All three NGOs face common weaknesses in addressing delays related to travel time, transportation, and cost. All three NGOs use a combination of facility-based and community-based health development strategies, and at least two are working to address sustainability issues. http://wbln0013/External/lac.nsf/Sector+Units/LCSHD/.

Private providers and TB. Studies have been conducted on the magnitude of private provider involvement in TB treatment in India, the Philippines, and Vietnam. These studies describe the approximate magnitude of private provider involvement in the treatment; the main problems in private treatment, especially the gap between expected standards and providers' practices and the implications for TB control in these countries; and some public-private mix strategies for involving private providers in TB control, particularly in complying with national TB program guidelines. Some of the recommended strategies include education, and contracting with private providers to deliver TB care. http://www.who.int/gtb/policyrd/TBPPM.htm.

Private providers and integrated management of childhood illnesses. The USAID-funded BASICS Project conducted

(Box continues on the following page.)

Box 2.7 (continued)

studies in Bangladesh, India, Indonesia, and Pakistan to identify appropriate strategies for involving private providers in the integrated management of childhood illnesses (IMCI). This was based on the rationale that, since the private sector is an important provider of child health services in these countries, success in implementing IMCI could not be achieved without involving private providers. As was the case for the TB studies these studies also focus on understanding the magnitude of child health services provided through the private sector, providers' current treatment practices for childhood illnesses, and provider incentives and motivations. Specific strategies focus on training the providers, contracting with them to meet IMCI standards, increasing consumer awareness of IMCI, and defining reasonable expectations for private treatment. These interventions were tested on a pilot basis in all four countries. http://www.basics.org.

Private providers and reproductive health services. Various USAID projects (such as SOMARC and PROFIT) have targeted their efforts at harnessing the private sector for delivery of quality reproductive health services (particularly family planning). Under these projects various private sector assessments have been undertaken to understand the range of demand- and supply-side factors affecting private sector delivery of family planning services. Demand- and supply-side interventions have been designed based on these studies. The sustainability of the interventions and the fact that donor support for harnessing the private sector was not sustainable have led more recent efforts in this area to take a close look at the environment for private sector participation, including government policies. http://www.tfgi.com/somahome.asp.

- The area and population targeted by the study (such as urban upper- to middle-class to support market segmentation policies, or the poor living in urban and rural areas)

- The types of strategies that have worked in addressing the particular area of concern and ways these lessons of experience can be used to develop local strategies

- Multipronged strategies that target various levels of the health system such as government (whether policies or programs), private providers, and consumers

Because the topics that might be covered under Part 3 of the PHSA are numerous, step-by-step guidance cannot be provided for each topic. A list of documents included in appendix 2.A also provides information on various country examples and case studies.

Conclusions

This chapter of the handbook has explained how to do a PHSA with an eye to working with a country's private sector to achieve health sector goals such as improved access, efficiency, quality, and cost-effectiveness. It encourages evaluators of the private sector to move from a broad perspective of the private sector's nature and characteristics to the identification of specific areas where the private sector can be mobilized. To recapitulate, the major steps in a PHSA are:

1. Get a broad picture of the organization, management, and financing of the health system.

2. Determine the structure and function of private health care markets. In other words, understand the demand, supply, and price characteristics in the private sector, the particular market failures, and key constraints in mobilizing the private sector for health.

3. Hold business consultations and stakeholder meetings to discuss and deliberate on the results of the private sector overview and

identify medium- and long-term plans for developing an appropriate public-private mix.

Appendix 2.A Conducting a Private Health Sector Assessment—Some Useful Sources

For PHSA, Parts 1 and 2

Berman, P., and K. Hanson. 1994. *Assessing the Private Sector: Using Non-Government Resources to Strengthen Public Health Goals: Methodological Guidelines*. Cambridge, Mass.: International Health Systems Group, Harvard University. http://www.hsph. harvard.edu/ihsg/topic.html#13.

Berman, P., K. Nwuke, R. Rannan-Eliya, and A. Mwanza. 1995. *Zambia: Non governmental Health Care Provision*. Cambridge, Mass.: International Health Systems Group, Harvard University. http://www.hsph.harvard.edu/ihsg/topic.html#13.

Berman, P., K. Nwuke, K. Hanson, M. Kariuki, K. Mbugua, S. Ongayo, and T. Omurwa. 1995. *Kenya: Non governmental Health Care Provision*. http://www.hsph.harvard.edu/ihsg/topic.html #13.

Bouhafa, M., and H. Waters. 1998. *Assessment of the Private Health Care Sector in Morocco*. Arlington, Va.: Population Technical Assistance Project. November.

Chawla, M., P. Berman, A. Windak, and M. Kulis. 1999. *Provision of Ambulatory Health Services in Poland: A Case Study from Krakow*. Cambridge, Mass.: International Health Systems Group, Harvard University. http://www.hsph.harvard.edu/ihsg/ topic.html#13.

Deloitte Touche Tohmatsu International. 1996a. *Consumer Survey on Preferred Source of Basic Health Care and Family Planning Services, Philippines*. PROFIT Project, Promoting Financial Investments and Transfers to Involve the Commercial Sector in Family Planning, Arlington, Va.

———. 1996b. "Attitudes and Practice Survey among Health Professionals in the Private Sector, Philippines." PROFIT Project.

Promoting Financial Investments and Transfers to Involve the Commercial Sector in Family Planning, Arlington, Virginia.

Hanson, K., and P. Berman. 1998. "Private Health Care Provision in Developing Countries: A Preliminary Analysis of Levels and Compositions." *Health Policy and Planning* 13 (3): 195–211.

Tembon, A. C. 1996. "Health Care Provider Choice: The North West Province of Cameroon." *International Journal of Health Planning and Management* January–March: 11 (1): 53–67.

Yesudian, C. A. K. 1993. "Behavior of the Private Health Sector in the Health Market of Bombay." *Health Policy and Planning* 9 (1): 72–80.

For PHSA, Part 3

Bang, A. T., R. A. Bang, and P. G. Sontakke. 1995. "Management of Childhood Pneumonia by Traditional Birth Attendants." *Bulletin of the World Health Organization* 72 (6): 897–905.

Iqbal, I., S. Pervez, and S. Baig. 1997. "Management of Children with Acute Respiratory Infections (ARI) by General Practitioners in Multan—An Observational Study." *Journal of the Pakistan Medical Association* 47 (1): 24–28.

Kanji, N., P. Kilima, N. Lorenz, and P. Garner. 1995. "Quality of Primary Outpatient Services in Dar-es-Salaam: A Comparison of Government and Voluntary Providers." *Health Policy Plan* 10 (2): 186–90.

Madden, J. M., J. O. Quick, D. Ross-Degnan, and K. K. Kafle. 1997. "Undercover Careseekers: Simulated Clients in the Study of Health Provider Behavior in Developing Countries." *Social Science and Medicine* 45 (10): 1465–82.

Mitchell, S. 1997. "Conducting a Private Sector Family Planning Country Assessment: The PROFIT Project: A Compendium of Experience and Findings." Arlington, Va.: Deloitte Touche Tohmatsu International, Promoting Financial Investments and Transfers to Involve the Commercial Sector in Family Planning (PROFIT), Arlington, Va.

Paredes, P., M. de la Pena, E. Flores-Guerra, J. Diaz, and J. Trostle. 1996. "Factors Affecting Physicians' Prescribing Behavior in the Treatment of Childhood Diarrhea: Knowledge May Not Be the Clue." *Social Science and Medicine* 42 (8): 1141–53.

Perez-Cuevas, R., H. Guiscafre, O. Munoz, H. Reyes, P. Tome, V. Libreros, and G. Gutierres. 1996. "Improving Physician Prescribing Patterns to Treat Rhinopharyngitis: Intervention Strategies in Two Health Systems of Mexico." *Social Science and Medicine* 42 (8): 1185–94.

Priti, D. S. 1994. *Case Studies of Mosque and Church Clinics in Cairo, Egypt.* http://www.hsph.harvard.edu/ihsg/topic.html#13.

Sherpick, A. R., and P. J. Hopstock. 1996. *Study of Romanian Private Pharmacists.* Deloitte Touche Tohmatsu International, Promoting Financial Investments and Transfers to Involve the Commercial Sector in Family Planning (PROFIT), Arlington, Va.

Sobti, J. C. 1992. "Treatment of Acute Respiratory Infection in Children by Practitioners in India." *Journal of the Indian Medical Association* 90 (September): 231–32.

Thaver, I., and T. Harpman. 1997. "Private Practitioners in the Slums of Karachi: Professional Development and Innovative Approaches for Improving Practice." In S. Bennet, B. A. McPake, and A. Mills, eds., *Private Health Providers in Developing Countries: Serving the Public Interest?* London: Zed Books.

Thaver, I., T. Harpman, B. McPake, and P. Garner. 1998. "Private Practitioners in the Slums of Karachi: What Quality of Care Do They Have to Offer?" *Social Science and Medicine* 46 (11): 1441–49.

Uplekar, M., S. Juvekar, S. Morankar, S. Rangan, and P. Nunn. 1998. "Tuberculosis Patients and Practitioners in Private Clinics in India." *International Journal of Tuberculosis and Lung Disease* 2 (April): 324–29.

Uplekar, M. W., and R. A. Cask. 1991. "The Private GP and Leprosy: A Study." *Leprosy Review* 62: 410–19.

Uplekar, M. W., and D. S. Shepard. 1991. "Treatment of Tuberculosis by Private General Practitioners in India." *Tubercule* 72: 284–90.

Appendix 2.B Interview Template Sample Survey for Primary Care

Interviewer: The purpose of these interviews is to get a better understanding of the environment, constraints, and experience of local participants in the health sector including providers of health services, pharmaceuticals, and medical equipment. This interview template is designed for use with both for-profit and non-profit primary care organizations.

During our discussion I'd like to touch on the following general issues related to your clinic and the environment in which you operate:

    I. Basic Information about the Clinic or Practice
   II. Sources of Funding for (Capital) Investments
  III. Sources of Revenues from Services or Patients
  IV. Service Quality and Regulation
   V. Obtaining Supplies
  VI. Infrastructure
 VII. Workforce Issues
VIII. Business Environment
  IX. Mid-Term Prospects: Overall Assessment
   X. Final Background Questions

I. Basic Information about the Clinic or Practice

Date of interview: _____

Position in organization: _____

Name (optional): _____

Number of clinics: _____

Location(s): _____

Please describe the main activity (or activities) of your clinic or practice:

Activity	*Rank in terms of proportion of volume of activities*
Services Curative	
General consultation	
Minor surgery	
Delivery	
Observation	
Laboratory	
Radiology	
Pharmacy	
In-patient (if so, number of beds)	

Activity	*Rank in terms of proportion of volume of activities*
Services—Preventative	
Vaccination	
Prenatal care	
Family planning	

Nutritional follow-up for children
Prevention of STDs/AIDS
Education Information Communication
Other (specify)

Do you perform services outside your clinic, such as home visits? _____

In what year did your clinic or practice first begin its operations? _____

How has your profile of activities changed in the past three years and why?

_____

_____

Can we discuss your workforce? How many people work at your clinic (or clinics, and other facilities)?

Doctor _____

Medical assistant _____

Qualified nurse _____

What about nonmedical staff? Such as.....

Technical administrators _____

Other _____

Could you describe any changes to staffing in the past three years (and why)?

_____

_____

Organization/Ownership

Who owns this clinic? _____

What kind of organization is that?   NGO   Business

Does your clinic engage in any other activities besides health services?   YES   NO

What portion of total activity is health services/supplies?

_____

Level of activity (over time, and by activity, if possible)

Number of patients per day/number of consultations per day (by doctors) (by nurses)

Patient data (if relevant/available)

Do more women come to your clinic than men? (male/female distribution)

More older or younger people, or children?

Would you say that over the past three years, the number of truly poor people you have been serving has gone up or down?

Please explain this trend.

In operating your clinic today, what are the three most important constraints you face?

1. _____

2. _____

3. _____

II. Sources of Funding for (Capital) Investments

Over the last year, has your firm invested in new plant
and equipment?   YES   NO

If yes, what was the source of finance?
Earnings? _____

If earnings, approximately what percentage of your firm's earnings did you invest?
_____ Percent

If donation, international or local? _____
Please describe nature of donation. _____

For your most recent major investment (in the last 2 years), what was the source (or what
were the sources) of the financing?

Percent of total investments

1. Financed through donors and/or charitable sources
2. Earnings
3. Government allocation
4. Personal or family resources or loans

Have you received investment funds from a bank, development finance institution, or NGO
in the last two years?
                    YES (specify source, term, interest, collateral)   NO

Source _____ Term _____ Interest _____
Percent Collateral _____
If more than one, list each:

Source _____ Term _____ Interest _____
Percent Collateral _____
If you received donations, are there specific
constraints as to the use of these funds?_____
_____

For-profits?

If you have not received loans in the last two years, why not?

a. didn't need loan b. interest too high c. application too difficult d. collateral too much e. bank refused f. no credit available

For all

How severely do the following credit factors constrain your clinic's operations?

Please do not select more than three items as "Very severe obstacle"

	No obstacle		Moderate		Very severe obstacle
Level of interest rates	1	2	3	4	5
Excessive collateral requirements	1	2	3	4	5
Too much paperwork, too many rules	1	2	3	4	5
Need for connections with bank officials	1	2	3	4	5
Problems with letters of credit	1	2	3	4	5
Problems with money transfers and checks	1	2	3	4	5
Lack of supplier credit	1	2	3	4	5
Corruption of bank officials	1	2	3	4	5
Donations reduced	1	2	3	4	5
Other (specify)	1	2	3	4	5

Do you plan a major investment in building or machinery and equipment over the next year?

YES (specify amount) _____ US$.   NO

If yes, for what? _____

For for-profits

In case of future investment projects, would
you welcome a financial equity partner?   YES   NO

If no, why not? _____

If yes, what share of equity would you be prepared to give to a financial equity partner?

_____ Percent

For non-profits

In case of future investment projects, how do you propose to obtain finance?

International donors
Local donors
Bank
Other (please specify) _____

III. Sources of Revenues from Services or Patients

At what percent of your full capacity are you now operating? _____ Percent
Has this increased or decreased in the past three years?

Why?

Have your prices gone up or down in the past year? _____

Could you please explain this trend? _____

_____

Has your revenue (from services) gone up or down in the past year? (by how much?)

Percent _____

Could you please explain this? _____

How severe are each of the following income problems for your clinic or center?

Non-payment by patients
Non-payment by government, health insurance fund
Non-payment by private insurance
Insufficient or unstable demand from paying patients
Too much competition from other doctors, clinics
Other (please specify)_____

Do you have any strategy for addressing this problem? _____

_____

What percentage of your total services to patients are:
Percent of total revenues
Direct out of pocket payments
Reimbursed by the health insurance fund
Covered through private insurance
Financed through donors or charitable sources
Services are explicitly free

Are there any services which you provide, for which you are the only provider in the area?

_____

Contracting

Do you have any agreement to provide services for
reimbursement by the government?   YES   NO

If so, for what services? _____

_____

If yes, could you please describe the process of contracting with them:

_____
_____
_____

How long does it usually take to be reimbursed?

_____

How was this arrangement initially established? _____

If there are difficulties with this agreement, what do you do?

_____

Do you have any suggestions for how this process might be improved?

_____

Private Insurance

Are any of your patients covered by private insurance?   YES   NO

If yes, when the patient is covered by private insurance,
how are you reimbursed? _____

Are payments made fairly quickly? _____

Is the process of reimbursement fairly straightforward? _____

Are all providers eligible for reimbursement by
private insurance?   YES   NO

If no, how does a provider become eligible
for reimbursement by private insurers? _____

Do private insurance companies check out your practice in any way?

Prices

Do any insurers or other payers pay a different price than your normal price?
Government health insurance fund? Private insurer?

Do these prices cover your costs?   YES   NO
Government health insurance fund
Private insurance

If the prices do not cover the cost of your services what do you do to cover your costs?

Does your revenue from patients cover your operating expenses (including wages and cost
of drugs, medical supplies, etc.?)

If not, how do you make up the difference?

IV. Service Quality and Regulation

Turning back to your services for a moment...

How many hours a week are you open? _____

Do you have personnel "on-call" during closed hours?   YES   NO

What is the average waiting time for consultation? _____

What proportion of patients who come
to your clinic receive a prescription? _____ Percent

How do patients procure the drugs you prescribe? _____

_____

_____

Do you have a therapeutic guide/medical practice protocol?

If yes, have personnel trained on its use?	YES	NO
Is it available in the consulting room?	YES	NO
Is it regularly consulted?	YES	NO
Has it been updated?	YES	NO

Adequacy of regulatory framework

Some people have said that private health services aren't regulated very much, so I'd appreciate it if you'd share your views on the regulatory framework.

What do you think is the biggest problem with the quality of primary care?

_____

_____

Initial Licensing of Clinic

Requirements? Enforcement? Sufficiency?

Renewing clinic license

Requirements? Enforcement? Sufficiency?

Initial Licensing of Doctor

Requirements? Enforcement? Sufficiency?

Renewing License of Doctor

Requirements? Enforcement? Sufficiency?

Is there any other external oversight of medical practice?

Please specify _____

Altogether, are these requirements sufficient to ensure the quality of medical practice?	YES	NO

If no, what is the biggest problem with them? _____

How many times a year is your clinic visited or monitored by someone from the government (MoH)? _____

If they come, what type of inspection do they do?

_____

_____

Are there any regulatory requirements regarding the *procurement* of specialized equipment (ex. certificate of need)?

Please specify _____

Are these regulations enforced?	YES	SOMEWHAT	NO
Are there any regulatory requirements regarding the *training and availability of staff operating* specialized equipment?	YES	NO	
Are these requirements enforced?	YES	SOMEWHAT	NO
Are these sufficient to maintain quality of operation?	YES	NO	
Are you satisfied with the quality of diagnostic services (includes equipment and personnel)?	YES	NO	

If no, what is the problem?

_____

_____

Regulations on operation/staffing of diagnostic equipment/labs?

Requirements? Enforcement? Sufficient to maintain quality of operation?

Are the drugs you obtain of sufficient quality?	YES	SOMEWHAT	NO

If no, what is the biggest quality problem? _____

Are these sufficient to maintain the quality of the drug supply?	YES	SOMEWHAT	NO
Are there regulatory requirements regarding the reporting of certain diseases (esp. infectious, communicable)?	YES	NO	
Do you think most clinics make these reports?	YES	NO	
Do you think the requirements are sufficient for public safety?	YES	SOMEWHAT	NO

_____

What are the main problems you experience in dealing with government agencies?

#1 _____

#2 _____

a. In operating your clinic which government agency is the most helpful?

   (specify agency and government) _____

b. What services has this agency provided?

_____

Is your firm exempted from any taxes or duties?

   YES (specify exemptions and start year)   NO

Some clinics have complained that they must compete with other clinics or centers that don't follow all of the formal rules. Do you have problems with informal or unfair competition?

YES   NO (skip to 55)

If yes, what are the most serious problems regarding the practices of other providers for you?

(a) They avoid sales tax or other taxes
(b) They do not pay duties or observe trade regulations
(c) They have preferential access to patients
(d) They have preferential access to inputs (drugs and so on)
(e) They unfairly charge prices below yours
(f) They avoid labor taxes/regulations (such as social sec'ty)
(g) They collude to limit your access to credit, supplies, equipment, or patients
(h) Other (specify) _____

In operating your business, how severe is the impact of each of the following government regulations? Please do not select more than three items with a "Very severe obstacle" ranking.

	No obstacle			Very severe obstacle	
Price controls	1	2	3	4	5
Labor/trade union regulations	1	2	3	4	5
High level of taxes	1	2	3	4	5
Tax administration, collection procedures	1	2	3	4	5
Functioning of the judicial system	1	2	3	4	5
Quality standards	1	2	3	4	5
Other (specify)	1	2	3	4	5

V. Obtaining Supplies

In general, do you have difficulty keeping any supplies in stock?

Drugs? _____

Other medical supplies? _____

Over the past three years, has this problem gotten worse or better? _____

	No obstacle		Moderate	Very severe obstacle	
Drug availability					
Drug quality	1	2	3	4	5
Consumables (other medical supplies)					
availability	1	2	3	4	5
Consumables quality	1	2	3	4	5
Equipment availability	1	2	3	4	5
Equipment quality	1	2	3	4	5

Prices of inputs	1	2	3	4	5
Reliability of supply of inputs	1	2	3	4	5
Availability of skilled labor, technicians	1	2	3	4	5
Availability of managers	1	2	3	4	5
Cost of labor	1	2	3	4	5
Attitude, motivation of labor	1	2	3	4	5
Lack of short term finance	1	2	3	4	5

What percentage of drugs and other consumables (by value) purchased or obtained by you are obtained from:

Source	Percentage of supply	Percentage of supply
State	_____ Percent	_____ Percent
Central Buyer	_____ Percent	_____ Percent
Wholesale distributor	_____ Percent	_____ Percent
International aid	_____ Percent	_____ Percent
Local Donations	_____ Percent	_____ Percent
Other (specify)	_____ Percent	_____ Percent

For your most important drugs/consumables, from how many organizations could you buy it:

_____ Today

_____ Two years ago

VI. Infrastructure

Does your clinic own or lease, rent the premises you occupy?

Are you secure in being able to occupy this space?_____

If not, what is your concern?_____

What problems do you have related to public services and infrastructure?

   (a) Problems of buying/leasing, accessing land
   (b) Problems of getting office space
   (c) Power breakdowns
   (d) Voltage fluctuations/frequency variations
   (e) Telecommunications problems
   (f) Water supply problems
   (g) Problems in waste water disposal
   (h) Problems in the disposal of garbage/medical waste
   (i) Quality/availability of transportation

VII. Workforce Issues

Do you experience problems in hiring certain categories of workers?   YES   NO

If yes, what types of workers? _____

What is the rate of absenteeism in your enterprise?
(percent of real workers absent/day) _____

How hard is it to dismiss a worker?   VERY   SOMEWHAT   NOT HARD

In your clinic, what are the most severe problems related to the recruitment/management of labor?

_____

_____

    (a) Low productivity of laborers
    (b) Missed work due to illness, or death in the family
    (c) Absenteeism due to closures
    (d) Lack of skilled labor
    (e) Lack of technicians
    (f) Lack of management skills
    (g) Restrictions on laying off local workers
    (h) Regulations on working conditions
    (i) Trade union activities, restrictions
    (j) Seasonal shortages of unskilled labor
    (k) Turnover related costs (i.e., training)

VIII. Business Environment

Do other providers near you have any advantages or benefits which you don't have, such as special access to critical supplies, special access to certain paying patients, low cost loans, subsidies, tax benefits, etc.? Is there fair competition among primary care providers?

Is it unreasonably difficult to start a practice or open a clinic?

If so, in what way?_____

_____

Problems related to obtaining capital _____

Policies (specify) _____

Technical skills, monopoly control (specify)

_____

Obtaining accreditation _____

Licensing of practice _____

Licensing of facilities _____

Other (please specify) _____

Is there an unfair restriction on competition, such as professional or union protectionism? Are there unreasonable licensing benchmarks (such as staffing norms or unnecessary equipment standards)?

Considering your most recent dispute with a patient or another practice, or supplier over debt or other matters, how was it resolved?

    (a) Negotiation
    (b) Legal action
    (c) Legal judgment
    (d) Collection agency
    (e) Mediation/arbitration

IX. Mid-Term Prospects

Do you expect your clinic's volume of activities to be larger, smaller, or the same in two years' time?

(a) _____ percent larger (b) _____ percent smaller (c) same size (if smaller or same skip to next question)

If you plan to expand, what steps have you taken for achieving your objective?

In the *medium term* (one to three years), how are the following factors going to constrain your clinic's future operations and growth in your country? Please do not select more than four factors as "very severe obstacle."

	No obstacle		Moderate		Very severe obstacle
Too little demand for services of your clinic	1	2	3	4	5
Increasing numbers of non-paying patients	1	2	3	4	5
Crowding out by public providers and clinics	1	2	3	4	5
Less financing from government/health insurance fund	1	2	3	4	5
Fewer privately insured patients	1	2	3	4	5
Problems with obtaining financing/donations	1	2	3	4	5
Cost and/or quality of the labor force	1	2	3	4	5
Availability or cost of inputs	1	2	3	4	5
Availability or cost of equipment, spare parts	1	2	3	4	5
Health policy uncertainty	1	2	3	4	5
Problems with infrastructure (land, electric power, roads, telephone, etc.)	1	2	3	4	5
Taxes and tax administration	1	2	3	4	5
All other regulations (licensing, price controls, labor regulations, etc.)	1	2	3	4	5
Economic policy uncertainty	1	2	3	4	5
Threat of war or border closures	1	2	3	4	5

X. Final Background Questions

Prices of key services
Services—Curative
    (a) General consultation
    (b) Minor Surgery
    (c) Delivery
    (d) Observation
    (e) Laboratory
    (f) Radiology
    (g) Pharmacy
    (h) In-patient (if so, number of beds)

Services—Preventative
    (a) Vaccination
    (b) Prenatal care
    (c) Family planning
    (d) Nutritional follow-up for children

(e) Prevention of STDs/AIDS
(f) Education Information Communication
(g) Other (specify) _____

Revenues (pre-tax) _____

Broad indication of recent growth. _____ percent change in revenue (or patients served, utilization of capacity—specify which)

What basic financial data for your organization:
(a) Income (yearly)
(b) Expenditure (yearly)

For-profits
(a) Assets
(b) Equity
(c) Debt

How helpful would you find each of the following changes in promoting the growth of private health care?

	Not helpful		Moderately helpful		Very helpful
1. Successful completion of elections	1	2	3	4	5
2. Repair of infrastructure	1	2	3	4	5
3. Rationalization of legal framework and policies	1	2	3	4	5
4. Improved laws for ownership of property	1	2	3	4	5
5. Enactment and enforcement of antimonopoly law	1	2	3	4	5
6. Reduction of tax rates	1	2	3	4	5
7. Rationalization of tax regulation	1	2	3	4	5
9. Privatization of public services	1	2	3	4	5
10. Banking reforms	1	2	3	4	5
11. Stabilization of laws	1	2	3	4	5
12. Easing of laws on employment, layoffs	1	2	3	4	5
13. Stabilization of prices	1	2	3	4	5
14. Completion of peace process	1	2	3	4	5
15. Increased volume of government contracting	1	2	3	4	5
16. Improved contracting process	1	2	3	4	5
17. Improved insurance market	1	2	3	4	5
18. Quality regulation	1	2	3	4	5
19. Accreditation	1	2	3	4	5
20. Increased economic growth	1	2	3	4	5

THE SURVEY ENDS HERE. THANK YOU FOR YOUR COOPERATION

Date of interview _____

Title of Interviewee _____

Appendix 2.C Private Health Sector Assessment Interview Template: Policymakers

Who This Interview Is For

Policymakers are defined as government decisionmakers and their advisers. They are likely to include senior government officials (from ministries of health, finance, economy) as well as others from academia, politics, and so forth.

How Public Policy Affects the Prospects for Private Sector Participation in Health

Government policy creates the environment for the private sector by establishing the framework in which the private sector may operate. The range of factors that determine the environment for the private sector include taxation, tariffs, regulation, licensing, and many more.

Governments increasingly look to the private sector to complement government-funded and -provided health care. However, "complement" may mean many different things, such as provide those services the government cannot or chooses not to provide, or absorb demand from wealthier classes so the government may concentrate on providing services to the poor, or other interpretations. This interview should provide a clear picture of how a government wishes to engage the private sector in meeting the nation's health sector goals. In some instances, there may be no explicit policy toward the private sector, or, as described below, a government may deliberately choose not to formalize its policies toward the private sector.

Policy may be articulated formally in written government policies and plans (for example, a five-year national health plan). It may also be expressed informally—an unwritten set of rules and understandings that have an equally powerful impact on private sector development. For instance, there may exist explicit and official criteria for the establishment of private ambulatory care clinics. In practice, however, new practices may be difficult to establish if additional informal criteria are invoked or quotas applied. The aim of this interview is to understand both formal and informal policies affecting private sector participation in health.

The interview should also identify issues associated with the private sector's involvement in health, from the perspective of policymakers, and to elicit recommendations on levers that can be addressed at this time to generate more effective private participation in the health sector.

The Objectives of the Interview

The interview is designed to obtain the following information:

- The normative policy process and the actual policy process (in relation to the private sector's role)

- The role and functions of individuals and groups in the policy-making process (who makes policy affecting the private sector in health, and how?)

- Current health sector objectives

- Critical problems impeding health sector reform or development

- The contribution of the private sector to these problems

- The desired role of the private sector in the nation's health system, including its contribution to meeting health sector goals

- Possible actions to increase private sector contribution to health sector goals

- Constraints to reform imposed by the private sector

- Recommendations for removing or averting these constraints.

Questions to Guide a Semistructured Interview

1. Please summarize the government's current health sector objectives. [Alternatively, confirm health sector objectives per latest national health plan.]

2. How does the private sector fit into these objectives at present? How do private and NGO service providers, and other suppliers, contribute to these objectives?

3. Does the government currently have a formal policy about the role of the private sector in health? If so, please describe. Informal policy?

4. What are your primary information sources about private sector activity in health services? [Ensure discussion covers all relevant sectors—acute care or hospital services; ambulatory services; specialist; and, diagnostic services]

5. Does the government have different policies for NGOs and for-profit private sector organizations?

6. What are the critical problems/challenges facing the health sector at this time?

7. How does the private sector contribute to these problems?

8. What role does the government propose for the private sector in health reform/development? How will this contribute to the achievement of the government's health sector goals?

9. How is policy concerning the role of the private sector made? Who influences the process? [Which government ministries are involved with the health private sector? Health? Treasury? Finance? Others? At what level?]

10. Do you rely on groups outside government to monitor or influence the private sector in health? Medical associations? Other professional groups? Private sector lobbying groups? Consumer or patient's organizations? Other? If so, how do you interface with these organizations? Do you oversee their activities in any area? Do you support their activities in any area?

11. Do you have any concerns about the private sector's current or future involvement in health? Please specify.

12. How do you wish the private sector to contribute to meeting government's health sector goals in future? How might the private sector constrain achievement of health sector goals?

13. If the latter, what measures might be taken to avoid or minimize the impact?

14. Governments usually rely on external advisers, such as academics or other professionals, but also political groups, for policy advice, including advice on the role of the private sector. Are there any policy advisers we should meet with to continue to explore the opportunities and issues concerning private sector involvement in health?

15. Any other comments?

Note: Relevant administrative and policy structure and flow charts are useful (Bloom 2002).

Notes

1. In this chapter, and throughout the *Handbook*, we use the term "private sector" to refer to both for-profit and not-for-profit health care providers, including hospitals, primary care physicians in solo or group practice, pharmacies, diagnostic facilities, and nongovernmental organizations (NGOs). This includes consumer groups and community-based organizations that provide health services.

2. The range of market failure typically noted with regard to health goods and services is public goods; externalities; competition failures; asymmetric information; and missing markets (World Bank 2000a).

3. We use the term "contracting" rather than purchasing because buyers and sellers of health care goods and services often have ongoing exchange that is grounded in a long-term contract or contracts, rather than simply bought and sold as a "one-off" deal. See chapter 3, "Contracting for Health Services," for elaboration.

4. The characteristics generating a certain level of buyability are also correlated with the effectiveness of other nonownership instruments. That is, services that are easier to buy are also easier to regulate, and it is easier to educate consumers about their proper use.

5. For ease of exposition, only contestability and measurability are plotted on the table. Interested readers are referred to the Preker, Harding, Girishankar (1999) paper for a more detailed discussion of the information asymmetry characteristics of health goods and services. For our purposes the reader may think of measurability as capturing much of the information asymmetry.

6. See Busse 2000 for a discussion of the different perceptions manifested in OECD health systems regarding the "buyability" of hospital services.

7. In many countries informal payments in public facilities are a major component of private, out-of-pocket payments; recent household surveys include questions on informal payments. If this information is available, it should be included.

8. The Private Sector Development page of the World Bank Web site contains extensive information about various areas of private sector development, including competitiveness indices for various countries, business environment, and other topics. http://www.worldbank.org/html/fpd/privatesector (Private Sector Development Web page through World Bank external Web site).

9. For further details on the types of laws and regulations that may positively or negatively affect nonprofit participation in the health sector please refer to the *World Bank NGO Handbook*, which can be downloaded from: http://www.icnl.org/handbook/index.html.

10. This module does not cover details related to conducting household surveys, since most countries conduct some type of household survey, and there are many other sources of information on conducting such surveys.

Bibliography

Berman, P. 1998. "Rethinking Health Care Systems: Private Health Care Provision in India." *World Development* 26 (8): 1463–79.

———. 1999. "Understanding the Supply-Side: A Conceptual Framework for Analyzing Health Care Provision with an Application to Egypt." Data for Decisionmaking Project, No. 82, Department of Population and International Health, Harvard School of Public Health, Boston.

Berman, P., and R. Rannan-Eliya. 1993. *Factors Affecting the Development of Private Health Care Provision*. Bethesda, Md.: Abt Associates, Inc. and Harvard School of Public Health, Health Financing and Sustainability Project.

Berman, P., and L. Rose. 1994. "The Role of Private Providers in Maternal and Child Health and Family Planning Services in Developing Countries." Data for Decisionmaking Project, Department of Population and International Health, Harvard School of Public Health, Boston. URL: http://www.hsph.harvard.edu/ihsg/publications/pdf/No-18.PDF.

Bloom, A. 2002. "Private Health Sector Assessment Interview Template: Policymakers."

Busse, R. 2000. "Hospital Governance and Regulation." Paper presented at European Observatory Summer Workshop, Dubrovnik, Croatia, August.

Chakraborty, S., A. D'Souza, and R. Northrup. 2000. "Improving Private Practitioner Care of Sick Children: Testing New Approaches in Rural Bihar." *Health Policy and Planning* 15 (4): 400–07.

Chawla, M., P. Berman, A. Windak, and M. Kulis. 1999. *Provision of Ambulatory Health Services in Poland: A Case Study from Krakow*. Cambridge, Mass.: International Health Systems Group, Harvard University. http://www.hsph.harvard.edu/ihsg/topic.html #13.

Griffin, C. C. 1989. *Strengthening Health Services in Developing Countries through the Private Sector*. Discussion Paper Number 4. International Finance Corporation, Washington, D.C.

Hanson, K., and P. Berman. 1994. "Assessing the Private Sector Using Non-Government Resources to Strengthen Public Health Goals. The Data for Decision-Making Project." Boston, Mass.: Harvard School of Public Health. http://www.hsph.harvard.edu/ihsg/ihsg.html.

Hong Ha, N., P. Berman, and U. Larsen. 2002. "Private Providers of Ambulatory Services in Vietnam: An Assessment of Utilization and Financial Burden." *Social Science and Medicine*.

Musgrove, P. 1999. "Public Spending on Health Care: How are Different Criteria Related?" *Health Policy* 47(3): 207–23.

Peters, D. 2001. *Better Health Systems for India's Poor: Findings, Analysis, and Options.* Washington, D.C.: World Bank.

Preker, A., A. Harding, and N. Girishankar. 1999. "The Economics of Private Participation in Health Care: New Insights from Institutional Economics." World Bank, Washington, D.C.

Simon, K. 1995. "Privatization of Social and Cultural Services in Central and Eastern Europe: Comparative Experiences." Paper presented at A Recipe for Effecting Institutional Changes to Achieve Privatization, Conference at Boston University, April 26.

Stone, A. H. 1999. "Private Sector Assessments: Best Practices and Pitfalls, Private Sector Development Department." PSD Note # 1. World Bank, Washington, D.C.

World Bank. 2000a. "Public Spending in a Market Context: The Efficiency Issue." Public Expenditure Knowledge Management Web site, Washington, D.C. http://www1.worldbank.org/publicsector/pe/efficien.htm.

———. 2000b. "Private Sector Development—Business Environment (Assessing Competitiveness)." Finance and Private Sector Investment (FPSI) Group, Washington, D.C.

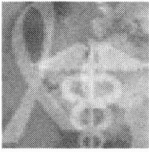

CHAPTER 3

Contracting for Health Services

Robert J. Taylor

Contracting is one of the principal instruments a government can use to harness private sector resources in order to help achieve national health objectives. Contracting is more than just buying health care services to provide access for patients (see box 3.1). It is also used to purchase employee training, health education, institutional cleaning, food services, and many other health-related services. More important, it is also used to enhance quality of priority services. This latter strategy is particularly important where private providers are the first point of contact with the health system for targeted individuals, such as tuberculosis (TB) symptomatics, sick children, or carriers of sexually transmitted diseases (STDs). In this context key public health programs can also be strengthened through contracting to enhance appropriate treatment or referral.

Use of contracting is growing in developing countries. While the requirement of financial resources constrains its use, private sector interest in remuneration enables a substantial portion of the burden of the interaction to be shifted out of government hands. Private sector contractors themselves can take on the tasks of collecting and delivering critical information about their activities—indeed, they are motivated to do so. The active cooperation of the contracted providers then makes contracting less onerous to implement than regulation in many settings.

Box 3.1 Contracting Defined

Contracting is a purchasing mechanism used to acquire a specified service, of a defined quantity and quality, at an agreed-on price, from a specific provider, for a specified period. In contrast to a one-off exchange, the term "contracting" implies an ongoing exchange relationship, supported by a contractual agreement. In this handbook we discuss contracting between the government (or government agency) as purchaser, and a private provider (or providers) of services. Internal contracting, between government entities, will not be discussed.

Nevertheless, contracting is a complex, structured process. Government officials must see themselves as directors and strategists for the whole health system, not just administrators of publicly owned health facilities. To ensure accountability for contracted services, both the contracts and the ongoing process of contract monitoring and negotiation must be done well. Contracting officials need new skills to perform these unfamiliar tasks. It is perhaps even more important that health services contracting be done in such a way that supports communication and the development of trust among the contracting officials, the providers, and the community served. The importance of service continuity, the difficulty of measuring and monitoring health services, and the common distrust between the public and private actors make it especially important that transparency, communication, and predictability characterize the interaction between the contracting agency and the providers. This chapter will review the principles and steps involved in health services contracting. It will also present the most common challenges associated with the development of government's capacity to implement and manage such contracts. See appendix 3.A for additional sources of information on contracting.

Contracting is usually utilized by itself to implement a specific program or initiative; we will discuss it in this context. It is also increasingly being seen as a strategy in and of itself, as an approach to reforming the health system in general (Carrin, Jancloes, and Perrot 1998). From this perspective contracting is viewed as a core element of a systemic reform, under which governments expand their attention in the health sector to include not only service delivery but also a range of additional roles. This shift adds the role of health services buyer to its traditional role of health services provider. In this context contracting gives government choices as to how it fulfills its responsibilities, and supports a more strategic approach to health sector policymaking.

Contracting as a Government Tool

Historically—for ideological, theoretical, and practical reasons—the governments of many developing countries have assumed responsibility for providing health services directly to their populations, creating extensive systems of hospitals, clinics, and programs with large and complex bureaucracies to oversee them. The role of the private sector in service provision has often been discounted, ignored, or even actively restrained. Recently, however, governments in many developing countries are finding that operating health service delivery systems imposes onerous managerial burdens and that, despite extensive public investments, such systems often fall short of their objectives. At the same time governments are giving greater recognition to the private sector's already substantial role in health care provision, and are selectively introducing reforms to build on their widespread utilization. As governments seek alternatives to direct provision of health services and to implementing programs exclusively through public facilities, contracting is emerging as a useful tool for harnessing private providers in order to help achieve national health goals.

Governments need money to support their contractual obligations so that they can take advantage of strategic contracting opportunities. A cornerstone of such contracting efforts is the transfer of money from the government (or government agency) as purchaser, to a private provider (or providers) of services, in exchange for specified deliverables. Opponents view such money transfers as enriching the private sector at the government's (the public's) expense. Although that might happen, ultimately the purpose of the money transfer is to achieve governmental objectives, and to do it through a combination of public financing and private means.

As discussed in chapter 1, "Introduction to Private Participation in Health Services," governments have an interest in ensuring adequate delivery of a range of health goods and services. However, saying a service merits public intervention does not dictate its production by the state. In most developing countries governments have a hard time financing the services they already provide; it can be a challenge to find the resources needed to support even clearly beneficial contracting opportunities. Freeing up money by cutting back on inefficient or low priority government-provided services is an obvious, but sometimes problematic, option.

One barrier to such efforts is that the ministries of health in many developing countries do not a have a clear idea of how much money they are spending for selected health services, or what benefits they are getting in return. More accurate cost finding might stimulate governments to reexamine their historic budgetary commitments, but in doing so might threaten entrenched government bureaucracies. Even so, in spite of this significant barrier, many developing countries are finding ways to secure financing, broaden their policy options, and improve health service delivery through contracting instead of pursuing national health objectives exclusively through public facilities.

Public Responsibility and Choice in Health Services Delivery

Contracting, together with information, regulation, and a variety of other methods, are the instruments a government can use to harness private sector resources to help achieve national health objectives. As seen in table 3.1, governments have a range of choices they can ex-

Table 3.1 Government Tools for Influencing the Private Sector

LEVEL OF INTRUSIVENESS	TOOL OR METHOD	APPLICATION
Most intrusive	Direct provision	• Public hospitals and clinics • Preventive services • Sanitation
	Financing	• Budgetary support • Subsidies • Concessions • Contracting
	Regulation and mandates	• Taxation • Licensure • Accreditation • Employee health insurance • Required immunization of school children
Least intrusive	Information	• Research—product testing • Provider information—treatment protocols, recommended medicines • Consumer information—provider quality comparisons, consumers' rights, dangers of smoking, rehydration methods, birth spacing

Source: Adapted from Musgrove 1996.

ercise to influence the private sector, ranging from highly intrusive (direct provision) to largely persuasive (providing information).

It is an important insight underpinning modern approaches to public sector management to recognize that governments have a choice about the ways they fulfill their responsibilities. While governments have a responsibility to ensure health services are available, they have a choice about whether to deliver those services directly or to use some other method, such as contracting, to ensure their availability through private providers.[1]

This trend toward the strategic consideration of the method or instrument to be used to ensure the availability or quality of health services is consistent with the emerging concept of stewardship. Stewardship places a broad responsibility on the state—to direct, coordinate, and oversee the entire health care sector; to protect the poor and vulnerable through monitoring, evaluation, and regulation of the health sector; and to ensure that all citizens have access to the health services they may need (Saltman 2000). Stewardship broadens the state's perspective beyond the public system to include the private sector and all it does or can do to help government address national health policy objectives. It de-emphasizes the state's obligation to provide health services as their only choice for ensuring access to priority services. This handbook applies this concept of stewardship in order to encourage policymakers to consider, wherever possible, the full range of options for pursuing their health objectives, and to consider the likely costs and benefits of using each option.

The use of contracting can be seen as providing public officials with an additional tool they can use to achieve health policy objectives—a tool that can help guide the behavior and development of the private sector in directions that support the achievement of national health goals. Contracting can be used to motivate private providers to structure their services in accordance with contracted provisions to capture revenues and to position themselves to take advantage of future contracting opportunities. The financial resources associated with the contracts can provide incentives for desired behaviors on the part of private providers who are in an advantageous position to serve priority public objectives.

Contracting can be used by governments as a strategic process to precipitate and reinforce health sector reform by introducing competition, offering alternative approaches to service delivery, and clarifying the relationship between health finance and provision. Contracting can be used as a mechanism to achieve certain targeted objectives, such as mobilizing private capital investments; limiting commitment to long-term recurrent costs; promoting access, equity, or improved quality; or other health sector objectives. Contracting can also be used to influence the supply of health services, such as the availability of medicines; or the demand for health services, such as an antismoking publicity campaign. In addition, contracting can help achieve broader social and economic objectives, such as increasing employment opportunities in rural communities, and thus indirectly discourage migration from rural to urban areas.

Contracting is also a management process—for purchasing a specified service, of a defined quantity and quality, at an agreed-on price, for a specified period. As such, contracting introduces disciplined managerial activities and encourages improved managerial performance by exacting greater precision, attention, vigilance, and action than are typically required of governmental officials. The contracting process is necessarily complex and time consuming, requiring a substantial capacity on the part of both government and the provider to plan, negotiate, implement, and monitor the contractual agreement.

Although contracting has many potential benefits, it is neither a panacea nor applicable in all situations; it can have substantial risks. Ultimately, the success of the contracting process is not just a reflection of how well the process is managed or how impressive the contracting agreement, but rather of performance—the achievement of measurable outcomes and results.

Market Failures and Limitations of the State

Governments are often hesitant to consider contracting as an option, especially if they see it as compromising its role as a health service provider or as endorsing providers of questionable quality. Their reluctance is understandable, since a government's role as a health services provider is often long-standing, and grounded in ideological, theoretical, and practical arguments.

- *Ideology*. Ideologically, many governments are politically and even constitutionally obligated to provide health care for all their citizens. Health care is seen as every citizen's right, and the government is seen as the guarantor. In addition, the private sector is often viewed with suspicion and mistrust, catering to the wealthy and neglecting or ignoring the poor.

- *Theory.* According to economic theory, a number of health-related activities are public goods, or goods with large externalities. These are health services that benefit the public at large as well as the individual consumer, and that would not be available unless supported by government (such as mosquito spraying as part of an antimalarial program). Further, market failures, such as the failure of private markets to serve the poor or remote geographic areas, are often cited as justification for public provision of health services.

- *Practice.* Practically, many developing countries have already developed extensive systems of hospitals, health centers, and programs and have created large bureaucracies to operate them. Budgetary allocations are well established and jealously guarded. Health personnel are entrenched and protected by civil service regulations. In addition, ministries of health often know very little about the private sector, making it hard to design or implement effective contracts. In many instances the health care provided by these private providers is of questionable quality, so it is necessary for the government to be well informed to avoid contracting for poor services.

Consequently, governments often seem locked into doing too much—especially in terms of production of health care services—with too few resources and limited capacity. Focused as they are on providing health services, governments often fail to devote adequate resources to their obligations to guide and direct the health system through policy development and regulation, providing adequate information, or ensuring adequate financing for public goods for the whole population. In essence, the governments' failure to fulfill their stewardship obligations is as common as market failures in the private sector. Regardless of motivation or intent governments must constantly struggle to overcome obstacles, both practical and theoretical, to fulfilling their obligations (Preker, Harding, and Girishankar 1999). They include:

- *Poor public accountability.* In any country the values and desires of its citizens are rarely homogeneous; it can be difficult for public officials to reflect the interests of the whole population, let alone safeguard minority interests. Citizens can also have conflicting desires—wanting governmental accountability, on the one hand, while wanting to retain their individual sovereignty, on the other.

- *Bureaucratic inefficiency.* The funding and delivery of health care in the public domain are subject to intense stakeholder politics. Politicians and government officials often lack a strong sense of ownership or responsibility, and have few incentives to promote the efficient allocation of public resources. At the same time, they risk swift retaliation from powerful stakeholders when they do take actions to promote that efficiency.

- *Information gaps.* In both the public and private sectors the flow of information is often inadequate between patient and health care professionals and health systems administrators on the one hand and between health care professionals and health systems administrators on the other. Policymakers often know little about what services are actually being delivered, of what quality, or how patients are being treated. Such gaps make it extremely difficult for administrators to effectively manage public delivery.

- *Abuse of monopoly power.* Public production of health care services often generates monopoly powers, exposing users to exploitation, and reducing potential performance pressures that might be brought to bear on providers. Monopoly power is created by legal restrictions against competition; access to subsidized capital and revenues, creating an uneven playing field; distribution at below-marginal costs to achieve equity goals; and production of public goods, or goods where markets are not viable. As is true of a monopoly in the private sector, a governmental monopoly can result in abuses such as informal user charges imposed by publicly employed doctors and other health workers in exchange for favorable treatment.

- *Failure to provide public goods.* Governments often neglect the very health-related services they are most responsible for providing, such as public goods (policymaking and information), goods with large externalities (disease prevention), and goods with intractable market failures (insurance). Justified or not, government health systems tend to emphasize hospitals and curative services (which are more like private goods) that require a substantial infrastructure and impose an ongoing budgetary burden.

Between private market failures and limitations of the state, there are neither saints nor demons. Private health providers cater to people who can pay, and often fail to adequately serve the needs of the poor and rural inhabitants. Left to their own devices, private providers will not adequately produce public goods with large externalities. It is not the private sector's job to ensure equity, however—that job belongs to government. Governments are often no better than the private sector in meeting these obligations. Unfocused public expectations, public officials with vested interests, and well-entrenched public infrastructure and bureaucracy combine to limit the government's ability to fulfill its responsibilities. Contracting can provide government with a means of bridging the gap between desired health objectives and performance.

Structuring Planned Markets

Through contracting governments can structure a planned or targeted market—with the intent of stimulating competition in the production of some desired health good or service. Such a planned market can be either an internal market, where one agency of government contracts with another, or an external market, the focus of this chapter, where government contracts with a private provider. Through the contracting process government interjects a number of market mechanisms—competitive bidding, financial incentives, and performance measures—to guide private providers toward delivery of services that contribute to fulfilling its national health objectives.

Competitive bidding. In market theory competition is seen as the key to securing a quality product at the lowest price. In structuring a planned market the government normally prefers as many qualified providers as possible eagerly bidding for its business. In reality, especially in a country with limited contracting experience, for any given contracting opportunity there may be few, if any, qualified providers and fewer still that are willing or able to enter into a contracting relationship. The ability of a bidder to enter the market—that is, the contestability of the market in economic terms—will be influenced by both the provider and the government. The provider's experience in providing the same or similar services, the provider's capacity to expand, and the need for capital investments or staff training will all affect the provider's ability to respond to a bidding opportunity. If the government has maintained a virtual monopoly in the production of the service in the past, if the regulatory environment is too restrictive, or if the terms of the proposed contract are too onerous, potential providers may be unable or unwilling to enter the market.

Even when structuring an internal market, where only governmental providers are invited to submit bids, providers may have difficulty responding competitively. To do so they need to behave much like private enterprises—tracking and controlling their costs, preparing bids, and monitoring their performance. These are managerial behaviors, where they may have limited experience. In open bidding—where governmental providers must compete against private providers—the difficulties for governmental providers of entering the market may be further accentuated.

Financial incentives. Contracting provides a mechanism for introducing a variety of financial incentives that can significantly influence the provider's and the market's behavior. The mere fact that the government will pay for a selected service creates an opportunity for new or expanded business. In addition, different payment methods provide different incentives. A capitated rate, for example, encourages increased enrollment; fee-for-service encourages increased volumes; and prepayment shifts the risk of increased service volumes to the provider.[2] Contractual concessions—such as tax holidays, land grants, or the lease of government land at favorable rates—can also encourage providers to enter the market.

Performance measures. What the government chooses to measure in a contract will greatly influence provider behavior. The performance parameters selected send a strong message to all bidders about what government values, and what it will pay for those valued goods and services. If government is concerned about the cost, quality, or volume of services provided under a contract, specific methodologies for measuring those parameters need to be stipulated in the contract—even if those measures are less than ideal. For the message to be heard, however, the government has to devote time and attention to monitoring and evaluating those parameters—which is not always an easy task, since parameters can vary widely in their measurability.

To Make or Buy Health Services

Government authorities can exercise their discretionary powers by weighing the comparative advantages of acquiring health services from a private source versus providing those services directly—much like the make or buy decisions faced by managers in other industries.

Ideally, the public and private sectors are each perceived to have certain strengths and limitations. As illustrated in table 3.2, the public sector, as compared with the private sector, is thought to be more concerned with ensuring equitable access for the poor and vulnerable and to be more attentive to issues of public health and prevention. In contrast, the private sector is perceived to have a greater ability to raise capital, to be more attentive to personal service, and to place greater emphasis on managerial and financial performance. The private sector is thought to be better than the state at adjusting to changing prices and technology. The private sector is also thought to offer greater flexibility in coping with changing demand, particularly with respect to labor, since workers in the private sector usually can be more readily hired, reassigned, and fired than public employees (McCombs and Christianson 1987, p. 191).

Any observer of the health sector knows that many of the idealized or perceived comparative advantages described in table 3.2 do

Table 3.2 Comparative Advantages and Disadvantages of the Public and Private Health Sectors: Ideal and Perceived

ISSUE	PUBLIC SECTOR	PRIVATE SECTOR
Equity and access	• Targets services for poor and vulnerable populations • Attentive to geographic disparities	• Individuals who can pay favored; the poor and vulnerable excluded or ignored • Services concentrated in population centers
Public health, preventive and curative care	• Emphasis on preventive and public health services (public goods with large externalities) • Extensive system of hospitals and curative care centers often maintained	• Little attention to preventive and public health services without special incentives • Emphasis on curative care services valued by paying customers (private goods)
Management	• General dependence on political and legislated direction • Difficulty recruiting qualified managers • Hierarchical bureaucracy with diffused accountability • Commitment to public service compromised by vested personal interests • Restrictive range of discretionary authority, less flexibility, less innovation	• Greater reliance on information for decision-making and planning • Recruitment of managers limited primarily by cost/benefit considerations • Smaller and more focused authority structures • Greater synergy between business and personal interests • Broader range of discretionary authority, greater flexibility, more innovation
Customer orientation	• Heterogeneous constituency with wide range of expectations • Limited attention to customer convenience and comfort • Indirect accountability for customer satisfaction	• Focuses on relatively narrow range of customer needs and wants • More attentive to customer convenience and comfort • More direct accountability for customer satisfaction • May exclude poorest and sickest
Flexibility	• Extensive infrastructure of owned facilities • Restraint of civil service system • Slow to respond to changing market conditions because of political and budgetary commitments to ongoing programs	• Adaptable access to infrastructure through rentals and leasing • Flexible employment and pay practices • Quicker response to changing market conditions

(Table continues on the following page.)

Table 3.2 (continued)

ISSUE	PUBLIC SECTOR	PRIVATE SECTOR
Financing	• Access to tax revenues • Weak incentives to be cost conscious or cost efficient • Programs financed primarily through historic budgetary allocations • Limited access to private capital or donations	• Dependent on revenue flows from sales or contracts • Attentive to cost and price • Needed but unprofitable services possibly curtailed or discontinued • Resources assigned to profit centers • Sensitive to cross-subsidization and cost shifting • Access to capital markets or donations
Competition	• Possible monopoly on selected services reinforced by regulation and subsidization	• Subject to competitive pressures from public and private providers • When entering the market, interested in increasing contestability and, once successful, interested in decreasing contestability (to restrain competitors)

not play out in reality. Governments, for example, are often not as attentive to ensuring access to health services for the poor or for rural populations as planners might hope, and managers of private health services are not always as skilled or as well motivated as idealized. It is debatable whether the perceived comparative advantages illustrated in table 3.2 can actually be realized—through any specific contracting initiative or other means. Still, the perception that comparative advantages might be gained may open the door to greater public-private interaction, although the actualization of that interaction will undoubtedly vary greatly from application to application.

Strategic Opportunities in Contracting

The comparative advantages of the public and private sectors may offer some encouragement to governments to consider greater private participation in health services delivery. Of greater relevance to the government's decision to provide a service directly or to purchase it from an alternative source will be the strategic objectives that can be achieved by a specific contracting opportunity.

As noted, contracting provides government with an additional tool—together with information, regulation, training, and other forms of outreach—for pursuing its strategic objectives in other ways than through direct service provision. Contracting can be used to address public health priorities, by enhancing the availability and quality of critical services, such as treatment of sick children, or appropriate treatment and referral of carriers of TB or STDs. Contracting is a means for government to introduce market mechanisms—competitive bidding, financial incentives, and performance measures—without giving up the ability to ensure the provision of essential public health services and the protection of the needs of the poor and vulnerable (McCombs and Christianson 1987, p. 191). From a longer-term perspective contracting can be used to structure planned markets—markets that are intentionally developed by public officials to achieve public sector objectives (Saltman and Ferrousier-Davis 1995).

Contracting can also be used to influence the supply of health services, or the demand for health services, or to help accomplish identified health sector objectives or priorities, or to contribute to broader social and economic goals outside the health care arena. Table 3.3 illustrates ways that contracting can be used to address a variety of strategic objectives.

For contracting to have value it must help the government achieve some strategic health objective. Such actions presuppose that the government has assumed an active role in providing strategic direction to the health system and is willing to exercise its options in fulfilling its stewardship responsibilities.

Purchasing Health Services through Contracting

When government exercises its option to use contracting as a tool it assumes the role of purchaser—expanding its range of alternatives

Table 3.3 Strategic Contracting Opportunities in Health

TARGETED AREA	STRATEGIC OBJECTIVES	CONTRACTING OPPORTUNITIES
Government administration	• Strengthen capacity to plan strategically. • Strengthen capacity to manage contracting process. • Strengthen capacity to monitor and evaluate contracting results. • Strengthen regulatory framework and business climate to encourage appropriate growth of the private health sector.	• Obtain technical assistance to set up management information and cost accounting systems. • Contract for training in policy formulation, planning, contract management, and monitoring. • Purchase contract management services from nongovernmental organization or other provider. • Decentralize or delegate contracting to regions or institutions. • Obtain technical assistance to study existing regulatory framework and business climate.
Physical plant development and capital investments	• Improve quality of facilities planning and design. • Oversee construction to assure quality of materials and conformance with plans. • Control or reduce construction costs. • Finance capital investments. • Improve appearance and function of existing public hospitals and clinics.	• Contract with specialized architect and engineering firms. • Contract for construction management services. • Tender bids for facilities construction or renovation, or both. • Lease facilities from private sources.
Hospitals (general and specialized)	• Reduce the number and size of acute public hospitals. • Reduce occupancy and length of stay in public hospitals. • Improve access and quality of specialized clinical services. • Improve efficiency or quality of support services, or both. • Strengthen public hospital management.	• Obtain technical assistance for rationalizing hospital system. • Contract with management specialist or company to oversee hospital operations. • Contract for training to strengthen internal managerial capacity and systems. • Outsource laundry, housekeeping, security, maintenance, and other support services.

Basic primary care and preventive services	• Improve access to basic package of primary care services. • Increase immunizations among school children. • Increase use of modern family planning methods. • Improve HIV screening and treatment. • Improve TB screening, treatment, and monitoring. • Decrease childhood deaths due to diarrhea. • Reduce malaria. • Decrease smoking.	• Outsource business office functions such as admissions, accounting, billing, personnel, and purchasing. • Franchise hospital radiology, clinical laboratory, or other diagnostic services to private providers. • Contract with day-surgery facilities for public-sponsored clients. • Contract with nongovernmental organizations to manage primary care services in specified regions (such as Cambodia). • Contract with private physicians to provide immunization. • Contract with midwives, traditional healers, and others to promote modern family planning methods. • Contract for social marketing campaign for HIV, TB, and awareness of the sources of diarrheal diseases. • Contract for mosquito spraying. • Contract for antismoking social marketing campaign.
Diagnostic services	• Increase availability of specialized diagnostic services. • Avoid capital investments for high-tech medical equipment.	• Contract with private diagnostic center to provide services to publicly-sponsored clients. • Refer specialized laboratory procedures to private laboratory.

(Table continues on the following page.)

173

Table 3.3 (continued)

TARGETED AREA	STRATEGIC OBJECTIVES	CONTRACTING OPPORTUNITIES
Extended care	• Encourage availability of extended care services for chronically ill. • Reduce number of elderly housed in hospitals.	• Contract with extended care facility to care for public-sponsored clients. • Contract with elder-housing facility to care for public-sponsored clients. • Contract to provide home-care services.
Ambulance and transportation services	• Avoid or reduce investment in vehicles. • Decrease ambulance response time.	• Lease vehicles under contract. • Contract with private transportation/ambulance services to respond to emergency calls in designated areas.
Pharmaceuticals, medical supplies, and equipment	• Increase access to quality medicines. • Reduce unnecessary multiple prescriptions. • Improve operation and maintenance of critical medical equipment. • Reduce investments in high-tech medical equipment.	• Contract for training medicine sellers, pharmacists, and doctors on proper medicine use. • Contract for social marketing campaign to inform consumers on proper medicine use. • Tender bids for bulk purchase of essential medicines and medical supplies. • Contract for medicine and medical supply warehousing and distribution services. • Contract for equipment maintenance. • Lease high-tech medical equipment.

Human resources, education and training

- Encourage doctors, nurses, and other health personnel to stay current on professional practice.
- Improve quality of medical and nursing education.
- Reduce or control number of personnel on government payroll.
- Encourage greater personal responsibility for disease prevention.

- Contract with medical associations to help develop treatment protocols.
- Provide technical assistance for curriculum development.
- Contract for development and implementation of accreditation program for educational institutions.
- Contract for temporary workers or a service staffed by private providers.
- Contract for social marketing campaigns on smoking, nutrition, diarrhea rehydration, AIDS, and other preventive measures.

Knowledge management

- Strengthen capacity for health policy research and development.
- Improve availability, quality, and utilization of information needed for planning, research, and quality management.

- Contract for technical assistance and training on policy research and development.
- Contract for development and operation of management information systems.
- Provide training for managers in planning and decisionmaking.

for achieving its strategic objectives in health services delivery. As a purchaser, rather than simply as a provider, government can be selective in what and how it purchases a service. Ideally, government should choose what health services to buy based on defined strategic objectives. Similarly, how government chooses to buy should be based on what purchasing mechanism will best achieve those objectives. Contracting, as one of several possible purchasing mechanisms, has a number of potential benefits—as well as risks and limitations—that must be evaluated in deciding when it is the option of choice.

The Government's Purchasing Role

One alternative to providing health services directly is for the government to assume the role of purchaser, providing or mobilizing the necessary financial resources but buying the needed services from other governmental or nongovernmental sources. By assuming the purchasing role the government maintains the responsibility for ensuring that health services are provided, but fulfills that responsibility by funding those services instead of providing them directly.

In health care, all governments already play the role of purchaser—by buying medicines, medical supplies, equipment, food, and other products and materials needed to support the operation of their public health systems. From that perspective, purchasing health services from private provider organizations simply broadens the government's purchasing role to include the acquisition of a wider array of management, support, and clinical services that may strengthen, augment, or substitute for publicly provided services. As a purchaser, government has to determine what services are needed, where they might be obtained, under what conditions, and at what price. Purchasing separates financing from provision and allows government to concentrate its energies on deciding which services are most needed and how much they will cost, while leaving most of the operational details to the service provider.

Contracting is a mechanism that can be used by the government to exercise its purchasing role in an orderly and disciplined way. Because all governments have some contracting experience, a number of official and unofficial rules and practices will have grown up around the contracting process. Efforts to extend contracting to new areas of activity should be mindful of such historic precedents. Managing the contracting function has two broad components: preparing for and issuing the contract, and monitoring the contractor's performance. These two functions can be performed by the same or different bodies and may be either centralized or decentralized. In developing countries these functions are usually highly centralized, with approval required by a central tender board. The functions may also be handled by the local health authority or by the individual institution. Some contracts naturally lend themselves to national tendering—purchasing of medicines, for example—while other tendering—such as building maintenance—is more appropriately handled at the local level (Hillman and Christianson 1984, as cited in Mills and Broomberg 1998).

The entity that is assigned the responsibility for purchasing health services may be the ministry of health, a parastatal health insurance fund, or some other governmental or nongovernmental agency. Having the ministry of health play the role of purchaser may create internal conflicts between objective selection of providers and vested interests within the ministry's own provider network. Ideally, the purchaser and provider roles should be separated. Governments often delegate the responsibility to undertake all contracts for health services to a parastatal agency (often a social insurance organization), thereby distancing themselves somewhat from the purchasing role. Such agencies often negotiate contractual agreements for services to be provided by either public or private providers.

Exercising Purchasing Selectivity

The power of the purchasing role lies in the purchaser's ability to exercise selectivity. As a purchasing mechanism, contracting is a proactive process quite distinct from the more passive, traditional budgeting process used to allocate financial support to established governmental programs. Budgeting takes governmental resources and allocates them primarily to ongoing services and providers, often with only perfunctory attention to service priorities or effectiveness. In contrast, contracting is based on exercising selectivity and taking a strategic orientation toward three critical factors: services, providers, and payment methods.

- *Services.* Regardless of whether health services are directly provided by the state or purchased, no government can afford to finance all the health services for which there is a demand; some rationing will thus always occur. Under public provision rationing is often hidden, or at least not recognized. Contracting often makes rationing more explicit, since the contracts must identify specific services or populations to be covered. A strategic orientation toward contracting requires the purchaser to target desired service outputs—such as volume, service mix, quality, price, and timing—while openly omitting other, less critical, factors.

- *Providers.* A strategic orientation toward providers involves allocating resources to organizations according to their ability to deliver the desired level and quality of services. Selective contracting requires comparative information about provider quality, efficiency, and effectiveness, as well as the freedom to not contract. In addition, once a provider has won a contract there is no guarantee that the contract will be extended or renewed after it expires. Selectivity and choice are key. If it were otherwise contracting would become another form of passive budgeting.

- *Payment methods.* The payment methods can and should underscore the government's strategic orientation. The contractual arrangement must match the fee structure to the purchaser's strategic objectives. As examined later in this chapter on page 191, different payment methods (such as block grant, capitation, and fee-for-service) will each influence provider behavior in different ways. Input-based payment mechanisms (mechanisms that base payments on staffing levels, facilities, and so on) have relatively little strategic power, as compared with output-based payment mechanisms (that base payments on volume or other measures of performance), thus encouraging providers toward efficiency and cost-effectiveness.

Alternative Contracting Options

Contractual arrangements can take many forms (table 3.4).

Typically, contracting does not refer to the autonomization or privatization of a government health facility or service. Autonomous institutions may remain under public ownership but may not be able to rely on governmental support. If privatized, a facility's or service's assets are turned over or sold to a private entity, and the facility or service becomes independent and financially self-sufficient. In either case the autonomized or privatized enterprise may enter into a contractual arrangement with government for one or more selected programs or services, as is true of any other private provider (Jenkinson and Mayer 1996, p. 9).

Contracting Benefits and Limitations

Jenkinson and Mayer (1996, p. 3) point out that the benefits of contracting fall into three categories: risk sharing, incentives, and protection against exploitation of specific investments. Through contracting, for example, the government can shift certain risks to the provider—such as under a fixed-price contract where the provider assumes the risk for cost increases. Contractual incentives, primarily financial, can promote changes in service volumes, efficiency, quality, or other provider behaviors. By assuring a provider that there is a continuing market for the duration of the contract, contracting can protect a provider's investment in needed infrastructure or personnel. In application, however, these functions of contracting, and their potential benefits and limitations, are likely to be perceived by the public and private sectors in quite different ways (table 3.5).

Box 3.2 offers an additional perspective on the challenges of contracting.

Table 3.4 Contracting Options for Purchasing Health Services

OPTION	APPLICATIONS
Contracting-out or outsourcing	Purchase one or more services from an outside source that provides the service to either a government entity or patients, using primarily an external work force and resources. Examples of services provided to government entities include sending linens out to a private laundry or securing clinical laboratory services from a private laboratory. Examples of services provided to patients might include contracting with a nongovernmental organization to manage a number of district facilities, or to provide a service package to identified users in their own facilities.
Contracting-in[a]	Purchase management services from an outside source that is assigned responsibility for managing an internal service or work force. Examples include hiring a private firm to manage a hospital's housekeeping staff (most of whom remain publicly employed) or external technical assistance to direct an internal task force.
Procurement	Purchase supplies or materials from one or more outside sources, as in the purchase of medicine, food, or medical equipment. Procurement contracts are typically used when a large volume of goods—in terms of number or cost—are to be acquired.
Lease or rental arrangements	Securing the use, but not the ownership, of facilities or equipment from an outside source under a lease agreement. Leasing is usually used for capital-intensive items. Examples include the leasing of buildings, specialized medical equipment, and vehicles.
Subsidy or subvention[b]	Direct or indirect financial support intended to alter the provision or production of a selected service. Direct subsidies include grants and budgetary support; indirect subsidies may be in the form of tax exemptions. Subvention is a form of subsidy commonly used in Africa where government provides financial support to religiously sponsored charity hospitals in areas not served by public facilities. These arrangements may or may not be formalized by contract.
Franchise	A contractor, or franchisee, is granted the right, which may or may not be exclusive, to provide specified services to a defined clientele or in a specified geographic region. The contractor is given the right to collect and retain revenues, but is required to pay a fee or a percentage to the government for the privilege of doing so.

a. Contracting-in should not be confused with internal contracts among governmental agencies. Contracting-in, as used here and in some countries (such as in Cambodia), refers to bringing in outside private management to operate an internal government service.
b. Subvention is also used as a public finance term in many Eastern European countries for reallocation of financial flows across geographic regions.
Source: Personal communication, Jack Langenbrunner, World Bank, e-mail, January 20, 2000.

Table 3.5 Benefits and Limitations of Contracting

	PUBLIC SECTOR PERSPECTIVE	PRIVATE SECTOR PERSPECTIVE
Benefits of contracting	• By introducing competitive forces, contracting puts pressure on both public and private providers to improve their performance in terms of both service and price. • Expanding the range of activities subject to contracting encourages the private sector to expand the services it provides in areas desired by government. • Contracting both requires and promotes better planning and policy development by improving the flow of information about volumes of goods, services, costs, quality, responsiveness, population served, health needs, and other issues. • Contracting provides government with a mechanism for purchasing needed health services at an agreed-on, and therefore predictable, price. • Contracting can provide government with an additional means of financing capital investments. • Contracting promotes transparency, constrains conflicts of interest, and reduces opportunities for graft and corruption.	• Contracting expands market opportunities to include public sector clients or customers. • Contracting allows a private provider to "capture" a market, to be protected from competitors, at least for the term of the contract. • Contracting can provide a reliable and timely source of revenue, encouraging investments necessary to support quality and innovation and ensuring longer-term viability—assuming the government has a functioning financing system in place and contractual terms are favorable. • The contract term may provide adequate time to justify investments in the capital and personnel needed to support contractual obligations.
Limitations of contracting	• Qualified private providers may not be available. • Qualified bidders may not be interested in contracting with government. • Competition may be weak or nonexistent. • Government may discourage bona fide bidders by shifting too much risk to providers.	• The costs of entering the market to compete successfully for government contracts may be too high. • The market may be too unstable, or the contract period may be too short, to support needed capital investments. • Transaction costs, the costs of securing and managing the contract, may be too high.

(Table continues on the following page.)

Table 3.5 (continued)

	PUBLIC SECTOR PERSPECTIVE	PRIVATE SECTOR PERSPECTIVE
Limitations of contracting (continued)	• Successful contractors could compete with the public sector for health personnel. • Governmental capacity to negotiate contracts may be weak. • Government's managerial and bureaucratic overhead may increase. • Government may agree to disadvantageous contract terms. • Long-term contracts may restrict government flexibility. • Contract financing may introduce unanticipated, even perverse, incentives. • Costs may be higher than anticipated. • Consumer choice may be limited as unsuccessful bidders are forced to close. • Equity may be threatened if providers select low-risk patients. • Public hospitals may be forced to behave more like private hospitals, focusing on profitable services and reducing unprofitable services.	• Government payments may be inadequate to cover operating or capital costs, or both. • Successful contract performance may depend on uncertain government performance such as government-provided medicines or supplies. • Government may not pay its obligations on time. • There may be no legal recourse if government fails to fulfill its contractual obligations.

Source: Mills 1996; Broomberg, Masobe, and Mills 1997; and Bartlett and LeGrand 1993, as cited in Mills and Broomberg 1998.

Contracting is not a panacea. Thomas Rice (1998), for example, offers the contrary view that market theory and competition should not be relied on as the basis for public policy in health. He postulates that economic theory—in terms of market competition, demand theory, supply theory, and equity and distribution—should be reexamined, when applied to health. Rice's observations deserve consideration. Still, the prevalence of contracting for health services in the highly performing social insurance health systems justifies its consideration alongside public provision.

Box 3.2 Challenges of Contracting

Expected savings. Contracting of nonclinical and clinical services is expected to generate savings for public purchasers by utilizing more efficient private firms and transferring financial risks to them to perform according to contractual obligations. Experience shows, however, that significant transaction costs are incurred by public sector agencies that are involved in designing, administering, and monitoring and evaluating contracts. By some accounts these costs range from 7 to 20 percent of the value of the contract.

Government capacity. A contract is only as good as its contents, with the implication that the contractor must be skilled at specifying expectations and outcomes, understanding how different contractual forms and payment mechanisms may affect performance, and ensuring satisfactory performance. Most studies suggest that steps should be taken to improve public sector management skills in contract preparation (Mills 1996; and Mills 2000).

Provider selection and capacity. Ideally, many private or nongovernmental organizations (NGOs) will bid for a contract and will provide sufficient information to allow the purchaser to make the best choice. In limited markets, though, or in countries where the health-related private sector is small or weak, the number and capacity of bidders may be limited. Assessments should be undertaken and assurances given that the contractor can indeed deliver on its obligations—that it has the human resources and financial sustainability to do so.

Level of detail and kinds of tasks. The level of detail in contracts, and the kinds of tasks selected, will vary with the na-

(Box continues on the following page.)

Box 3.2 (continued)

ture of the service and the ease of specification. Nonclinical services such as catering, laundry, and vehicle maintenance are relatively straightforward in terms of quantity of items, activities anticipated, and quality standards to be met. The same does not apply, however, to clinical services, especially when it is necessary to link their provision to outcomes.

Requirements of the regulatory framework. Because public agencies increasingly transfer responsibility for delivering services to private organizations (by means of contractual agreements), commensurate attention must be given to the regulatory framework. On the one hand, public agencies will have to ensure that contractors are aware of and abide by regulations pertaining to private markets—such as minimum wage laws. On the other hand, the public sector must devise and enforce new regulations that ensure that opportunistic behaviors or information problems do not undermine health service provision. Confidence must be strong that government regulatory agencies can assume increasing responsibility in guiding the private actors who are engaged in service delivery.

Complexities of price setting. By contractually agreeing to provide a range of services for an agreed-on amount, the contractor runs the risk of incurring a financial loss if more money is required to deliver the services than had been anticipated. While this is part of the appeal of contracting—to shift the financial risk from the purchaser to the provider—contractors are aware of the potential costs and risks and will demand some form of built-in compensation. Usually this takes the form of a larger contractual amount than would be justified by the cost of providing the agreed-on services alone. It is important to understand such complex-

Box 3.2 (continued)

ities of price setting—and these complexities will vary according to the way the contractor is paid—which include fixed price, cost and volume, or capitation basis.

Monitoring and evaluation. In contractual arrangements funds and human resources must be dedicated to ensure that performance is sufficiently monitored and evaluated. Such information is critical to appraising whether outcomes are achieved, to enforcing contracts, and to undertaking mid-course corrections if performance is failing. Virtually all studies of the contracting process conclude that this important dimension is given inadequate attention or is poorly implemented.

Contracting learning curve. While it is necessary to consider the costs and benefits of contracting and to seek evidence on its performance, it is important to recognize that the initial phase of contracting will likely be the most problematic. Over time, as public officials become more familiar and effective in their new tasks, the costs will fall and the benefits will rise. There is some evidence of spillover effects; as public officials become more adept at holding private providers accountable, they often utilize these skills in order to hold public providers more accountable, as well.

Source: Several points have been adapted from Shaw 1999, p. 69.

Evaluating Contracting Risks and Benefits

Many governments intuitively recognize the inverse relationship between ease of contracting and potential impact, as measured by efficiency, quality, and accessibility. The levels of risk and benefit vary with the service being contracted,[3] as well as with whether the ser-

Table 3.6 Contracting Risk-Benefit Continuum

CONTRACTING DIFFICULTY	HOSPITAL-RELATED CONTRACTED SERVICE	CONTRACTING IMPACT
Easier	Hotel or ancillary services: housekeeping, catering, maintenance, security	Low
Medium	Clinical support services: pathology, radiology	Medium
Difficult	Core clinical services: hospital inpatient and out-patient care	High

Source: Abby Bloom 2000.

vice to be contracted for is currently publicly provided or is "new." As Domberger (1998) points out, "There is no unique set of costs and benefits associated with a particular contracting decision: there are a large number of them. . . ." As proposed by Abby Bloom, based on her experiences in Australia, table 3.6 illustrates these relationships in terms of a "risk-benefit continuum," using examples drawn from establishing contractual relations for existing hospital-related services, although the principles also apply to a wide range of health services.

When contracting for hospital-related services, Bloom postulates, it is often easier to test the waters by contracting for "hotel services" (such as cleaning, maintenance, and food services) than for services more central to the provision of health care ("core clinical services"). Generally, ancillary or support services are less threatening to the core of government health provision and are unlikely to threaten powerful stakeholders such as doctors, nurses, and administrative personnel. Not only is the outsourcing of hotel services less controversial, it also delivers a modest impact in terms of efficiencies and structural reform.

At the other end of the spectrum are core clinical services. In many communities, for example, the public hospital is among the largest employers, and the prospect of outsourcing basic patient care services would be synonymous with the loss of guaranteed employment. More important, it may mean the loss of strategic control over a highly specialized work force that generates much of the cost of providing services. "Clinical support services" (such as pathology, radiology, or a blood bank) occupy the middle ground of the continuum because they begin to encroach on "clinical" functions, yet they present only modest risk. They also entail services whose availability, quality, and efficiency can only be addressed through significant capital investment, providing benefits to the government, doctors (who get better diagnostic tools), and patients (who value the benefits). Not included in the continuum is contracting for the management of entire hospitals; that would vary in risk according to local circumstances.

In some circumstances contracting for a few pilot services is attractive simply because, although some risk is involved, it is manageable. In such cases the government can experiment with the practical and political consequences of contracting but reserves the option to revert to full government provision.

Contracting as a Strategic Process

Contracting is a strategic process that government can use to guide the activities of private providers, thus achieving targeted national health objectives. To ensure that contracting is used strategically—to introduce market mechanisms while ensuring that essential public services are provided and the needs of the poor and vulnerable are protected—the government needs to recognize that contracting is a powerful process, a purposeful methodology, not just a cluster of independent transactions. As a strategic process contracting sends strong messages to the market, and to the public sector. The contracting process can promote more thoughtful planning and provide greater transparency in government purchasing. In addition, contracting utilizes direct financial incentives to encourage specified provider behaviors. On the other hand, contracting carries risks, including the potential risk to skew the supply of health services. This means that contracting initiatives must be regulated and monitored at the highest level of government, by experienced and astute policymakers, economists, and operational personnel.[4] The routines of contract management may be delegated to a contracting unit or units, but national policy objectives must guide the strategic decisions.

The contracting process involves several critical steps:

- Define contract goals and performance expectations.

- Determine contract payment strategy.

- Select a provider or source of service.

- Negotiate contract terms and conditions.

- Mobilize and implement the contract.

- Manage contract performance.

The list of critical steps described here differs in specifics but not in spirit from the "seven steps to successful contracting" described by Mills (1996) in her study of contracting experiences in several developing countries.

Because all governments have some contracting experience, most will already have some guidelines and protocols—possibly even regulatory requirements—that govern how contracting is to be conducted. Contractors may be required to post a performance bond. Licensure or accreditation may be required. Regulations may specify bidding requirements or other aspects of the tendering process. Whatever the existing regulatory climate, the steps listed above and outlined below are generic to all contracting activities and should be viewed as augmenting or focusing a government's current contracting practices, not supplanting them.

Each step of the contracting processes requires disciplined attention to a number of important tasks. Also important, each step offers opportunities and options that can help advance government's strategic health objectives.

Define Contract Objectives and Performance Expectations

As a purchaser of health services the government needs to lay the groundwork for contracting well before bids are solicited or negotiations are undertaken. The objectives of this advance work are threefold—to identify the specific service to be contracted, to assess the potential benefits and risks involved, and to provide information that supports the government's ability to negotiate successfully. Several tasks need to be addressed during this period of advanced preparation:

- *Identify health policy objectives and government service or program needs*. Deciding whether to contract, and which services to contract for, entails analysis of what government hopes to accomplish through contracting (Mills 1996). Clarity on governmental objectives will help determine which tools to use, in what combination, and where contracting might have a strategic advantage over other governmental interventions. If contracting is being considered in the context of a specific program (rather than as a systemic reform), then information is needed about which private providers are relevant for achieving the program's objectives.

  For systemic contracting initiatives:

- *Focus on the service or services that have contracting potential*. Contracting includes setting priorities among services that might be contracted-out, and defining the service or a package of services to be included in the contract (Mills 1996). In cases where government has relatively little experience in contracting, less complex services (such as hospital security, equipment maintenance, laundry) might be targeted instead of clinical services, such as imaging technology or coronary bypass surgery.

- *Evaluate whether to make or buy the needed service or services*. A key parameter in a make or buy decision is the comparative cost—what would the same or similar service cost if provided by government as opposed to purchasing the service on the open market. Both the costs included in the contract and the related transaction costs—the costs of managing the process—need to be considered (Mills and Broomberg 1998). Often, governments are not sophisticated in cost estimating and do not know their in-house production costs or the quality received for the money spent. Similarly, they may lack good data on internal transaction costs. Still, given attention, better costing is possible and contracting may provide the impetus for government to pursue improved cost-finding capabilities.

For program-based initiatives:

- *Determine which private providers are critical to the program objectives.* The contracting strategy will need to be effective in reaching the targeted individuals, illnesses, or interventions. To enhance child health for poor slumdwellers, for instance, contracts might be undertaken with a number of private providers in that area, conditional on their application of the integrated management of child illness (IMCI) strategy. If the program objective is to expand access to health care in specific rural areas, contracts might be undertaken with NGOs who are currently operating in those areas to deliver a "basic package" of services for inhabitants.

- *Mobilize stakeholder understanding and support.* Contracting cannot be done in isolation. Everyone who will be affected by the contracting effort, or who might influence its progress or results, has to be informed and involved. While opening up the contracting process to politicians, bureaucrats, and public and private providers—as well as to consumers and financial benefactors—has some obvious dangers, attempts to shield the process from these influences are both short-sighted and futile. Especially in the early stages, when contracting is still an unfamiliar tool, special care should be exercised to gain stakeholder understanding, even if full endorsement is not obtainable. In some instances the government may wish to engage a panel of private providers to help identify contracting opportunities, or to offer advice on the content, size, and even the financing of potential contracts.

- *Define service specifications, expectations, and performance measures.* For purchases of tangible goods (such as medical supplies or equipment) physical characteristics and functional parameters can be specified with reasonable accuracy. Defining specifications for services can be more difficult and can be either performance-based or method-based (Walsh 1995). Performance-based specifications (such as would be found in a contract for housekeeping services) define the desired outcomes but leave the method up to the contractor. Method-based specifications state the process or inputs to be used, but are less precise about results and are used where outcomes are not easily defined (such as would be found in a contract for a clinical service). The more closely specifications can be tied to measurable outcomes, the better.

- *Determine contract duration.* Contracts can be in force for years. Short-term contracts, for one or two years, can increase competition and make it easier to replace an unsatisfactory contractor. At the same time, contractors may be reluctant to invest in needed equipment or staff training if those costs cannot be amortized over the contract's life. Transaction costs for the contractor also increase because of frequent retendering. With longer-term contracts the purchaser and the contractor have the time to build a collaborative relationship, which can reduce both monitoring and transaction costs (Mills and Broomberg 1998).

- *Prepare bidding documents.* Bidding documents have three main purposes: (a) to communicate the purchaser's needs and expectations to potential providers; (b) to describe the contractual terms to govern the relationship; and (c) to prescribe the conditions for submitting qualified bids. Service specifications and performance expectations, as defined by the purchaser, need to be clearly and realistically described. Contractual terms need to be detailed, usually by including a copy of the proposed agreement. If the conditions for submitting a qualified bid are too loose, unqualified buyers will be encouraged to submit proposals. If too tight, even qualified bidders may be reluctant to respond.

Determine Contract Payment Strategy

How a provider is paid has more potential to shape results than any other contractual provision. The form of payment, not just the amount, strongly influences provider performance. The introduction of financial incentives into the contract is the purchaser's principal mechanism for shaping the contractor's behavior. Financial incentives can take different forms, each with potential advantages and disadvantages. The challenge to the purchaser is to select the payment strategy that best achieves the desired results. Table 3.7 illustrates major payment strategies, anticipated results, and potential contract applications.

As a rule, purchasers lacking experience in contracting are likely to select payment methods that are simple to administer (such as block grants, or cost and volume payment), with lower transaction costs, but also minimal attention to their strategic possibilities. More sophisticated payment strategies, with higher transaction costs, require greater capacity to gather and use data and to monitor and evaluate results; these are tasks that may be beyond the capacity of purchasers with little contracting experience. Purchasers commonly introduce more sophisticated payment strategies as they gain experience and capacity. There are exceptions, however, as in the United Kingdom National Health Service, which has moved to more simply administered payment methods.

Once a payment strategy has been selected it must be incorporated, with other service and performance expectations, into the contract-bidding documents. The bidding documents—including instructions to bidders, eligibility requirements, the expected content of the technical and price proposals, and other bidding requirements—are then ready for distribution to prospective bidders as a request for proposals (commonly known as an RFP).

Select a Provider or Source of Service

Ideally, any purchaser prefers to face a number of potential providers who are highly motivated to be chosen as the contractor. Hence, a major strategic objective of contracting over the medium to long term is to promote competition among qualified or targeted providers on service and price, even though that objective may be compromised for any individual contracting opportunity. Studies in the United Kingdom have shown that:

> [T]here is an important interaction among competition, prices, and quality. Competition between providers gives health authorities information about costs of provision to which they

Table 3.7 Optional Contract Payment Strategies

PAYMENT STRATEGY	ANTICIPATED RESULTS	CONTRACT APPLICATIONS
Block grant or fixed price—payment of a single fixed amount (including direct and indirect costs and profit) for all specified services for a specified period. A block grant functions much like a global budget.	• Provider assumes risks of changing or un-known costs. • Provider may reduce or terminate services if costs increase. • Information needs are minimal. • Contract is easy to administer.	• Contract for technical assistance • Contract for delivery of package of basic health services • Useful where purchaser has limited experience or limited ability to project or monitor actual costs
Labor and materials—payment of total direct costs (labor and materials) with an additional percentage for indirect costs, management, and profit.	• Purchaser assumes risk of increased costs. • Recognizes uncertainty or rapid changes in the cost of labor and materials. • Recognizes uncertainty in service specifications. • Gives provider little incentive to control inputs. • May encourage "padding."	• Contract to remodel an older hospital • Contract for hospital management where labor costs are determined by government, not the contractor
Cost and volume—payment of a fixed amount for a specified volume of service. Excess volume may be paid on a fee-per-case basis.	• Encourages increased volume of covered services. • Encourages increased volume of services with greatest profit margins. • Provider may neglect less well-reimbursed services.	• Contract for laundry services based on cost per pound of linen • Contract for food services based on an agreed-on price per patient day

(Table continues on the following page.)

193

Table 3.7 (continued)

PAYMENT STRATEGY	ANTICIPATED RESULTS	CONTRACT APPLICATIONS
Fee-for-service—payment based on an agreed-on price per procedure or test.	• Provider assumes risk of increased unit costs. • Purchaser assumes risk of increased volume. • Encourages increased volume of covered services. • Encourages increased volume of services with greatest profit margins. • Provider may neglect less well-reimbursed services.	• Contract with private doctors to provide specified health promotion or preventive services • Hospital services
Capitation—payment based on an agreed-on amount per person covered or enrolled for a specified package of covered services.	• Provider assumes risk of increased costs. • Purchaser assumes risk of increased volumes. • Encourages enrollment. • May encourage provider to reduce quantity or quality of service.	• Primary care services • Hospital services
Set price—purchaser establishes payment amount in advance and asks bidders to propose how much they can provide for that price.	• Provider assumes risk of increasing costs or cost overruns. • Provides purchaser with a range of volume and quality options. • May encourage low quality.	• Support services (housekeeping, catering, laundry)
Prepayment—payment provided in advance for specified services to be rendered. Akin to "hard" contracts (Saltman and Ferrousier-Davis 1995).	• Provider assumes risk of increased volumes. • Discourages overutilization of covered services.	• Various
Indemnification—payment provided after service has been rendered. Akin to Saltman's and Ferrousier-Davis' (1995) "soft" contracts.	• Encourages increased volume of reimbursed services. • Purchaser retains risk of increased volumes.	• Health insurance plans where the range of covered services and exposure is limited

194

might otherwise not have access and affects the degree of bargaining power between purchaser and provider . . . where there are few providers, competition may be so restricted that large surpluses can be earned by providers (Jenkinson and Mayer 1996, p. 5).

In many developing countries, however, where health markets are immature, identifying even one qualified provider, let alone several, may be problematic. In such situations contracting with a sole-source provider may be a necessary alternative. In some cases contracting directly with a single provider can be advantageous (such as an NGO or a nonprofit agency) where mutual trust and respect are strong and both sides see the benefits of working together (Bartlett and LeGrand 1993; and Gilson and others 1997). More commonly, though, through the tendering process the government hopes to identify or stimulate the entry of multiple competitors.

Selecting a qualified provider involves three important tasks: qualifying bidders, writing guidelines for tendering bids, and deciding upon guidelines for evaluating bids.

Qualifying bidders. Open bidding and prequalification are the two principal methods for identifying qualified bidders.

- *Open bidding.* As a strategy for encouraging competition, especially in a country where contracting for health services is relatively new or where qualified bidders are difficult to identify, government may wish to use an open bidding system even though it may require additional work to sort out unqualified proposals. Open bidding allows any provider to submit a proposal, can signal the government's intent to use bidding as a financing strategy, and may encourage providers to gear up for current and future bidding opportunities. Contracting with inexperienced contractors, however, may require more careful monitoring and lead to higher transaction costs.

- *Prequalification.* Where qualified bidders are numerous or easily identified, the purchaser may wish to prequalify bidders, selecting

196 • Private Participation in Health Services

a number of providers thought to have the capabilities of providing the contracted service successfully. Prequalifying bidders involves a few basic steps:

- *Develop criteria for bidder qualification.* Determine what characteristics a provider needs to perform successfully for a specific contracting opportunity.

- *Identify possible bidders.* Solicit, through promotion and referral, a list of interested providers.

- *Screen potential bidders for their ability to perform.* The purchaser can request that potential bidders submit letters of interest documenting their qualifications. A short list of qualified bidders can be compiled from these responses.

Guidelines for tendering bids. The bidding process is designed to encourage bidders to submit their best proposal in terms of technical performance and price. Sealed bids, submitted by a stipulated deadline, help increase transactional transparency by reducing opportunities for government officials to exercise undue influence and minimizing collusion among providers. Tendering bids involves a few basic steps:

- *Distribute bidding documents.* The bidding documents, prepared earlier, are distributed to potential bidders upon request, or to a list of prequalified bidders.

- *Set deadline.* A specified amount of time—depending on the complexity of the requested services—is allotted for bidders to prepare and submit their proposals. Typically, a date is specified by which the purchaser must have physically received sealed bids, at a designated location. If an extension is allowed to any bidder, it must be granted to all bidders.

- *Answer bidder inquiries.* In fairness, information provided to one bidder should be provided to all bidders. A bidders' conference, held shortly after release of the bidding documents, can often address most questions.

- *Request separate technical and cost proposals.* Bids should be submitted in separate, sealed, envelopes. Separating technical and cost proposals allows all bids to be evaluated first on technical merit. Cost proposals are then evaluated only for those bids that qualify technically.

Guidelines for bid evaluation. The objective of the evaluation process is to select the vendor with the greatest potential to fulfill the objectives of the contract in terms of service, performance, and price. Price, though important, should not be the sole criterion for accepting a vendor's bid, but it can help differentiate among otherwise qualified bidders. Evaluating bids involves a few basic steps:

- *Empower a Bid Evaluation Panel to review submissions.* The panel must be knowledgeable enough to evaluate the bids fairly, and as free from political and bureaucratic influence as possible. The participation of one or more objective outsiders is desirable.

- *Define evaluation criteria.* Typically, the criteria used to evaluate the technical portion of a proposal include three broad areas: the contractor's prior experience, the qualifications and experience of the personnel who will staff the project, and the quality of the plan for managing the project. Evaluation criteria should be determined in advance and included in the bidding documents distributed to bidders.

- *Maintain bid confidentiality and security.* Sealed bids should be requested and, once received, should remain sealed until they are opened in the presence of the Bid Evaluation Panel.

- *Evaluate technical compliance first.* Technical bids are opened first and evaluated according to the predetermined criteria. To reduce the chance of undue influence, each proposal should be evaluated independently by each member of the panel and the results pooled. Bids should be ranked by technical merit. Technically unqualified proposals should be eliminated.

- *Evaluate cost proposals.* The sealed cost proposals submitted by the qualified bidders can then be opened. Typically, the cost and technical portions of the proposal are weighted according to a prede-termined formula—again made known to all bidders in advance. Bids are than ranked accordingly and bidders notified.

Negotiate Contract Terms and Conditions

Once a successful bidder has been identified, negotiation of final contract terms can begin. It is essential that both the purchaser's and the bidder's representatives in negotiations have the power to exe-cute a contract. Contract negotiations usually include the following tasks:

- *Complete draft contract.* Typically, a draft contract is included in the bidding documents. The contract usually covers a variety of fac-tors such as starting date, term, dispute settlement terms, payment terms, and contract termination terms. Negotiations are usually limited to a few specific technicalities. Any perceived discrepan-cies in the contractor's ability to perform as specified—as in the loss of a key person included in the bidder's proposal—must be rectified.

- *Clarify terms of reference.* The specifics of the work to be performed are usually spelled out in the terms of reference and appended to the contract itself. The date and approach for mobilizing the con-tractor's team or resources must be determined and made part of the terms of reference.

- *Finalize details with provider or providers.* The next step is to final-ize all details about the contracting and service provision arrange-ments. In finalizing the arrangements and contract terms, it may happen that the purchaser cannot reach agreement with the suc-cessful bidder after a good faith effort. In this event, the purchaser may exercise the option to terminate negotiations and begin dis-cussions with the second-highest-ranked bidder.[5]

- *Sign the contract.* Once agreement has been reached, both parties should sign the contract at the earliest opportunity. Delays are costly and, if prolonged, should be subject to indemnification.

- *Notify stakeholders.* While stakeholders who will be affected by the contract should be kept informed at each stage of the tendering process, an official notification should be distributed when the contract has been finalized.

Mobilize and Implement the Contract

Once the contract has been signed the purchaser and the contractor, working together, begin to mobilize the resources and arrangements necessary to implement the agreement. Typically, contract implementation involves the following key activities:

- *Hand over authority.* The purchaser should pass authority to the contractor as specified in the contract.

- *Arrange payments.* The contractor should provide any financial advances and should arrange for ongoing payments. If advances are specified in the agreement, they should be paid promptly. Criteria for ongoing payments should be unambiguous and should be paid promptly when authorized.

- *Acquire resources.* The contractor should acquire workspace, furniture, and equipment.

- *Identify and mobilize personnel.* Key staff who have been specified in the contractor's proposal should be mobilized; sources of additional staff should be identified in advance, and that staff mobilized.

- *Establish contractor's presence and set start date.* The contractor needs to make its presence known to all affected stakeholders and constituents. Mobilizing and maintaining stakeholder support will require ongoing attention throughout the contract to ensure they are informed and supportive.

Manage Contract Performance

The strategic objective of managing contract performance is to ensure that underlying service objectives are met, and, if not, whether the contractual terms, the provider's performance, or the government's performance, or all three, should be adjusted. Monitoring and evaluation play important management roles in informing the purchasing process and strengthening the capacity of both the purchaser and the provider to contract more intelligently. In addition, the relationship between the purchaser and the provider, whether collaborative or distrustful, will color how the contract is managed. Finally, because contracting for health services is still considered experimental in many regions of the world, lessons learned from contracting experiences in one country can prove valuable for governments attempting similar activities elsewhere. Given these important contributions, contract management is often not given the time and attention it deserves. Four major contract management activities deserve particular emphasis—monitoring, evaluating data, resolving differences between expectations and performance, and contract extension or renewal.

Monitoring. At its most fundamental level monitoring is simply keeping track of what is happening. To be significant, however, monitoring requires measurable parameters that directly or indirectly reflect performance. Meaningful monitoring requires that the purchaser and provider:

- *Establish monitoring and evaluation parameters in advance.* Decide early what constitutes success (such as quality, volume, or cost) and how these factors can be measured. These performance measures should be incorporated into the bidding documents and purchasing contract. Where possible, baseline data against which advances can be measured should be established.

- *Measure performance, not inputs.* Emphasize results by establishing output targets rather than inputs and processes. Monitoring outcomes, instead of contract outputs, is problematic, since outcomes are often long-term and may be influenced by factors not under the control of the provider. Develop direct or indirect measures of the most relevant quality indicators (such as application of IMCI, correct diagnostic procedures for TB symptomatics, cleanliness of facilities, waiting times, and patient satisfaction). Identify the actual recipients of contracted services and the number of services provided.

- *Make monitoring and evaluation a collaborative exercise.* Monitoring and evaluation are most effective when the purchaser and providers are engaged in deciding what parameters will be used for determining success and how those parameters will be measured. It is also best to monitor locally, as close to the performance of the service as possible.

- *Solicit patient input.* Users of services can play an important role in monitoring, because they have first-hand knowledge of the physician-patient interaction, as well as the general environment prevailing in the facility at the time of their visit. Government can strengthen the impact of patient perceptions by collecting and comparing information from user questionnaires or surveys as part of the monitoring arrangements for the contracted providers (Van de Van and Van Vliet 1992).

- *Set up monitoring systems.* Initially, the data-gathering capacity of both the purchaser and the provider may be rudimentary. Because of the inherently complex nature of health services and the lack of information technology support systems, measuring and monitoring either public or private sector activities can be extremely difficult. Further complicating verification is the fact that, while the government contracts and the contractor provides, it is the patient who receives the service. The need for improved information—which is driven by the need to make informed decisions about the contracting process—will encourage greater sophistication in data gathering over time.

- *Collect routine and episodic data.* Data gathering is time consuming and expensive. Decide what parameters should be measured continuously (such as expenses and revenues) and what parameters are better measured episodically (such as household expenditures for health services).

Evaluating data. Deciding what the collected data mean brings power to the monitoring and evaluation process. If data are simply compiled and filed but not utilized (a disturbingly common practice), the effort of monitoring and evaluating ultimately erodes the quality and integrity of the data collected, in addition to reducing the incentives to perform at the levels specified. Data evaluation includes:

- *Tracking progress.* One of the simplest uses of the information collected from contracted providers is to compare their performance over time, while avoiding the more complex calculations needed to allow comparison across providers who treat different types of patients or who may be dealing with different health-related challenges among their patients. New contracting initiatives benefit greatly from substantive impact analysis, which requires collection of baseline data, and the establishment of control groups whenever possible.

- *Evaluating contract costs.* Ideally, costs should be evaluated from two perspectives: a comparison of actual with contracted costs and, more broadly, a comparison of the costs of contracting the service—including transaction costs—with the costs of providing the service directly. However, public accounting systems may be inadequate to make accurate comparisons. Clinical contracts may be particularly prone to manipulation by providers and particularly difficult to monitor (Mills and Broomberg 1998).

- *Benchmarking.* It is increasingly common to utilize benchmarking, comparing results across contracted providers. Benchmarking can also compare the performance of contracted providers with standardized performance indicators, when these exist. An increasing number of databases of performance measures for health providers have been established, though most of them are based on experience in countries of the Organisation for Economic Co-operation and Development.

- *Lessons learned.* While measuring results is the principal emphasis of evaluation, an analysis of the way results were obtained can be useful for improving future performance. Linking methodology with results, however, should be approached with some caution since the cause-effect relationship may be tenuous.

- *Reporting and information dissemination.* Regular progress reports submitted to the purchaser can help signal discrepancies early and allow both purchaser and provider to make timely adjustment. Regular reporting of progress and lessons learned also keeps stakeholders informed and allows others to benefit from the contracting experience.

Resolving differences between expectations and performance. One product of the evaluation process is the identification of needed contract adjustments. Walsh (1995) makes a distinction between punishment-based contracts and cooperative contracts. Punishment-based contracts assume the purchaser and contractor have different interests and each seeks to exploit the other. Sanctions are required to discourage the contractor from failing to deliver. Cooperative contracts assume the parties have interests in common and that the contractor's performance is often affected by events outside its control. The following guidelines should be given consideration:

- *Discover deviations early.* Wherever possible, deviations from expected performance should be discovered before they worsen, and should be resolved through collaborative discussions between purchaser and provider.

- *Resolve disputes quickly.* Both parties should aim to minimize disputes and, when they occur, to resolve them quickly and amicably. Where differences cannot be resolved between the parties, they can be submitted to mediation where a neutral party can help reach a mutually endorsed settlement. If mediation fails, adjudication should be used, after both parties have agreed to abide by the decision of a neutral arbitrator.

- *Use penalties as a last resort.* Sanctions or penalties may be useful motivators but should be administered as a last resort, sparingly, and only for just cause. In Papua New Guinea, for example, termination was the only option provided for in a contract, and since termination would have left the hospital without the contracted service, managers were reluctant to request it. Contract arrangements in Thailand were more effective—financial sanctions were available but never used because the contractor had other incentives to keep equipment functioning (Mills and Broomberg 1998).

Contract extension or renewal. When a contract nears the end of its term, the purchaser must decide whether the contracted service is still needed, that it still addresses an important objective, and that contracting is still the preferred mechanism for its achievement. Allowing a contract to lapse assumes that the contracted service is no longer a priority or no longer needed, or that it will be provided in some other way. If the government wishes to continue contracting for a service, however, the purchaser must decide whether the contract should be extended, renewed, or opened up for rebid.

- *Extension.* Under certain circumstances a contract extension of a few months, or even years, may be offered to a provider—usually under the same terms as the original contract. Typically, an extension is offered when the provider has generally performed satisfactorily but where unavoidable or excusable delays have been experienced in reaching a contracted goal or conclusion. An extension may also be offered as a way to bridge a gap between the current contract and some future alternative—such as a new contract or a contract rebid.

- *Renewal.* Where a contracted service is still needed and the contracted provider has performed satisfactorily, the parties may elect to renew a contract—usually under terms specified in the original contract. Typically, a renewal is open to renegotiation of price and quantity, although these terms or their calculation may be specified in the original contract.

- *New tender.* Opening up a lapsing contract to the bidding process is time consuming and expensive and, without a compelling reason, both the purchaser and the provider may be reluctant to incur the heavy transaction costs involved. In fact, thoughtful contract extensions or renewal can be satisfying, cost-effective, and performance enhancing. Still, where market conditions or service needs have changed, where the contractor's performance has been unsatisfactory, or where a substantial improvement in contracted costs can be achieved, a rebidding may be worth the extra effort. Failure to rebid a contract when it is needed is ultimately no different from a passive budgeting exercise.

Strengthening Contracting Capacity

Contracting for health services is demanding work, requiring both the purchaser and the contracting provider to gather and analyze sophisticated information and to apply skills in planning, negotiation, and management at each step in the process. Government needs access to good data and the ability to analyze such information to plan effectively, to negotiate and manage contractual arrangements, and to monitor and evaluate contract performance. The government also has a critical need for the capacity to finance any purchasing arrangements it chooses to enter into. Private providers also need the capacity to provide the services desired by the government and to successfully compete for contracting opportunities. Private providers need the ability to prepare realistic proposals and to successfully manage their contractual obligations once a contract has been signed.

Working through the critical steps in even a simple contracting opportunity can be challenging and time consuming. Even when a history of experience has been accumulated, several months, even years, may be required to prepare for and conduct negotiations, followed by a period of implementation typically covering years. From table 3.8 it is easy to infer how even the simplest of contracts can take from 8 to 12 months, or longer, from conception to implementation.

In many developing countries building the capacity of the government and private providers to perform these numerous tasks well will require an investment in time, training, and experience.

Building Government's Capacity to Manage Contracting

All governments have some experience in contracting in the health arena, but public sector agencies often lack the critical skills needed

Table 3.8 Contracting Tasks and Time Line

1	2	3	4	5	6
DEFINE OBJECTIVES AND PERFORMANCE EXPECTATIONS	DETERMINE CONTRACT PAYMENT STRATEGY	SELECT PROVIDERS OR SOURCES OF SERVICE	NEGOTIATE CONTRACT TERMS AND CONDITIONS	CONTRACT MOBILIZATION AND IMPLEMENTATION	CONTRACT MANAGEMENT
• Identify policy or program objectives Systemic initiatives: • Focus on contracting potentials • Decide whether to "make or buy" relevant services Program initiatives: • Identify providers utilized by target group • Mobilize stakeholders • Define specifications • Decide on contract duration • Prepare bidding documents	• Block grant • Labor and materials • Cost and volume • Fee-for-service • Capitation • Set price • Prepayment • Indemnification	• Qualifying bidders: open bidding, prequalifying bidders • Tendering guidelines • Bid evaluation guidelines	• Complete draft contract • Clarify terms of reference • Finalize details with provider(s) • Sign contract • Notify stakeholders	• Hand over authority • Pay financial advances and prepayments • Acquire office space and equipment • Mobilize personnel • Commence work	• Monitoring • Evaluation • Dispute resolution • Contract extensions, renewal, or rebidding
2–6 months	1–3 months	2–6 months	1–2 months	1–3 months	Over 1- to 5-year life of contract, plus extensions

206

to manage the contracting process at the level of sophistication needed to achieve the full strategic potential of contracting. Skills are needed in: designing, costing, and evaluating health services; negotiating and managing contracts; and developing payment systems that ensure timely payments to providers. Efficiency gains from contracting appear to be contingent on government capacity to act as an efficient purchaser, and, more specifically, to make appropriate decisions about whether and when to utilize contracts, to design efficient contracts, and to effectively monitor contractor compliance. Conversely, lack of this capacity may lead to inefficiency through exploitation by contractors, through distorted resource allocation (Bennett, McPake, and Mills 1997), or through uncontrolled expansion of the private sector, creating further problems of fragmentation and inequity (Saltman and Ferrousier-Davis 1995). Lack of capacity in these areas can lead to a deterioration of trust between the public and private sectors and to a lessening of cooperation in future programs.

The process of contracting—which is designed to alter fundamental structures and reveal useful insights about purchasing and provision—will logically change the role, function, and orientation of health officials and their ministries. Some government officials, because of recent health reform efforts, have gained valuable experience and insights into the workings of the private sector. Too often, however, public employees do not have the depth of experience or knowledge needed to negotiate with their private counterparts on equal terms (see box 3.3). Failure to prepare for these new roles is one of the most predictable lapses observed in other contracting experiences (Bloom 2000).

To better fulfill their role as purchasers of health services governments need to develop increased capacities in several vital areas: data collection and analysis; effective planning; negotiating and managing contracts; and monitoring and evaluating contract performance.

Collecting and analyzing data. Governments' need to improve their data management capacities is not new, but it is accentuated by the demands of the contracting process. In fact, the failure of governments to improve data availability often reflects a weak management

---

Box 3.3 Government Contracting Skills

Some analysts have pointed to a generic set of skills and resources that governments need in contracting, including
skills in planning, economic analysis, and contract design
and negotiation, as well as suitable information systems and
sophisticated government regulatory capacity to carry out
functions such as licensing and accreditation. Not surprisingly, current evidence suggests that most developing countries lack all or most of these capacity requirements. However, evidence is still limited on the relative importance of
these various aspects of government contracting capacity or
of their specific impact on contractual efficiency.

Source: Mills and Broomberg 1998.

---

structure in which managers have little authority to make decisions
and therefore little reason to need good information. Improvements
in data availability are usually driven by the demands of managers
who need to make decisions, such as decisions that are required during the contracting process.

Planning effectively. Effective planning helps identify and evaluate
suitable contracting opportunities. Where government has been unable to develop a coherent medium-term health service–planning
horizon, it may settle for short-term, ad hoc contracts. Short-term
contracts may discourage providers from making the investments
needed to support service delivery in areas where they might otherwise make a positive contribution to broad health sector objectives.
Achieving potential cost savings and enhancing service quality require a longer-term planning perspective.

Negotiating and managing contracts. The contracting agency's ability
to manage the contracting process is crucial to success (see box 3.1).

In South Africa, for example, health department staff had allowed contracts to persist that were highly favorable to contractors but that were concurrently unfavorable to the health department. The same was true of some medical equipment contracts in Bangkok. Weak government planning capacity can also lead to late payments, which is likely to make contractors more reluctant to bid for future public sector contracts (Mills and Broomberg 1998).

Monitoring and evaluating contract performance. Identifying appropriate and realistic performance indicators; gathering data and measuring progress; identifying and evaluating progress; and finding constructive ways to deal with discrepancies and disputes all require considerable managerial sophistication. Over the last few years, international experience in measuring performance in health has been growing, with an expanding library of materials on monitoring and evaluation techniques. Developing countries should tap into these resources to support their local efforts and to begin to add their own experiences to the growing international pool of information.

Governments' capacities will be different, depending on the nature of the task, the type of service being contracted out, and the nature of the contractor. Contracting for a package of basic services poses greater challenges than contracting for delivery of health education or nutrition services in terms of the information required for designing and monitoring the contract. Yet as Mills (1996) points out, in some of the case studies examined, problems frequently arise around even such basic functions as paying contractors on time and keeping records of contracts negotiated. The external environment within which contracting takes place is also critical: in particular contracts embedded in slow-moving, rigid bureaucracies face substantial constraints to successful implementation.

Poor governmental administrative capacity in many developing countries suggests that contracting may not produce the hoped-for transparency. Similarly, although contracting will encourage some managerial decentralization relative to direct public management, the general lack of managerial expertise in developing countries may prevent decentralization from being actualized among the majority of providers, even where it is formally introduced (Mills and Broomberg 1998).

Building the government's capacity to manage the contracting process depends largely on acquiring experience—which usually takes years. As described in table 3.9, which is based on experience in Australia, governments often go through several phases as they build contracting experience—starting with simpler and less-threatening contracting opportunities, learning from the inevitable errors, and then, as they gain skill, expanding into larger and more complex contracting opportunities.

In the early stages, to jump-start its contracting capacity, a government can contract with technical assistance for temporary support, or may contract out its contract management activities with an agency or company that specializes in contract planning, tendering, negotiations, and management.

Government's Capacity to Finance Contracted Services

Finding the financial resources to support the government's contracting obligations can be difficult. Limited budgets in poor countries often mean fewer or poor-quality health services. As a result, contracting out a service may require an increase in public expenditures. For example, in Jamaica, a contract for cleaning and related services cost 25 percent more than the hospital's previous costs but resulted in services of increased quality and scope (Mills and Broomberg 1998). Essentially, the funds needed to finance contracted services can come from three sources: reallocation, new revenue sources, or external donors.

Reallocation. Simply reallocating governmental health funds is often problematic and might bump up against historic budgetary allocations, vested interests, and competing priorities waiting in line for limited resources. Still, improved costing data, where government can more precisely identify how it is spending its health budget and what it is getting for its money, may help leverage support for contracting alternatives. At the local level contracting alternatives can

Table 3.9 Phases of Building Contracting Capacity: Key Features

PHASE 1 PREPARATION	PHASE 2 TRIAL AND ERROR	PHASE 3 CONSOLIDATION AND REVIEW	PHASE 4 EXPANSION	PHASE 5 REFINEMENT
YEAR 1	YEARS 2 TO 3	YEARS 3 TO 4	YEARS 4 TO 6	YEAR 6+
• Analysis of current costs and utilization • Data warehouse established • Training • Recruitment	• Contracting pilots initiated • Contracting for non-core services begun • Minor and major setbacks	• Analysis of private sector performance • Identification of government's own gaps and weaknesses • Result: more effective contracts, contract management; better value for money	• Contracting expanded to: larger scale; clinical support or core services, or both • Data collection and analysis routine used for monitoring and management • Result: improved contract performance	• Predictability • More dynamic and responsive private sector • Good understanding of contractors and ongoing interaction with private sector • Public-private competition for contracts routine • Result: better scope for stable partnership between government and private sector

Source: Abby Bloom 2000.

211

also be encouraged if institutional managers and local authorities have discretionary power to reallocate budgetary funds among line items.

New revenue sources. The introduction of new revenue sources, through new taxes, user fees, or other sources, may be desirable but may also be problematic. Contracting opportunities may arise where social health insurance schemes have been introduced, funded by increased payroll taxes, although the competition for such revenues is likely to be fierce. In some cases revenues may be generated through the contract, such as where the contractor is allowed to collect user fees. The contract should specify how such revenues are to be allocated, whether exclusively to the contractor or shared with the purchaser.

External donors. Occasionally, donors provide funds to support contracting initiatives; this is true, for instance, in Cambodia, where proceeds of an Asian Development Bank loan are being used to fund contracts for the delivery of basic health services in rural areas. External support can be particularly helpful in motivating provider interest in situations where the government or health ministry has a poor reputation in terms of timely payment. External support can also be critical in countries where the government has generally negative attitudes about interactions with private providers. Assuming donors are funding priority services or users, however, the government must allocate budgetary resources to sustain these efforts.

Private Sector Capacity

The government's ability to successfully contract with the private sector for health services depends on the availability of qualified and willing private providers. Although most developing countries have numerous private health providers, many are individuals or small enterprises with limited ability to respond to contracting opportunities. To strengthen the private sector's ability and willingness to respond to contracting opportunities, three issues must be addressed:

market contestability, provider capacity and capability, and provider willingness.

Market contestability. In most developing countries private health providers are likely to face significant barriers to pursuing contracting opportunities. The historic dominance of the government as the principal provider of other than very basic health care services, which endow government providers with important competitive advantages, often leaves the majority of private providers comparatively small, weak, and undercapitalized. Regulatory and financial factors can also inhibit private sector growth. In any case, the government has an obligation to examine how its own behavior may restrain or enhance competition.[6]

Provider capacity and capability. Private providers can do much to strengthen their ability to win government contracts. There is strength in numbers in the health industry, as there is in other industries. Where individual practitioners band together—to form a group practice, for example—they are likely to gain both professional and economic leverage, enabling them to be better financed and to serve a larger constituency. Financially successful providers find they can attract better-qualified employees, further broadening the scope and improving the quality of their services. Theoretically, providers that can attract investment capital are able to improve the quality of their facilities and equipment and invest more in training and education. Realistically, however, such gains can be hard won and tenuous.

Provider willingness. Even when qualified providers exist they may be reluctant or unable to pursue government contracts. They may consider government contracts to be insufficiently profitable or the process of preparing a bid too onerous. A rapidly growing private market may offer easier and more predictable opportunities. Private providers that do prosper are likely to cater to the urban wealthy and may not be particularly interested in providing the services that have government priority. When economic growth slows, however, as in

South Africa, there may be more interest in government contracts (Mills and Broomberg 1998). One government option is to look for willing providers among NGOs and other nonprofits. In Cambodia, for example, the government identified a number of international NGOs with enough local expertise and experience to successfully bid on opportunities to manage the delivery of basic health service in several rural districts.

Enabling Environment for Contracting

The success of contracting initiatives is contingent on the broader enabling environment as well as on government actions directly related to the program. Elements of the institutional environment that positively influence contracting efforts include low incidences of corruption and a social context in which private and public actors communicate and share commitment to social responsibilities as well as mutual compliance with contracted obligations. Another important element of the institutional environment is a legal and regulatory system that generates predictable sanctions for noncompliance. Where such conditions are absent contracts may be inappropriately awarded, and contractors may exploit them, undermining efficiency (Mills and Broomberg 1998).

Many of these institutional issues can be addressed only through broader public sector reform efforts, and may go well beyond the narrow focus of most health service contracting initiatives. Even so, awareness of these factors is important. Particular problems in the enabling environment may need to be addressed within the contracting program, or may even render contracting unwise. In addition, it is useful for policymakers who are involved in contracting initiatives to consciously seek to contribute to the improvement of the overall enabling environment.

Appendix 3.A Other Sources of Information on Contracting

BASICS Project, Health Service Contracting in Africa, Conference Proceedings, USAID/REDSO/ESA, September 1997.

Ellis, R., and M. Chawla. 1993. "Public and Private Interactions in the Health Sector in Developing Countries." Health Financing and Sustainability Project, Management Sciences for Health, USAID.

England, R. 1997. "Contracting in the Health Sector: A Guide to the Use of Contracting in Developing Countries." Institute for Health Sector Development.

Epp, J. 1999. "A Guide for Bank Operations on 'Contracting-Out' for Reproductive Health Services." World Bank, Washington, D.C.

Griffin, C. 1989. *Strengthening Health Services in Developing Countries through the Private Sector*. Discussion Paper No. 4, International Finance Corporation.

La Forgia, G., Levine, Brenzel and Couttolenc. 1993. "Health Policy Reform in Latin America, Framework and Guidelines for Health Sector Assessment." A Manual Presented to the Inter-American Development Bank, The Urban Institute, June 30.

Lal, D. 1994. "The Role of the Public and Private Sectors in Health Financing." Human Resources Development and Operations Policy (HRO), Working Paper.

Lewis, M. 1988. The Private Sector and Health Care Delivery in Developing Countries: Definition, Experience, and Potential." Resources for Child Health Project (REACH), USAID.

McPake, B., and E. Ngalande Banda. 1994. "Contracting Out of Health Services in Developing Countries." *Health Policy and Planning* 9(1): 25–30.

Over, M., and N. Watanabe. Forthcoming. "Evaluating the Impact of Organizational Reforms in Hospitals." In A. Harding and A. S. Preker, eds., "Innovations in Health Care Delivery: Organizational Reforms within the Public Sector." Annex. World Bank, Washington, D.C.

Preker, A. S., and A. Harding. Forthcoming. "Conceptual Framework." In A. Harding and A. S. Preker, eds., "Innovations in Health Care Delivery: Organizational Reforms within the Public Sector." Annex. World Bank, Washington, D.C.

Rice, J. A. 1995. New Contracting for Health Gain: A Discussion Paper for Developing Health Insurance and Health Services Purchasing. ZdravReform Project, USAID.

Rosen, J., and S. Conly. 1999. "Getting Down to Business: Expanding the Private Commercial Sector's Role in Meeting Reproductive Health Needs." Population Action International.

Rosen, J. E. 2000. *Contracting for Reproductive Health Care: A Guide.* Health, Nutrition and Population Publications Series. World Bank, Washington, D.C.

Schieber, G., ed. 1997. "Innovations in Health Care Financing." Proceedings of a World Bank Conference, March 10–11, 1997. World Bank Discussion Paper No. 365, World Bank, Washington, D.C.

Slater, S., and C. Saade. 1996. "Mobilizing the Commercial Sector for Public Health Objectives: A Practical Guide." BASICS and UNICEF, USAID.

Torres, G., and S. Mathur. 1996. "The Third Wave of Privatization: Privatization of Social Sectors in Developing Countries." Private Sector Development Department, World Bank.

World Bank. 1993. "Investing in Health." *World Development Report 1993.* New York: Oxford University Press.

———. 1999. "Health Sector Goods." Procurement Technical Note, Final Draft. Washington, D.C.

Zinn, J., and E. Balotsky. 1994. "Selecting International Markets: Lessons from For-Profit Hospitals." Hospital and Health Services Administration. Spring.

Notes

1. Throughout this chapter and the handbook, the phrase "private provider" is used to refer to all providers outside the government sector, including both for-profit and nonprofit providers.

2. Optional contract payment strategies, and their anticipated results and potential applications, are discussed in greater depth later in this paper, and summarized in table 3.7.

3. Personal communication, Abby Bloom 2000. Health Innovations International, Sydney.

4. Personal communication, Abby Bloom 2000. Health Innovations International, Sydney.

5. The provision establishing for this eventuality should be clearly stated in the request for proposal.

6. For more on the impact of governmental regulation and incentives, see chapter 4, "Regulation of Health Services," in this handbook.

Bibliography

Bartlett W., and J. LeGrand. 1993. *Quasi-markets and Social Policy*. Basingstoke: MacMillan.

Bennett, S., B. McPake, and A. Mills. 1997. *Private Health Providers in Developing Countries: Serving the Public Interest?* London: Zed Books.

Bloom, A. 2000. Personal communication based on experience in Australia. Health Innovations International, Sydney.

Broomberg, J., P. Masobe, and A. Mills. 1997. "To Purchase or Provide? The Relative Efficiency of Contracting Out versus Direct Public Provision of Hospital Services in South Africa." In S. Bennett, B. McPake, and A. Mills, eds., *Private Health Providers in Developing Countries*, chapter 13. London: Zed Books.

Carrin, G., M. Jancloes, and J. Perrot. 1998. "Towards New Partnerships for Health Development in Developing Countries: The Contractual Approach as a Policy Tool." *Tropical Medicine and International Health* June 3 (6): 512–14.

Domberger, S. 1998. *The Contracting Organization: A Strategic Guide to Outsourcing*. New York: Oxford University Press.

Gilson, L., J. Adusei, D. Arhin, C. Hongoro, P. Mujinja, and K. Sagoe. 1997. "Should African Governments Contract Out Clinical Health Services to Church Providers?" In S. Bennett, B. McPake, and A. Mills, eds., *Private Health Providers in Developing Countries*, chapter 13. London: Zed Books.

Hillman, D., and J. Christianson. 1984. "Competitive Bidding as a Cost-containment Strategy for Indigent Medical Care: The Implementation Experience in Arizona." *Journal of Health Policy, Politics and Law* 9 (3): 427–51.

Jenkinson, T., and C. Mayer. 1996. "The Assessment: Contracts and Competition." *Oxford Review of Economic Policy* 12 (4): 9.

McCombs, J. S., and J. B. Christianson. 1987. "Applying Competitive Bidding to Health Care." *Journal of Health Politics, Policy and Law* 12 (4): 703–22.

Mills, A. 1996. "Government Capacity to Contract with the Private Sector: Health Sector Experience and Lessons." *Briefing Notes*. HEFP.

Mills, A., and J. Broomberg. 1998. "Experiences of Contracting: An Overview of the Literature." *Macroeconomics, Health and Development Series*, Technical Paper No. 33. Geneva: World Health Organization.

Musgrove, P. 1996. "Public and Private Roles in Health: Theory and Financing Patterns." Human Development Department, World Bank, Washington, D.C.

Preker, A., A. Harding, and N. Girishankar. 1999. "The Economics of Private Participation in Health Care: New Insights from Institutional Economics." World Bank, Washington, D.C.

Rice, T. 1998. *The Economics of Health Reconsidered*. Chicago: Health Administration Press.

Saltman, R. 2000. "The Concept of Stewardship in Health Policy." *Bulletin of the World Health Organization* 78 (6): 732–9.

Saltman, R., and O. Ferroussier-Davis. 1995. *Applying Planned Market Logic to Developing Countries' Health Systems: An Initial Exploration*. Discussion Paper No. 4. Geneva: World Health Organization.

Shaw, R. P. 1999. "New Trends in Public Sector Management in Health." Washington, D.C.: World Bank Institute. April.

Van Vliet, R., and W. van de Ven. 1992. "Towards a Capitation Formula for Competing Health Insurers: An Empirical Analysis." *Social Science and Medicine* 34 (9): 1035–48.

Walsh, K. 1995. *Public Services and Market Mechanisms: Competition, Contracting and the New Public Management*. Basingstoke, U.K.: Macmillan.

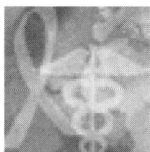

CHAPTER 4

Regulation of Health Services

Nihal Hafez Afifi, Reinhard Busse,
and April Harding

When health services are part of the government, issues such as quality, efficiency, and access can be dealt with administratively. Hence, where public provision predominates, health regulation plays only a minimal role.

In most health systems, however, public and private providers deliver services; consequently regulation is an essential instrument of government policy. Regulation is critical for harnessing private sector activities to contribute to social objectives; the unique character of health care as both a private and social good means that untempered market forces will generate a wide range of problems. The task of regulating health services, however, is a challenging one. In developed countries, with mixed delivery systems, highly sophisticated regulatory "networks" have emerged—where government, along with professional and provider associations, community groups, and increasingly, patients' organizations, play significant and complementary roles in guiding private activities toward social goals. In many developing countries, private providers are also widespread. In most of these countries, however, neither health authorities nor the other potential actors are playing an effective role in guiding private sector activities.

While most developing-country governments have passed substantial legislation related to health care and health care providers, these governments often lack institutional capacity, and have not succeeded in the challenging task of implementing and enforcing regulation. The other potential regulatory actors, such as professional and provider associations, may be present, but rarely have assumed significant responsibility for monitoring or ensuring quality. Patients' organizations are emerging in developing countries, but they usually lack the leverage needed to influence service delivery to any significant degree. Left to their own devices private service providers generate numerous concerns, related not only to clinical quality but also to broader issues such as efficiency and financial protection for poor patients.

What can governments do?

Each developing-country government will have its own priorities in improving the regulatory regime for health service provision. Nevertheless, the first phase of improving the regulatory regime often requires the same actions—collecting information about the role the private sector is playing; and establishing an ongoing dialogue among health policymakers, the private sector, and representative bodies, such as provider or community associations. Most developing-country health ministries have little or no information about the private health sector. Without this information they can neither enforce existing regulations nor establish priorities for improving the regulatory framework. Effective regulation of any kind requires policymakers to communicate with regulated entities, and the health sector is no exception. In countries with effective regulatory frameworks this dialogue is institutionalized and takes place in a wide range of forums. The interaction, or dialogue, allows policymakers to understand the likely impact or weaknesses of regulations under consideration; it informs health service providers about upcoming regulatory developments, aiding compliance; and it enables policymakers to work with groups who have similar interests (and often better information) to achieve regulatory goals.

Beyond these basic actions any government that is attempting to improve the contribution of the private sector to health goals will have to address the weaknesses in the existing regulatory framework and identify priority problems and actions to resolve those weaknesses. The contents of this chapter are intended to support this exercise and will cover the rationale for health sector regulation, the range of regulatory instruments or strategies, the targets and mechanisms of regulation, and the institutional structures of regulation, and will conclude with some recommendations. While this chapter and the handbook itself are intended to support improvement in government health sector policy and management, it is clear that other actors are critical to the functioning of the overall regulatory framework. Users of this handbook are thus encouraged to address any regulatory reform action within this broader context—to complement the government's capacity, within its own limits.

Section 1 Defining Regulation

In health care, as in other sectors, the government usually has broad responsibility for regulation. Hence, the literature on health care regulation often focuses on activities directly undertaken by the government. This handbook is intended to support development of effective public policy, so we will also review instruments and strategies commonly used by governments. However, in health systems throughout the world it is clear there are a number of other actors that influence the practice of health care. Medical and health care educational organizations are perhaps the most obvious, but other organizations that strongly influence health care include professional and provider organizations, patients' organizations, and community groups.

Given the insufficient capacities and scarce resources in developing countries, the premise underlying this handbook is that governments need to prioritize, and focus their efforts. In addition, they need to build wherever possible on the existing or potential capacity of other actors. Thus, this chapter will seek to indicate where international experience indicates tasks that can be performed by other actors in partnership or collaboration with the government. Hence, for our purposes, we will use the following definition of health regulation:

Health regulation is the range of factors exterior to the practice or administration of medical care that influences behavior in delivering health care (Brennan and Berwick 1996).

Despite wide-ranging definitions and contradictory rationales, there is broad agreement about the general mechanisms of regulation referred to as regulatory instruments. There are, however, many ways to view and group these instruments. In the second section of this chapter regulatory instruments are viewed in light of the underlying rationale for regulation. In the third section regulatory instruments are grouped by their governing strategy—whether control or incentive-based. In the fourth section instruments are categorized by the aspect of the health system being targeted (such as price, volume, quality). Regulatory instruments are discussed in terms of the type of health provider being regulated in the fifth section and in terms of the organizational form of the regulator in the next section. The last section presents practical considerations for operationalizing and implementing regulation.

To understand these categories, consider the Certificate of Need (CON) programs (in the United States) that review hospital plans to expand, modernize, and buy equipment. These programs issue approvals or denials of certification based on the merits of each case, inquiring whether the community requires the proposed project.

CON programs can be viewed from any of the following angles (each of which will be discussed later in this chapter, as noted):

- *Rationale for regulation.* CON programs aim to improve allocative efficiency and ensure geographic equity (section 2).

- *Regulatory instrument.* CON programs are categorized as legal restrictions, or a command-and-control instrument (section 3).

- *Target of regulation.* CON programs address health sector capacity by controlling the volume and distribution of services (section 4).

- *Regulated provider.* Hospitals are regulated under CON programs (section 5).

- *Regulatory body.* The state is the regulator under CON programs (section 6).

To avoid unnecessary duplication, relevant information for the context of more than one section may be included only once. Regulation of pharmaceuticals and technologies is beyond the scope of this chapter. Health insurance regulation is covered only if it is relevant within the context of the above-mentioned topics.

Section 2 The Rationale for Health Sector Regulation

A range of rationales is commonly applied to determine and analyze the state's role in regulating health services. Regulation is an essential element in guiding private activity within every sector of a modern economy. The unique character of health care as both a social and a private good reinforces the importance of active government regulation in the health sector (Saltman and Busse 2002).

Regulatory systems attempt to protect the public by countering market failures, bringing efficiencies to areas in which the market has been retarded, or correcting the market's emphasis on a single dimension (such as cost). Some regulatory roles can have an economic focus, to address provider monopolies, combat scarcity of certain necessary services (such as primary care), or curb wasteful service utilization in insurance arrangements.

Broadly speaking, the government bears responsibility for the achievement of what Saltman and Busse (2002) term the "social and economic policy objectives" (of government regulatory activities).

- *Equity and justice* by providing fair and needs-based access to health care for the whole population, including the poor, rural, elderly, disabled, and other vulnerable groups

- *Social cohesion* by providing health care through a national health care service or a social health insurance system

- *Economic efficiency* to contain aggregate health expenditures within financially sustainable boundaries

- *Health and safety* by ensuring the appropriate delivery of effective, high-quality services

- *Informed and educated citizens* by educating citizens about clinical services, pharmaceuticals, and healthy behavior

- *Individual choice* by allowing users to select provider and insurer (within the limits of the other objectives).

An appropriate mix of supply-side interventions at both the microeconomic (organizational) and the macroeconomic (system) levels has to be found in order to achieve a sustainable balance between different social and economic policy objectives. Such regulatory measures are health sector management–oriented, practical, operational, and largely technical in nature.

Regulating quality and effectiveness
- Assessing cost-effectiveness of clinical interventions
- Training health professionals
- Accrediting providers

Regulating patient access
- Gate keeping
- Copayments
- General practitioner lists
- Rules for subscriber choice among third-party payers
- Tax policy
- Tax subsidies

Regulating provider behavior
- Regulating capital borrowing by hospitals
- Rationalizing provider interactions and referrals
- Regulating acquisition of technology

Regulating payers
- Setting rules for contracting
- Setting prices for health care services
- Introducing case-based provider-payment systems
- Regulating reserve requirements
- Capital investment patterns as well as other activities of private insurance companies

On the demand side (which is not the focus of this chapter), all governments work to steer the financing process. Direct intervention in financing is critical to maintaining access in mixed delivery systems if solidarity is to be maintained.

With the emergence of bodies concerned with patients' rights and other user concerns, a new challenge for policymakers is to channel "patient power" in directions that reinforce whatever mix of instruments may be in place to both achieve solidarity and constrain costs.

Besides this two-level framework of the rationale for regulation in health care that emphasizes the social foundations of health care, other frameworks emphasize economic rationales such as "preventing windfall profits." Table 4.1 lists rationales for and the main objectives of health care regulation and lists applications.

Section 3 Regulatory Instruments and Their Governing Strategies

Different regulatory instruments and their governing strategies involve distinct methods of intervention. Baldwin and Cave (1999) offer eight—partly overlapping—categories (table 4.2, column 1). Market-harnessing controls include competition laws, concessioning (putting service provision or management under open tendering for certain periods of time), and contracting. Table 4.2 provides an overview of the strengths and weaknesses of these instruments and provides examples from the health care area (Baldwin and Cave 1999).

Regulation with respect to the institution or profession has two different orientations: to achieve compliance and disclosure and to achieve deterrence. Measures for health sector regulation can therefore be categorized as either:

- *Legal restrictions or controls.* Participants must conform to legal requirements or face punishment.

- *Incentives.* Participants, responding to incentives (policy-created payoffs or penalties), change their behavior. Their behavioral changes lead to changes in the target variable (such as price or

Table 4.1 Rationale and Main Objectives of Regulation

RATIONALE	MAIN OBJECTIVE	HEALTH CARE APPLICATION
Distributional justice	Distribute according to public interest.	Health insurance and universal public funding
Universal access to continuously available services	Ensure socially desired (or protect minimal) level of essential service.	Accident and emergency services (nights, rural areas); orphan drugs[a]
Scarcity and rationing	Allocate scarce commodities according to the public interest.	Organ transplants; waiting list regulations; benefit catalogue (Oregon)
Public goods	Share costs where benefits of activity are shared; prevent free-riding.	Support for immunizations; basic health care infrastructure (assure availability in case of need)
Moral hazard	Prevent excessive unnecessary consumption.	Health payment measures such as utilization review; co-payments
Social policy and paternalism	Prevent undesirable behavior or results, or both.	Mandatory seat belt use
Unequal bargaining power	Protect vulnerable interests (such as unorganized, informal employees) where markets fail to do so.	Occupational health care
Information inadequacies	Inform consumers to allow market to operate (and to protect their health).	Pharmaceuticals, devices, health care providers (such as accreditation, labeling, and quality assurance)
Monopolies and natural monopolies	Counter tendency to raise prices and lower output. Harness benefits of scale economies. Avoid exploitation of monopoly power.	Hospitals
Anticompetitive behavior and predatory pricing	Prevent anticompetitive behavior.	Many areas (such as hospitals, pharmaceuticals, and professional associations)

Table 4.1 (continued)

RATIONALE	MAIN OBJECTIVE	HEALTH CARE APPLICATION
Rationalization and coordination	Secure efficient production where transaction costs prevent market from obtaining network gains or efficiencies of scale.	Office-based physicians
Externalities	Ensure adequate production and delivery of health goods and services with positive consumption externalities (such as those generated by immunization).	Public funding for health goods and services with positive externalities (such as vaccines and immunization programs).

a. Orphan drugs are those that treat rare diseases and hence face low demand, which motivates the need for government regulatory intervention to ensure access.
Source: Baldwin and Cave 1999.

quantity). These incentives can be in both financial and nonfinancial forms (Kumaranayake 1997).

Control-based measures will be briefly reviewed in this section and discussed in further detail in section 4, where instruments are grouped by the target of regulation (capacity and market structure, prices, and quality of services). Incentive-based schemes will be entirely covered in this section. Self-regulation as an alternative strategy will also be covered in section 3. No single section covers market-harnessing controls, but aspects of it are covered in section 4. Appendix 4.A summarizes the major forms of regulation, classified according to the target and strategy (control as opposed to incentive-based).

Control-Based Regulation

Regulatory controls are traditionally premised on government's ability to mandate compliance with its decisions (which in turn flows from the sovereign rights of the state). The government can establish its requirements in three forms, one for each of the three branches of government: as legislation (legislative), as an administrative decree (executive), or as a judicial order (judicial). Each of these can be gen-

Table 4.2 Strengths and Weaknesses of Regulatory Instruments

STRATEGY	STRENGTHS	WEAKNESSES	HEALTH CARE EXAMPLE
Command and control	Force of law; fixed standards set minimum acceptable levels of behavior; screens entry; prohibits unacceptable behavior immediately; seen as highly protective of public; use of penalties indicates forceful stance by authorities	Undermines good management; prone to capture; complex rules tend to multiply; inflexible; informational requirements severe; expensive to administer; setting standard is difficult and costly; anticompetitive effects; incentive to meet standard not to do better; enforcement costly; compliance costs high	Hospital licensing
Incentives	Low regulator discretion; low-cost application; low intervention in management; incentive to reduce harm to zero, not just to standard; economic pressure to behave acceptably	Rules are required; poor response to problems arising from irrational or careless behavior; predicting and measuring outcome from given incentive difficult; mechanical and inflexible; regulatory lag; fails to prohibit offense	Better pay for physicians who agree not to take under-the-table money; contracts for accredited institutions
Self-regulation	Access to superior information about clinical quality; interest in and value of reputation enhances impact; high ownership may reduce enforcement costs	Professionals frequently lax in disciplining members; may lack interest in important elements of health care quality	Peer review model in licensing, credentialing, accreditation
General competition laws	Responses to market driven by industry not bureaucrats; regulatory economies of scale if general rules are used; low level of intervention; flexibility for firms	No expert agency to solve technical or commercial problems in industry; uncertainties and transaction costs; courts slow to generate guidance; principles develop sporadically	Hospitals, community or long-term care institutions, review of professional association licensing rules

	Advantages	Disadvantages	Examples
Information dissemination	Low intervention; allows consumer to decide issues; lower danger of capture	Information users may make mistakes; cost of producing information may be high; risks may be so severe as to call for prohibition; policing of information quality and fraud may be required; information may be in form undermining its utility	Pharmaceuticals (consumer information), hospitals (dissemination of comparative performance indicators)
Planning	Assures efficient distribution and acceptable level of provision; allows state to plan long-term investments	Fairness of planning decisions may be contentious; government planning officials may favor public providers; innovations may be stifled	Governmental provision/planning of health care provision
Rights and liabilities laws	Low intervention; initially low cost to state	May not prevent undesired events resulting from accidents or irrational behavior; individuals may not enforce due to costs; difficult to produce evidence of misbehavior; legal uncertainties reduce enforcement; victims may lack resolve, information, and resources to proceed so that deterrence effect is weak; difficult for courts to deter efficiently; insurance may reduce deterrent effects	Right to health, health care, and health care of certain quality

Source: Adapted from Baldwin and Cave 1999.

229

erated in many different forms and formats, particularly administrative decrees, and with various levels of authority (such as advisory regulations, guidelines, or emergency measures). Most regulatory measures promulgated by the executive branch in a democratic system can be challenged in court—usually by those who fear they will be adversely affected. Often regulations are challenged on the grounds that they exceed legal authority or violate other laws; they can be overruled by judicial order. Litigation is expensive and time-consuming, however, and in a well-functioning system is undertaken only in the most serious situations. The use of these basic controls belongs to the realm of instruments.

A review of the international experience with control-based regulation finds that all developed countries and most low- and middle-income countries (LMCs) have basic legislation on health personnel such as registration and licensing requirements, the establishment of professional councils, and restrictions against dangerous or unethical clinical practice (Bennett and others 1994). Legislation regulating health facilities is less abundant in LMCs than laws governing health personnel, and is generally less demanding than legislation in developed countries.

Even when they do exist the degree to which regulations are enforced and effective in LMCs is low (Asiimwe and Lule 1993; Mujinja, Urassa, and Mnyika 1993; and Yesudian 1993). For example, personnel licensing fails to ensure quality in most LMCs for two main reasons:

1. The enforcement of regulatory controls is often lacking or weak, with limited funding available to the professional bodies that are responsible for regulating the profession.

2. Even if professional bodies have adequate resources, they can be reluctant to take action against their own membership.

Bennett and Ngalande-Banda (1994) found that the enforcement of regulatory controls is often weak or lacking in Sub-Saharan Africa. They presented the case of the Zimbabwean Medical Council, which has not publicized any cases of malpractice for fear of damaging the profession's reputation. The Thai experience reinforces this finding. Although Thailand has extensive legislation applying to the health sector they have substantial problems enforcing these laws, particularly due to the small number of staff used for monitoring and enforcement. Despite widespread problems the Thai Medical Council has received only a few complaints about physician performance (Roemer 1991).

In light of many countries' limited success with legal interventions, interest has been growing in the use of incentives to affect private health care provision. Cassels (1995) concludes that legal regulation alone has little influence on the behavior of for-profit providers and that complementary solutions such as incentives and competitive contracts are needed.

Appendix 4.B presents the major types of control-based regulations, distinguishing between those aimed at influencing health care facilities and those aimed at personnel.

Incentive-Based Regulation

One of the major changes in regulatory practice during the 1990s has been the development of softer, market-style, incentive-based instruments to encourage (or discourage) certain behaviors.

Incentives have the advantage of being voluntary, thus predisposing providers to offer information on their behavior, to actively demonstrate compliance. Developed countries have successfully used incentives in sectors such as telecommunications and utilities. Few studies have been devoted to the long-range role of incentive-based instruments within the health sector. One study examined targeted payments to physicians for cervical smears performed in the National Health Service (NHS). They found that the introduction of the targeted payments did lead to a short-term increase in the number of smears (Hughes 1993). In the long term, however, physicians reorganized their activities so that they would continue to receive the payments, without delivering the extra services.

Incentives, in general, attempt to avoid much of the informational, administrative, and political constraints that control-based interventions entail. An experiment on incentive regulation of nursing homes in the United States found much lower transaction costs associated with incentives than with legal interventions (Norton 1992). The above two studies, however, point out the need for continuous monitoring and relatively sophisticated design so that the incentives affect provider behavior in the manner desired. Nevertheless, the fact that incentive systems require less bureaucratic support and are less costly to maintain than control-based instruments makes them an important regulatory option for many LMCs.

Most incentive-based instruments mechanisms rely on one of three methods: taxation, selective contracting, or subsidies transfers to providers by means of the government. Transfers can take several forms, including direct subsidies, government loans at low interest, government guarantees for borrowing on private markets, and transfers of public inputs (Laffont and Tirole 1993).

Governments have an array of incentive options for influencing providers' behavior in ways consistent with their national health sector goals (table 4.3). These incentives can be economic (financial), noneconomic, or a mix of both.

Financial Incentives

Access to capital. Many investments in the health sector require substantial access to capital to finance buildings, equipment, and other startup costs. At the 1994 Kenya Conference of Private and Nongovernment Providers, it was reported that the lack of long-term lending to the health sector contributed to the domination of the sector by small clinics, and that ". . . private providers are constrained by the high capital outlays for establishing facilities, running day-to-day operations, paying advance rent, paying malpractice insurance premiums, holding an adequate supply of drugs, and others" (Hursh-César and others 1994, p. 9). Lack of access to reasonably priced credit has serious implications for health providers who must import goods. Unless they have sufficient capital to pay the full cost of the imported goods, they are forced to purchase in small quantities. Besides being inefficient, this situation makes it harder to maintain adequate supplies of medicines and other essential supplies. In

Table 4.3 Policy Options for Influencing Provider Incentives and Behavior

FINANCIAL INCENTIVES

Capital markets
- Provide government loans at low interest.
- Provide government guarantees for borrowing on private markets.
- Improve access to low-cost credit and simplified loan application processes.
- Provide access to foreign currency.

Taxes and tariffs
- Introduce tax waivers, exemptions, and deductibles.
- Provide favorable tariffs and duty-free imports of medical equipment and supplies.

Other subsidies
- Give direct government subsidies targeted to public health objectives.
- Provide government grants targeted to public health objectives.

Provider payment
- Selective contracting
- Ensure appropriate provider payment mechanisms.
- Assure reasonable profit margins (if prices are controlled by the government).
- Pay government obligations to providers in a timely manner.
- Protect overdrafts in response to government payment delays.
- Give bonuses to serve in underserved areas (box 4.6).

NONFINANCIAL INCENTIVES

Regulatory environment
- Improve ease of entry to the market.
- Improve regulatory processes and reduce bureaucratic controls (box 4.7).
- Disseminate information on regulations and laws.

Market and business environment
- Purchase selectively.
- Grant access to use government facilities and equipment.
- Provide consumer and market information
- Support development of an adequately skilled work force.

Human resource development
- Open training and professional development opportunities to private participants.
- Improve career path for private specialties that are in short supply.

Public-private sector relations
- Assure clarity and predictability of performance expectations.
- Promote public and private sector provider dialogue.
- Formal partnership where appropriate (such as engage private providers in public health programs).
- Enable referral across public and private.

many countries the problem is caused not only by low availability to credit but also by the complexities of the loan services.

Low-cost loans. Low-cost, or subsidized, loans are a direct business-development incentive that has been employed to accomplish health policy goals. Loan programs can be targeted to fund development in underserved geographic areas, such as small towns and rural areas, and can be designed to avoid concentration and duplication in saturated areas. For example, a program of loans for hospital construction, which operated in Brazil from 1974 to 1985, resulted in a substantial increase in the number of private hospitals. Another example is the Pakistan's Small Business Finance Corporation, which has a special loan rate for rural hospitals. Favorable loans can also be targeted to specialties such as family practices, or to providers who are willing to devote a significant portion of their services to preventive and primary care.

Tax incentives and other subsidies. Tax exemptions are useful tools to influence private sector behavior in support of public health policy and have wide appeal in the business community. Use of incentives requires a reasonably effective taxation system. The most frequently used forms of tax incentives are exemptions, waivers, and income tax contribution deductibles, often in some combination. Benefiting from a tax exemption is relatively straightforward, since the exemption directly reduces the tax burden of eligible organizations. When criteria are established that make an organization eligible for a tax waiver, the organization must still submit an application to receive the actual waiver. Waivers have not been very effective in influencing the behavior of private actors, because the administrative burden associated with receiving the waiver has been too high (PHR 1999). Countries as diverse as Cambodia, Indonesia, Malawi, and the Philippines established complex waiver procedures that required the participation of several agencies. Eligible organizations were required to submit and maintain numerous documents, and the response times were extremely long. In the Philippines, for example, private buyers, nongovernmental organizations, and for-profit providers must contend with five different agencies or institutions to obtain import duty waivers on contraceptives. If all goes smoothly, the process takes between 9 and 13 working days.

Such experiences suggest that policymakers should consider their tax incentive options very carefully, using tax exemptions where possible. If waivers are used the administrative procedures associated with their approval should be as simple as possible.

Since tax revenue has many important potential uses, the benefits of the incentive under consideration must be weighed against the cost of the foregone revenue.

Tax deductibility of contributions is often used to encourage the health-related activities of nonprofit organizations, although developing countries have difficulty in monitoring eligibility and compliance. Another direct incentive is to simplify the tax structure and procedures, which are often at cross-purposes with efforts to encourage the private sector.

Low-cost loans and tax incentives are a very common form of government subsidy. Other forms of government subsidy are often combined with them, such as when loans are forgiven or tax-free grants are used to accomplish public health objectives. Loans for medical education in the United States are forgiven in exchange for the doctor working in underserved areas. The government in Romania provides free buildings and equipment to doctors settling in rural areas, with the value of the investment paid off by service time. Subsidies can be built into contracts to support desirable practices such as training, which leads to increased revenue, and to improve access to particular services. In some cases where government pays private hospitals for public patients, a capital cost reimbursement component is included. Grants are the ultimate subsidy. Matching or direct grants can be used to supplement investments by the private sector. In some countries company-based clinics have received grants to expand services, sometimes to include families and residents of surrounding communities.

An oversupply of physicians in capital cities can be balanced by offering incentives to invest in private hospitals in smaller cities, as has occurred in the Philippines. These could be in the form of tax incentives or government subsidies.

High tariffs and import duties on medical equipment and supplies are a major constraint to private sector participation in many countries (box 4.1). Reductions of such tariffs have been successful in expanding access and utilization of critical health goods and services, such as bednets and condoms (boxes 4.2 and 4.3). The effect may also be an increase in the supply, which enables the private sector to buy at lower cost, thereby lowering consumer prices, if savings are passed on (PHR 1999). As noted above, the tradeoff with fiscal prudence is important to consider.

Mechanisms to control staff mobility. Governments have used a wide range of mechanisms to control mobility of staff and counteract "brain drain." Many governments stipulate that doctors, nurses, and paramedics trained at the expense of the state must complete a certain period of public sector service before transferring to the private sector (or to other countries). Specific financial incentives are sometimes offered in order to retain public sector staff. Nepal, Pakistan, and Thailand all have a nonprivate practice allowance. In Thailand special incentive payments were introduced to give public sector

---

Box 4.1 Senegal: High Taxes and Import Duties Impede Private Participation

In Senegal, high corporate and income tax rates (up to 35 percent and 50 percent, respectively) and high import duties on medical equipment are significant impediments to opening private medical practices.

Importers face complex and lengthy customs clearance and high import duties, resulting in medical equipment prices that are three times the cost in Europe.

Source: Knowles, Yazbeck, and Brewster 1994, p. 46.

Box 4.2 Philippines Contraceptives: Ease of Importation and Sale Can Facilitate Private Participation in Family Planning Programs

Exemption and waiver procedures directly influence the impact of tax concessions; while the Philippine government exempts contraceptives from import tariffs, obtaining the exemption is extremely time consuming. The main regulatory constraint reported by importers in the Philippines is the paperwork and administrative process for obtaining a government exemption from duty on contraceptives. One manufacturer's representative stated that the duty exemption process often takes up to seven weeks. These delays contribute to short-term stock shortages. Importation procedures become further complicated if a company's sales exceed its expectations and higher quantities of products than projected must be imported. Quantities over those initially reported to the responsible government agency create additional bureaucratic delays in the importation process.

Source: Ravenholt 1996, p. 9.

doctors extra payment according to the number of patients seen—an imitation of private sector payment mechanisms.

Contracting and provider payment. Contracting arrangements generate powerful incentives that affect the way providers produce and deliver health services. Allocating contracts based on important qualifications or performance indicators, or "selective contracting" is the most powerful form of incentive regulation. Payment mechanisms may induce movement toward or away from improved efficiency, equity, quality, consumer satisfaction, and health status. Interested readers should refer to chapter 3 for an overview of the various contracting arrangements and payment structures and their strengths and weaknesses.

Box 4.3 Ghana: Regulatory Reforms to Promote Private Sector Participation in Public Health Programs

As part of a bilateral population project, legal and regulatory reforms were enacted in Ghana to expand the private sector's role in family planning activities. These included the expansion of the list of essential medicines to include oral contraceptives, elimination of duties on commercial import of contraceptive products, and elimination of price controls on contraceptive commodities.

Source: Kenney 1993, p. 25.

Nonfinancial Incentives

Nonfinancial incentives to enhance private sector participation and behavior are often overlooked, but evidence is mounting that they merit a place in a comprehensive strategy.

Credentials. Professionals and other health workers value credentials that recognize accomplishment, for purposes of either marketability or status among their peers. In India, for example, a successful effort to expand and improve private sector tuberculosis care included awarding "expert" status in recognition of completing a course of continuing medical education. The enhanced status motivated physician participation (Porter and Grange 1999).

Social marketing programs. Private providers and suppliers can be motivated to serve public health goals by tying these objectives to commercial incentives in unconventional ways such as enhancing demand for their existing products and services. Examples of successful social marketing programs abound (such as soap, condoms, and mosquito nets).

Patient movement between the public and private sectors. The stimulation of patient movement between the private and public sectors can be designed as an incentive. There are many examples of government contracting with private facilities to provide services to public patients. Rules regarding referral systems can also increase private sector participation, especially abolishment of regulations prohibiting private doctors from referring their patients to public hospitals.

Training. Private providers may be motivated to improve the quality (i.e., integrated management of childhood illness) of priority health care services if the government supports appropriate training. Another opportunity for government to stimulate the private sector to enhance quality and efficiency is to provide management training in fields such as hospital accounting, auditing, health information systems, and government reports management.

Public-private alliances. Finally, building public-private alliances can help advance public health objectives (Slater and Saade 1996). Governments can collaborate with professional associations in ways that serve mutual interests. For example, collecting up-to-date information on the private sector (such as number and characteristics of private hospitals, pharmacies, or practices) can serve common interests, since associations need the information for membership and service purposes. The government can sponsor annual listings or directories assembled by the associations. The government can offer to provide speakers and workshops at annual meetings, signaling a desire to engage the broadest possible constituency in the discussion. Several developed-country governments frequently give associations small contracts to assemble data of interest to both, providing a source of revenue as well as enhancing the associations' status.

Self-Regulation

A complementary strategy to both control- and incentive-based regulatory instruments is self-regulation. This allows a group of professionals or providers to set standards for its members' behavior, for example, by leaving it up to them to decide whether they want to apply controls or incentives. Self-regulatory arrangements vary considerably in terms of the degree of governmental oversight. Self-regulation can be viewed as a continuum, with purely private arrangements (with no governmental oversight or involvement) at one end and various forms of publicly mandated and supervised self-regulatory arrangements at the other. Some professional organizations and voluntary organizations exercise private self-regulation, but usually compliance cannot be enforced. Therefore this type of regulation is often too weak to sustain many important social and economic objectives. Typically, publicly mandated and overseen self-regulation in health care is undertaken by professional associations, and, sometimes, by producer associations, as in the case of the hospital industry (such as in Germany).

Table 4.4 summarizes the potential advantages and disadvantages of self-regulatory arrangements by delegation.

Ayres and Braithwaite (1992) further distinguish forms of self-regulation by the degree of government involvement. In enforced self-regulation, enforcement is mandated and monitored by the government. When government ratification of (privately written) rules is necessary, it is referred to as coregulation.

Some European health care systems utilize private self-regulation without state enforcement, but publicly mandated self-regulation is more common, usually coupled with the threat of ultimate pub-

Table 4.4 Self-Regulation: Potential Advantages and Disadvantages

POTENTIAL ADVANTAGES	POTENTIAL DISADVANTAGES
• High commitment to rules • Well-informed rule making • Low costs to government • Close fit of regulatory standards with those seen as reasonable by actors • Potential for rapid adjustment • Enforcement potentially more effective • Potential for combining with external oversight	• Self-serving • Impetus toward monopolistic behavior • Exclusion of public from rule-making procedures • Laxness of enforcement toward providers • Public distrust of enforcers • Problematic legal oversight • Public preference for governmental responsibility

Source: Baldwin and Cave 1999.

lic enforcement. Self-regulatory activities frequently are conducted jointly by nongovernmental actors with potentially conflicting interests—for example, health care payers and providers. This joint self-regulation can be seen as a strategy to overcome some of the weaknesses of self-regulation (such as self-serving rules, weak enforcement, or problematic legal oversight) while retaining its strengths. The prototypical example for this type of regulation is Germany (box 4.4).

Section 4 Targets and Mechanisms of Regulation

Above, in section 3, we discussed regulatory strategies and the underlying mechanisms by which the strategies influence private activities in health. In this section we review the targets and mechanism of health regulation.

Regulating Capacity and Market Structure

The production of health care can be seen as a multi-stage process (figure 4.1). In the first stage inputs (facilities, manpower, equipment, and medical products) are produced. In the second stage providers use these inputs to produce curative care, and preventive and diagnostic services. In the third, and final, stage patients utilize these health care services to produce or improve their health. Traditionally, regulation has focused on the first two stages, the quality and quantity of inputs and the production process, as well as their regional distribution. More modern approaches of regulation focus more on the third stage, the delivery and use of health services.

Regulating capacity and distribution of services. Regulation often takes the form of establishing the ground rules for participants in the health system. Most prominently this involves establishing conditions for entry into health care provider markets by controlling admissions to medical schools and licensing personnel and facilities (box 4.5). All licensing procedures, though primarily intended to regulate quality of care (section 4), also indirectly regulate capacity by simultaneously

Box 4.4 Government Collaboration with Other Regulatory Actors: The Joint Self-Regulation Model in Germany

The German health system includes institutionalized collaboration between the government and other key regulatory actors. Laws specify who has the right or obligation to establish regulatory requirements in various areas, and to supervise compliance. They further specify requirements for relationships between the actors involved. Such arrangements are often referred to as joint self-regulation.

Important regulatory powers have been delegated to health insurance funds, their representative associations, as well as similar associations of providers. Most of these actors have not only been charged with public tasks but have also been established by law and exert legal powers over their membership. Called "corporatist," these bodies are neither "private" nor "public" in the standard sense of the terms. They are a unique hybrid, combining private status with public functions.

Legislation also gives joint self-regulation bodies the right to abolish certain mechanisms introduced by law (a prime example is the spending caps for pharmaceuticals [§ 84]).

"Joint self-regulation" in Germany mainly occurs in two different forms: (a) negotiations followed by contracts and (b) decisions by joint committees. Depending on the nature of the issue, and the interests of the negotiating parties, different decisions are allocated to different forums. While some delegated tasks always require decisions by joint committees (such as the definition of benefits), others are decided only by joint committees if no agreement is reached in open negotiations (such as negotiations on the budget for ambulatory care). In still others, a joint committee is the first level of appeal against another joint committee's decisions (such as in the case of claims review).

Supervision of self-regulatory decisions is a multilayered endeavor, involving self-regulatory institutions, the government, independent agencies, and the social courts. "The government" in this case in Germany is the Federal Ministry of Health for federal associations of sickness funds and providers, joint institutions between them, and their decisions and contracts. An independent agency, the Federal Insurance Office, supervises countrywide health insurance funds. For actors, decisions, and contracts on the state level "the government" is the health insurance unit within the state ministry responsible for health.

Supervision and enforcement can be divided into several levels. Level A is the formal governmental approval of decisions made by self-regulatory bodies; Level B is the governmental right to substitute for self-regulatory decisions if they are not made according to law; and Level C are legal threats to institutions that do not fulfill their prescribed tasks.

On Level A the responsible governmental unit must ensure that self-regulatory decisions and contracts fulfill social objectives. In practice, most emphasis is put on the sustainability of financing or cost containment.

Level B enforcement relates mainly to obligations of joint regulatory bodies. For example, the Federal Minister of Health may step in if the appropriate joint regulatory body fails to establish adequate regulatory guidelines for medical equipment quality and dissemination.

On Level C, the first threat to provider associations is the installation of a state commissioner, if the association fails to fufill its legal responsibilities (§79a).

While government review and action is an important "check" on the behavior of self-regulatory bodies, both can be subjected to judicial review, providing yet another check in the system.

Figure 4.1 The Production of Health Care

Health system

| System inputs | Health production | System output |

Facilities

Personnel

Equipment and supplies

Health providers

Health services

Patients

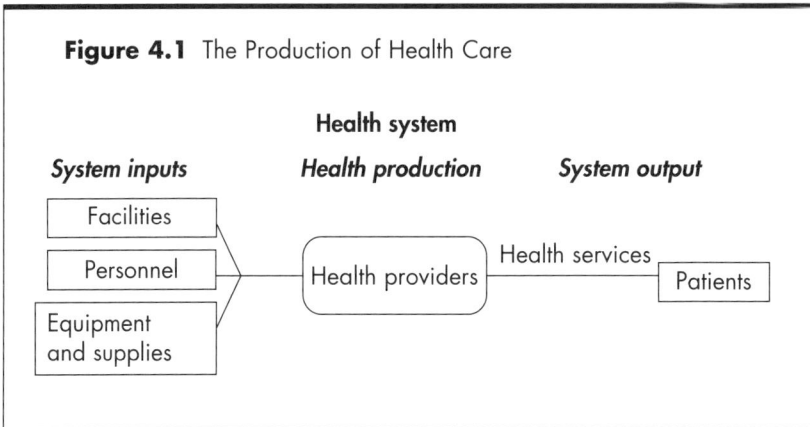

defining the right of entry into the medical care market and by determining who is eligible to provide services. Another tool for controlling capacity is to restrict who receives a contract with the main payer of health care in the region, such as social insurance systems do.

Many countries have adopted additional forms of regulation aimed at limiting health system capacity. The underlying rationale for such regulations is that uncontrolled expansion of health system capacity will lead either to supplier-induced oversupply of health care or to the waste of scarce resources. Typically, governments enact legislation and create agencies with the statutory administrative power to approve or block proposals to create new health infrastructure. In many countries rules regarding the criteria for expansion regulate health system capacity. Table 4.5 provides some examples of such instruments. Many direct mechanisms, despite their differing names, are quite similar.

The patterns of regulation of health sector capacity vary from one part of the world to another.

In the United States until the 1960s hospitals could be freely built or enlarged as long as they met state licensure requirements. As bed-population ratios increased and voluntary insurance for hospitalization expanded, this changed. New York was the first state to enact a law, in 1961, requiring construction of new hospital beds, not only

Box 4.5 Britain: Regulating the Supply of Physicians

In the United Kingdom the supply of physicians, through admissions to medical schools, has been traditionally controlled by the central government. Prior to 1991 four separate committees reviewed the supply of medical personnel and made recommendations about medical school admissions. In 1991 coordination of these recommendations was enhanced, with the establishment of the Medical Manpower Standing Advisory Committee. Committee members are appointed by the secretary of state for health. The committee is a permanent body that monitors the market continuously and makes recommendations to the health secretary.

to meet the licensure standards but also to satisfy the state government that there was a social need for the additional beds. CON laws were soon passed by many other states. In 1974 a national law was enacted (the National Health Planning and Resource Development Act) requiring every state to have legislation controlling the supply of hospital beds and their quality standards. The U.S. experience with CON programs is mixed. Too often the criteria determining which investments should and should not be allowed are not clear. In addition, a ban on hospital investment in one type of equipment may produce a "squeezed balloon" effect, with resources flowing into other types of capital items.

After the enactment of the federal-provincial hospital insurance program in Canada the government realized that the entire population would bear the cost of any new-bed construction under the social insurance system. The provincial government accordingly started exercising control over all new hospital construction or hospital expansion, requiring evidence of a definite need for any additional beds. Moreover, some provinces, faced with spiraling hospital costs, were ordered to close certain small hospitals to limit bed availability.

Table 4.5 Direct and Indirect Mechanisms for Regulating Capacity

MECHANISM	DESCRIPTION	EXAMPLE (COUNTRY)
Direct		
Planning boards or advisory panels	Act as specialized bodies for review and approval of new facility construction or technology procurement.	Australia
Certificate of Need (CON) programs	Ensure that any new facility construction or expansion is based on a local community need for the service provided by the facility.	United States
Health system agencies (HSAs)	Review expansion and modernization plans to determine their eligibility for capital reimbursement from the central (federal) government.	United States
Health maps (cartes sanitaires)	Plan the diffusion and geographic distribution of health facilities and technology.	France, Spain
Indirect		
Global budgets	Set an expenditure limit that ties premiums and provider-payment rates to the national health budget or sectoral budgets, and therefore control expenditures.	Most developed countries (except United States)
Contracts (selective)	Limit capacity by not contracting the whole range of available infrastructure (such as only 90 percent of hospital beds).	Netherlands, Germany, United States

In Western Europe the amount of legislation controlling number of beds or bed-population ratios depends largely on the type of health care system within each country. Typically, NHS-type systems, where all or most hospitals are public entities, do not necessitate any CON-type regulation, because the government directly controls expansion, usually by means of the public investment program. Since social insurance systems have a mix of public and private (not-for-profit and for-profit) hospitals, they require well-developed regulatory mechanisms to constrain capacity, because the entire population would bear the cost of any construction of new beds (Busse, van der Grinten, and Svensson 2002). The primary means of regulating (restricting) ca-

---

Box 4.6 Africa: Economic Incentives Can Influence Geographic Dispersion of Private Providers

Unless government intervenes the growth of private for-profit health care will often exacerbate existing biases—concentrating in urban areas and delivering services to higher-income groups, according to a study of private sector behavior in four African countries. Through various economic incentives, reduced drug and equipment taxes, loan guarantees, apprenticeship requirements, and regulatory relaxation, governments found they were able to increase private sector growth in underserved rural areas.

Source: Hursh-César and others 1994, p. 13.

---

pacity in social insurance systems is usually the allocation of several contracts from health insurance organizations. The eligibility standards for reimbursement are usually the same for both public and private hospitals.

Japan has a system of open staff hospitals and fee remuneration of doctors for inpatient care. The national government exercises direct control over all new hospital construction or enlargement, requiring demonstration of need for any additional beds.

In many developing countries, the severe shortage of health facilities makes the issue of capacity regulation irrelevant for the time being.

Several countries have attempted to influence the location of private providers (box 4.6) as a way of complementing public facilities and reducing access problems. In Tanzania applications to open a private practice or hospital must state the location, size of population served, distance from the nearest health facility, and number of staff to be employed. This is to avoid redundant capacity and rural-urban inequities. Box 4.7 reviews some lessons from the international experience with capacity regulation.

Box 4.7 Capacity Regulation: Lessons from International Experience

When governments directly control capacity, the issue can end up being thrown into the political realm (Rodwin 1997; and Schut 1995). Where local hospitals are important to citizens and politicians, central government attempts to limit growth in the hospital sector may be thwarted. This can be especially true in decentralized settings, where the central government does not control the entire health budget. The same issues arise if the central government tries to use its financial leverage as a payer in the system to influence capacity through the reimbursement rules. For example, budget-capping attempts in social insurance systems often run into opposition from local or regional interests.

Individual hospitals may also, for political, economic, or prestige reasons, seek to expand in ways that conflict with government attempts to regulate the sector. The strong influence of the medical profession can also make regulation of capacity difficult (Saltman and de Roo 1989). The success of mechanisms such as special planning boards depends on the regulating body's political and economic strength, not just its technical expertise.

Lack of integrated control over health system finance and planning makes capacity regulation much harder. When capital financing is fragmented among different levels of government, constraining capacity in one part of the system (for example, hospitals but not outpatient clinics, or only the private sector) often encourages the unregulated parts of the system to expand in ways that are inconsistent with the goals of regulation (Wilsford 1995).

In countries where health system capacity is regulated by rules on expansion (usually limited by units per capita), these rules often become the subject of controversy related to rationing (see appendix 4.E, the section on Germany).

There is some evidence that containing costs by means of capacity regulation comes at the expense of reduced incentives for providers to innovate and respond dynamically to changes in health care technologies.

Competition and antimonopoly regulation. Government regulation can also target the structure and functioning of health provision markets. The primary objective of such policies is to reduce cartel-like behavior of providers. Physicians and hospitals are the two most common health care markets where such behavior occurs.

The involvement of professional associations in the establishment of licensure, certification, and accreditation standards is an important component of quality assurance in all health systems. Nevertheless, physicians groups often manipulate these standards to generate unnecessary barriers to entry from potential competitors—whether they be new medical school graduates, foreign physicians, or practitioners of alternative forms of medicine (Anderson et al. 2000; Evans 1976). Hospitals more frequently seek monopoly power through mergers, which can give them the ability to increase prices and otherwise extract rents from patients and other payers.

Monopoly power is frequently overlooked in health care, since it is often supposed that the influence of markets on the price, supply, and quality of health care is weak. The health care sector is likewise frequently exempted from compliance with economy-wide competition law and policy, with the United States being the notable exception (box 4.8). In the past 10 years, however, physician and hospital markets have come under increasing scrutiny. In 1996, the Australian government initiated the application of national competition policy to health care services (Wooldridge 1996). A number of OECD countries have acted to reduce unnecessary restrictions related to physician licensure requirements and the number of medical school entrants.

Box 4.8 United States: Antitrust Regulation and Merger Evaluation

The methodology used to evaluate mergers in the United States is relatively well developed. First, the relevant market is defined in terms of products and geography. The geographic market definition suggested by the U.S. Department of Justice for assessing the impact of competition on social welfare is that a geographic market should be comprised of the smallest geographic area over which a hypothetical monopolist could profitably impose a small but significant and sustained increase in prices.

Second, the likely consequences of any changes in competition that would result from the proposed merger are assessed. According to the merger guidelines, this part of the evaluation process typically involves identifying the competing firms and summarizing the likely changes in the extent of competition in terms of a quantitative index. The most widely used index is the Herfindahl-Hirschman Index (HHI), defined as the sum of squared output shares of the firms in the market. The impact of the proposed merger on welfare is viewed as a function of the change in the HHI that would occur as a result of the merger. Other factors (such as efficiency gains or the avoidance of closure) that might mitigate or enhance the impact of market-structure changes are also considered. All else being constant, mergers that result in large increases in the HHI are considered to be more socially harmful than mergers that do not, and hence are more likely to be subject to veto under antitrust law.

Source: Kessler and McClellan 1999.

Government regulatory activities can address monopolistic behavior in health care in a number of ways. If generic competition policy exists, supporting application to health care provision can be useful. If physicians groups or hospitals are exhibiting cartel-like behavior (licensure standards, constraints on medical school placements, hospital mergers), health authorities will need to either apply existing antimonopoly regulations or establish health sector–specific policies.

Regulating Prices

Regulation of capacity and distribution of service providers is one way to address equity and efficiency issues. Prices are another common target of such efforts. The common rationale for governmental regulation of prices is either equity-based—to ensure affordable services and access to all income groups—or efficiency-based—to control the cost of care and overall health system expenditures. Efficiency-based regulation is more prevalent in developed countries. Examples of government instruments that constrain the prices of health goods and services include centrally determined fees (box 4.9). In Rwanda the government publishes the official fee schedule in the government gazette. Providers are obliged to post a complying fee schedule on their door (Data for Decision-Making Project 1993).

If the prices providers charge are capped, additional attention must be devoted to quality and patient selection. If the income a service can generate is constrained, the providers will be under pressure to reduce their costs. One way of reducing costs is to reduce service quality or intensity. Another way to reduce service costs is to treat the patients who require fewer services, a practice often referred to as "cream skimming."

Regulating Quality of Care

Quality is a core health policy concern that is pursued by means of regulation. Since professional and provider organizations, as well as patients, share this concern most quality regulation is implemented by government in collaboration with these actors. It is difficult and costly for government to collect and evaluate information about service quality; hence governments rely on these other actors to generate and use information to exert pressure to enhance various aspects of quality. It is a critical task to identify the areas where professional or other organizations share government objectives related

Box 4.9 Price Regulation: Lessons from International Experience

Price regulation is not common in LMCs. The lack of information about private sector costs makes it difficult to identify appropriate price-setting formulas for all providers.

Price control alone is not sufficient if the goal is to limit overall expenditures and costs. Regulation of prices must therefore be supplemented by an effort to control volume (Berg 1999).

Price regulation to control costs must adopt a comprehensive program, encompassing all payers, services, and providers, in order to avoid cost shifting (allocating some costs to other services and charging patients higher prices). Cost shifting can be eliminated when all purchasers face the same price structure, imposed through governmental regulation (Wallack, Skalera, and Cai 1996; and Anderson, Heyssel, and Dicker 1993). The all-payer hospital rate-setting system used by the U.S. state of Maryland illustrates this situation, which is also found in many West European countries (see appendix 4.E, the section on Maryland, United States; and Weill and Battistella 1998). Even when controls make costs more difficult to shift, reductions in care may result.

to quality, but it is also challenging to work effectively with them. The role of government in coordinating the activities of these actors is discussed further in section 6, "Institutional Structure of Regulation." In the remainder of this section we discuss health care that is targeted by quality regulation.

Quality regulation traditionally encourages quality care by ensuring the quality of the inputs of the health production process, namely, the physical facility, medical personnel, equipment, and supplies. Over the years the scope of quality regulation grew beyond inputs to encompass the process through which care is provided.

Table 4.6 Structure-, Process-, and Outcome-Oriented Quality Regulation

STRUCTURE-ORIENTED REGULATION OF HEALTH SYSTEM INPUT QUALITY	PROCESS-ORIENTED REGULATION OF HEALTH SYSTEM PROCESS QUALITY	OUTCOME-ORIENTED REGULATION OF HEALTH SYSTEM OUTPUT QUALITY
Health facilities • Facility licensing	*Health provider performance* • Facility accreditation • Personnel specialty certification and recertification	• Facility accreditation
Health personnel • Personnel licensing	• Utilization reviews and medical audits • Peer review • Professional standards review • Clinical practice guidelines and clinical protocols	• Peer review

Process-oriented quality regulation incorporates issues such as the organization of care and clinical performance. Newer approaches to regulating quality have shifted from asking, "Do providers have the capability to produce quality care?" to asking, "Are they actually providing quality care?" The move from structure and process to outputs and outcomes is based upon the recognition that certain mixes of inputs and processes may produce as good or better results than others. The three approaches to quality regulation—structure-, process-, and outcome-oriented—are summarized in table 4.6.

Licensing, accreditation, and certification are the most commonly used instruments for regulating the quality of health care. Although the three terms are commonly used interchangeably, in a health care context these methodologies refer to specific regulatory approaches with sometimes subtle, but important, differences.

Licensing of facilities or personnel is structure-oriented, whereas both accreditation and certification are process-oriented. Licensing serves as a screen to prevent entities (facilities or personnel) who lack minimum structure or qualifications from delivering any medical services. Accreditation and certification are publicly visible "seals of approval" of the technical practices of health care providers (both facilities and personnel), based on rational criteria. In bestowing such recognition they increase patients' abilities to judge a provider's level of technical quality. In requiring compliance with a well-developed set of quality standards the accreditation and certification processes not only judge technical performance but also provide facilities and caregivers with important information on practices that improve the delivered care, and in essence create an institutional feedback mechanism. Certification is essentially synonymous with accreditation, except that certification is often applied to individuals (certifying a medical specialist), whereas accreditation is applied to institutions or programs (accrediting a hospital or a medical education program).

The three instruments are also different in terms of who defines quality standards and how they are monitored. Licensing is a direct application of the public regulation model, where the state takes direct responsibility for setting standards and inspecting health care facilities, and where compliance is a condition for continuing to operate and, sometimes, for receiving public funds. Most facility accreditation and personnel certification systems worldwide are based on the self-regulation model, where an independent agency both defines and monitors the standards of institutions and individuals who choose to participate in the system. Some accreditation systems incorporate both self- and public-regulatory features to varying degrees. The Joint Commission on Accreditation of Health Care Organizations (JCAHO) in the United States is an illustration of this structure (box 4.10).

Structure-Oriented Quality Regulation

Structure-oriented or input quality regulation can be pursued in a variety of ways, focusing on either the personnel or the facility (see table 4.7).

Facility licensing. Facility licensing is the process of judging a health care facility or practice against a set of standards that specify the minimum structure that must be present in order for the facility to operate (figure 4.2). Licensing standards specify the equipment, staff, and physical facilities that are essential for delivering medical care. If the facility meets these standards it is granted a license, which represents the government's permission for the facility to be open

Box 4.10 U.S. Health Facility Accreditation—Self-regulation, Self-interest, and the Public Interest

The U.S. JCAHO was initiated as a model of self-regulation by the health care industry. In 1917 the American College of Surgeons established a program to ensure that the hospitals having the highest standards be recognized before the profession and the public, and that those with inferior standards might be motivated to improve the quality of their care. Three of the five standards developed dealt with the organization of the medical staff. A fourth standard dealt with medical records, and the fifth sought to ensure the availability of technical resources—the appropriate diagnostic and therapeutic facilities.

Over time the number of hospitals submitting themselves to the accreditation process rose. By 1950 more than half the hospitals in the United States were involved. The program became too expensive for the American College of Surgeons to run and so the Joint Commission on Accreditation of Hospitals—renamed JCAHO in 1988— was born. The medical profession continued to dominate the organization until 1993 when the JCAHO added four more seats to its member board—three seats for public members and one for nursing.

In principle, the JCAHO has maintained key characteristics of a self-regulation system. The processes of defining and monitoring standards remained independent, and participation by health service organizations remained voluntary. Over time, allocation of public funds and other government decisions have become increasingly tied to accreditation. Federal and state regulations were drafted

(Box continues on the following page.)

Box 4.10 (continued)

to follow many JCAHO standards. Some of the JCAHO standards on safety issues have been tightened in response to government pressure. Hence, in many ways, JCAHO accreditation has become part of the public regulatory system.

Source: Scrivens, Klein, and Steiner 1995.

and to provide care to patients (figure 4.3). A facility lacking any of these requirements is not allowed to operate.

Unlike accreditation—which is voluntary and primarily administered by nongovernmental bodies—licensing of health care facilities is mandatory and government imposed. The core idea behind licensing is the recognition of quality levels below which patient care should be prohibited. Since licensing is based on the minimum quality level, licensing standards are written to define the resources that must be present in order for the hospital to safely treat patients. The goal of licensing is not to define desirable quality; rather, it is to define the minimum acceptable level of capability.

Standards for licensing health care facilities vary from one country to another, according to level of development. Hospital licensing standards developed for the Kyrgyz Republic represent the minimum structure that must be present in a facility in order for it to operate as an acute-care facility (box 4.11). Most other governments have more sophisticated and stringent requirements than these minimum standards. The application of these measures also varies with a country's overall political ideology and regulatory capacity.

In the United States health facility licensing began in 1917, when, as a condition for federal grants, each state was required to enact a hospital licensure law. Under these laws all hospitals were periodically

Table 4.7 Licensing, Certification, and Accreditation: Typical Characteristics

	LICENSING	CERTIFICATION	ACCREDITATION
Applied to	Health care facilities Health care personnel	Health care personnel	Health care facilities or educational institutions
Granting body	Government agency	Peer organization, government agency, payer organization, or mix	Peer organization, government agency, payer organization, or mix
Required for	Entry into practice	Professional status and possibly reimbursement	Professional status and possibly reimbursement
Purpose	Restricts entry into field to personnel or facilities meeting minimum standards	Recognized qualification to practice at higher level	Public assurance of desired level of quality of care
Duration	Permanent	Permanent or fixed term	Fixed term
Type of standards	Minimum quality "Structure" Minimum qualifications (education)	Qualifications (education and experience)	Optimal quality: "Structure," "Process," and "Outcome"
Indicator of high quality	No	Yes	Yes
Performance based	No	Sometimes	Yes
Administration	Simple	Moderate	Complex
Renewal	Usually not necessary or automatic; possibly dependent on certain conditions	Continuing education; possible exam	Complete reinspection

Figure 4.2 The Licensing Concept

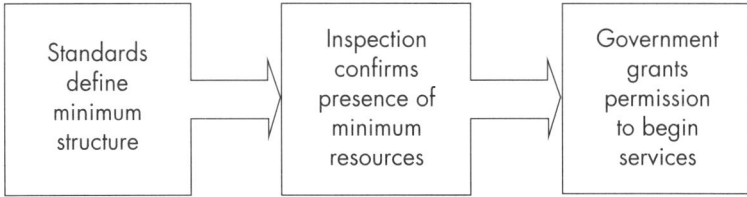

Figure 4.3 The Licensing Process

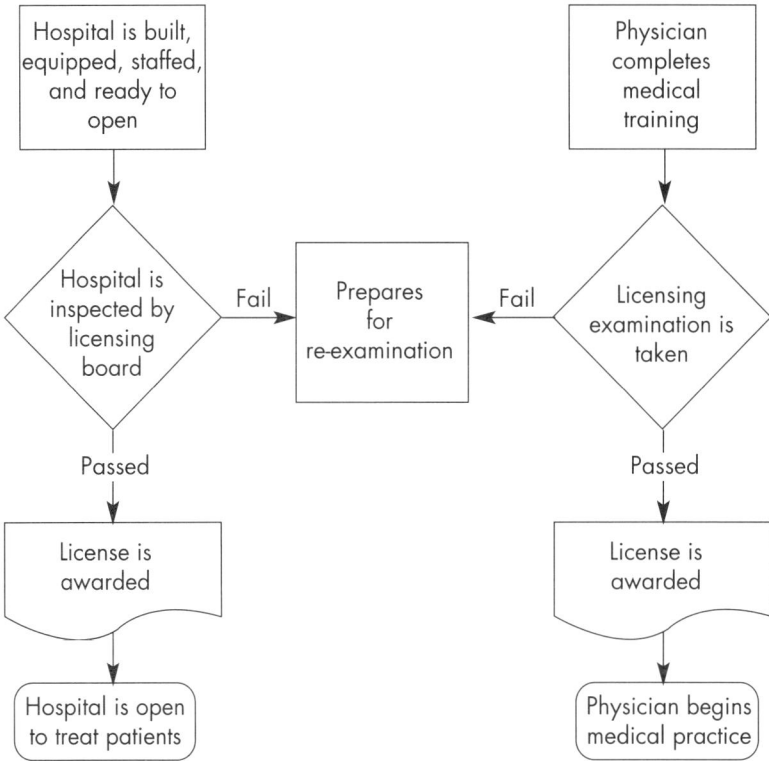

Box 4.11 The Kyrgyz Republic: Hospital Licensing Standards

In order for a hospital to receive a license in the Kyrgyz Republic, the following standards must be met:

- A licensed physician who is responsible for assuring that every patient is diagnosed as to the nature of his ailment and receives either effective therapy to alleviate the malady or palliative care in cases where effective therapy is not available.
- Nursing care any time there are patients at the facility.
- A bed that is occupied by a single individual, except in situations of extreme need. At no time may more than one person occupy a bed when such sharing would result in an adverse medical outcome for any of the persons.
- The minimum set of medical equipment and surgical instruments required by existing norms.
- Linens, bed supplies, and other "hotel" service necessities.
- Sanitary facilities adequate to prevent the spread of communicable disease.
- Safe drinking water.
- Food service providing meals appropriate to patients' needs, adequate kitchen facilities, or arrangements with outside contractors to provide food for patients.
- Transport, or regular and reliable access to transport.
- A working telephone in each facility.
- Compliance with public health and environmental standards.

Source: Becker, Ente, and Standards Development Committee 1995.

inspected for evaluation of their physical standards, laboratory facilities, kitchen sanitation, fire safety, radiological hazard protection, and related matters. Enforcement of these laws was, however, weak, since the staffing of the state inspection authorities (usually the state's department of health) was generally meager. Moreover, most of the state laws stressed standards connected with the hospital's physical features and demanded little in the way of standards for the functioning of the staff. The U.S. JCAHO was established in 1950 to compensate for this deficiency (refer to box 4.10).

In Western Europe the level of government authority responsible for facility licensing differs from one country to another. In both the British and French systems the national ministries of health promulgate quality standards for both construction and operation of hospitals, but regional or provincial authorities monitor them. In the United Kingdom, where most hospitals are owned and controlled by the central government, this task is performed directly through public sector administration. In France, where the government sponsors a large proportion of hospital beds, but not all, the implementation of standards is particularly challenging for the nongovernmental minority (Roemer 1977).

Hungary established minimum hospital standards in 1997 that are implemented by the regional offices of the ministry of health. Even though 35 percent of Hungarian hospitals have failed to reach the minimum standards, none has been closed (Scrivens 2001), a fact that underscores the importance of ensuring standards are relevant in the local setting. The impact of setting standards is undermined when a large portion of hospitals cannot meet them, since noncompliers feel relatively less concern about enforcement if they represent a substantial portion of the sector.

In China's decentralized model the provincial authorities authorize operation of new hospitals or health centers, but the facilities may voluntarily obtain advice on technical standards from the central health ministries. In practice, hospital beds are so badly needed and the resources to build them so limited that the impact of standards has been low.

Box 4.12 Germany: Regulating Nursing Staff Numbers

In Germany the 1993 Health Care Structure Reform Act established mandatory nursing time standards that directly translated into necessary nursing personnel. According to that regulation a daily documentation of nursing activities put every patient in one of nine categories with a standardized amount of necessary nursing time. The total amount of minutes per ward and per hospital was used to calculate the necessary nursing staff. Nursing time standards were introduced to end the period of (perceived) nursing shortages. It was expected that 13,000 new jobs would be created. After the regulation had led to 21,000 new nursing jobs in only three years, it was abolished as too costly and restrictive for hospitals.

Sources: Busse and Schwartz 1997; and Busse 2000.

In most LMCs, ministries of health are charged with licensing new health facilities. However, licensing is mostly a one-time process, and disciplinary controls are rarely exercised if a hospital fails to meet central government standards.

Germany used a form of structure-oriented regulation in the mid-1990s to increase the amount of nursing resources available in the delivery of acute-care services. They did so through establishing mandatory norms for staffing (in this case, the nursing intensity of patients treated). The new standards brought about a direct increase in the number of nurses employed in the facilities (box 4.12).

Personnel licensing. Personnel licensing is the process by which legal permission is granted by a competent, usually public, authority to an individual to engage in a practice or an activity that is otherwise unlawful. Licensing is thus mostly mandatory. A license is usually granted on the basis of examination or proof of education, or both, rather than on measurement of actual performance. The agency, by issuing a license, certifies that those licensed have attained the minimal degree of competency necessary to ensure reasonable protection of public health, safety, and welfare. A license is usually permanent but may be conditional on annual payment of a fee, proof of continuing education, or proof of competence. Grounds for revocation of a license usually include incompetence, commission of a crime (whether or not related to the licensed practice), or extremely immoral behavior.

The scope of responsibilities of licensing agencies varies from one country to another but may involve some of the following activities:

- Examination of applicants' credentials to determine whether their education, experience, and moral fitness meet statutory or administrative requirements

- Administration of examinations to test the academic and practical qualifications of medical graduates against preset standards

- Granting of licenses on the basis of reciprocity or endorsement to applicants from other localities or foreign countries

- Issuance of regulations establishing professional standards of practice

- Investigation of charges of violation of standards established by statute and regulation; suspension or revocation of violators' licenses; and restoration of licenses after a period of suspension or further investigation.

Personnel licensing practices vary from one region of the world to the other. In the United States and Canada individual states or provinces (not federal authorities) have the legal authority to license practitioners, a practice that is relatively uncommon around the world. The states and provinces generally coordinate their activities through voluntary membership in national associations (the Federation of State Medical Boards in the United States and the Federation of Provincial Medical Licensing Associations in Canada). The requirements for li-

censure typically include graduation from an accredited medical
school; postgraduate training in an approved internship or residency
program; and passing a national examination—in the United States,
the U.S. Medical Licensing Examination (USMLE) or, in Canada, the
Medical Council of Canada Licensure Examination. The USMLE is
administered by the nongovernmental voluntary National Board of
Medical Examiners, which standardizes licensure standards nationwide
through this unified exam.[1] Over the years reciprocity gradually grew
among U.S. states and among Canada's provinces in recognition of one
another's licensees, thus permitting mobility of doctors. Reciprocity
between the two countries is more complicated and depends on the
state and province involved (HEW 1977).

In Germany standards are set nationally by law, but the states
(in German, "Länder") do the licensing. In the United Kingdom
personnel licensing is a function of the General Medical Council
(GMC) and is available only to graduates of accredited institutions.
In Australia licensing is done by the state (or territory) medical
boards. These boards make decisions about the qualifications of applicants seeking licensing. Applicants whose credentials are not acceptable must pass an examination, which is currently conducted by
the Australian Medical Council.

In Eastern Europe and in most developing countries governmental personnel licensing is limited to granting entry permission with
no attempt to assess competence. Licensing of physicians with the
ministry of health follows automatically from completion of prescribed courses of training—without any additional licensing examination. In Colombia's ministry of health, for example, there is a
council of professional practice that registers all physicians and other
health personnel who have completed training at a recognized
school. Physicians must also show proof of a one-year hospital internship, plus a second year of service in a public health post or a
rural facility. Many Latin American countries require the latter form
of service as an approach to solving the shortage of rural doctors.
Nurses and allied health personnel are registered in essentially the
same way as physicians. Beyond these formal licensing procedures,
physicians, dentists, and others engaged in individual practice must

join a professional society for purposes of ethical control over their behavior. These societies may also engage in bargaining with government agencies on rates of payment for services, or they may establish parallel nongovernmental bodies for such purposes.

Process-Oriented Quality Regulation

Structure or input-oriented regulation is the most basic form of health services regulation. It is clear that health care delivery can still be of poor quality even if all needed inputs are available, however. Policymakers therefore utilize more sophisticated forms of regulation that focus on the actual process of producing and delivering health care, as well as the output, or service. In the rest of section 4 we discuss the process; in section 5 we discuss regulation of service outputs.

In health care, process-oriented regulation is applied to providers as well as to educational programs and organizations. It is applied both prospectively and retrospectively.

Facility accreditation. Accreditation is the formal process by which an authorized body evaluates health care facilities according to a set of standards describing the structures and processes that directly contribute to desirable patient outcomes. These standards provide guidance on achieving the highest level of care quality that is possible with the available resources. When a hospital meets or exceeds the structure, process, and outcome standards of the care delivery system it earns the honor of accreditation (figure 4.4). Accreditation is the most common form of external review for health care facilities.

The earliest attempt to set and monitor standards for health care organizations was initiated in the United States in 1917. Although full-fledged accreditation programs have been established in only a few other countries (such as Australia, Canada, and New Zealand), recent experience suggests that accreditation programs can be instituted in many more countries if the standards reflect realistic conditions in local facilities.

The definition of quality in accreditation models has evolved in recent years from standards monitoring to continuous quality improvement (CQI) or total quality management (TQM). The notion

Figure 4.4 The Accreditation Process

```
┌─────────────────────┐              ┌─────────────────────┐
│   Standards define   │              │ Survey evaluates     │
│  optimal performance,│─────────────▶│ facility             │
│   given existing     │              │ operations and       │
│     resources        │              │ provides             │
│                      │              │ recommendations      │
│                      │              │ for improvement      │
└─────────────────────┘              └─────────────────────┘
                                                 │
                                                 ▼
┌─────────────────────┐              ┌─────────────────────┐
│                      │              │ Accreditation body   │
│  Facility is awarded │◀─────────────│ determines if facility│
│    accreditation     │              │ has earned           │
│                      │              │ accreditated status  │
└─────────────────────┘              └─────────────────────┘
```

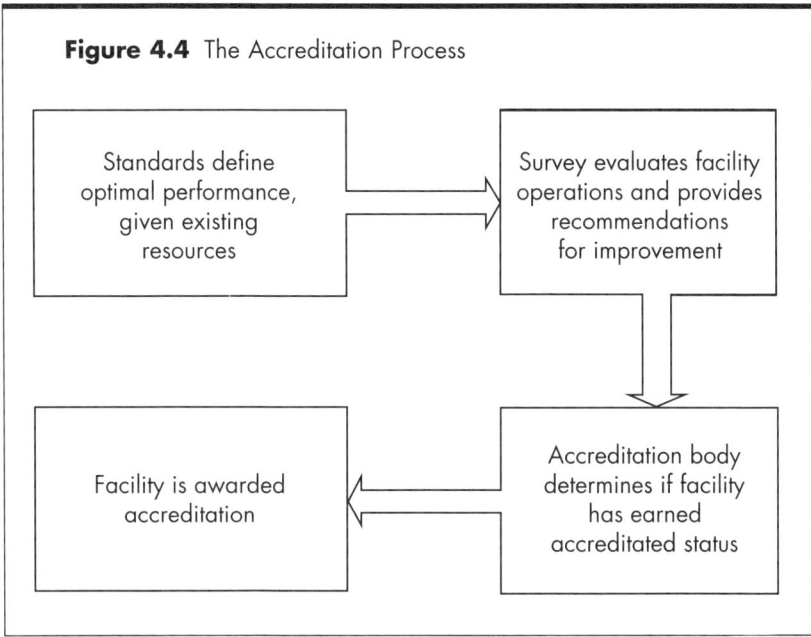

of standards implies fixed points in the definition of quality—points that may, from time to time, be revised and upgraded but that provide clear-cut criteria and well-defined targets.

The notion of quality, as interpreted in the CQI and TQM approaches, implies a continual process of self-examination, a never-ending effort to improve without a fixed end point. The concept of quality as something in a continuous state of evolution is now being incorporated into modern accreditation models.

Accreditation models in Australia, Canada, and the United Kingdom are reviewed in boxes 4.13, 4.14, and 4.15. The review shows a case study in the international propagation of models in the health policy arena. The U.S. model of accreditation directly shaped the systems in Australia and Canada and indirectly influenced developments in Britain. In each case, however, the model had to be adapted to national circumstances. As a result, despite their common ancestry, there are revealing differences in these four countries' systems. However, they are also converging in the way that they are revising their approaches and standards. All accreditation systems are devising or considering outcome indicators that measure the quality of

Box 4.13 Australia: Health Facility Accreditation

The Australian Council on Hospital Standards (subsequently renamed the Australian Council on Health Care Standards) was launched in 1974 in Victoria, subsequently extending its functioning to other states.

The Council was the product of a long campaign by the Australian Medical Association and the Australian Hospital Association. The influence of the U.S. JCAHO model in shaping this initiative was widely acknowledged. As in the United States (pre-1993) the medical profession dominates the membership, although nurses, allied health professionals, and consumers are also represented (albeit sparsely). Like its North American counterparts, the Australian Council has adapted its accreditation processes over the years. Two developments, in particular, are noteworthy. First, the Australian Council puts much emphasis on reviewing the quality assurance activities of the facilities being accredited, as part of its emphasis on promoting continuing improvement in the quality of care. Second, like the JCAHO, the Australian Council, in cooperation with the medical colleges, has been developing a set of clinical outcome indicators, the first of which were used in accreditation reviews during 1993.

Source: Scrivens, Klein, and Steiner 1995.

care provided more directly than the traditional review of inputs and processes. The focus is also shifting toward assessing quality in terms of the patient's experience, and a growing emphasis is being put on quality improvement rather than assurance.

Striking differences emerge, however, in other respects, particularly between the U.K. and the U.S. systems. In the United States the JCAHO has become a quasi-governmental accrediting body.

**Box 4.14 Canada: Health Care Facility Accreditation—
The Peer Review Model**

The Canadian Council on Hospital Accreditation (renamed the Canadian Council on Health Facilities Accreditation in 1988) was founded in 1958. Like the JCAHO, it is an autonomous body. Unlike the JCAHO, it was officially recognized from the start, receiving its letter patent from the secretary of state. It is the sole authority to accredit hospitals in Canada, and its accreditation activities embrace not only general hospitals but also long-term, mental health, and rehabilitation facilities.

The Canadian Council's history, like that of the JCAHO, is one of steady expansion. By the end of the 1980s it was accrediting around 1,300 facilities annually. The results of accreditation visits are graded from nonaccreditation to a four-year accreditation, with four intermediate awards. It also engages in a continuous process of standards revision. In 1990 a marked shift in the standards occurred, which reduced the number of questions and marked a move toward outcomes instead of inputs and processes.

Unlike the situation in the United States, there is not strong financial pressure to receive accreditation. The council's emphasis is on organizational education and self-development. The client for accreditation in Canada is the individual health care provider. The accreditation process is designed to act as a yardstick by which health care organizations can measure their own performance against national standards. However, the Canadian Council has permitted some moves toward regulation, at least for training purposes, in that it is required of hospitals wishing to train medical interns and other health professionals.

(Box continues on the following page.)

Box 4.14 (continued)

The Canadian system is less bureaucratic and legalistic than the U.S. model, and the accreditation documentation much less complex. Less emphasis is put on trying to reduce the discretion of surveyors by elaborate scoring systems. The Canadian system is also much closer to a professional peer review model than the U.S. original.

Source: Scrivens, Klein, and Steiner 1995.

Though theoretically voluntary, it has become a prerequisite key to accessing public funds, and is therefore virtually merged with government regulation. In contrast, accreditation in Britain is still predominantly an exercise in self-improvement, and can be seen as an offspring of the quality movement rather than an instrument of public policy. Australia and Canada are somewhere in between the U.K. and U.S. models. In neither Australia nor Canada has accreditation become a condition for access to public finance, but in both cases—in contrast to Britain—a national body uses national standards to accredit hospital activities.

Efforts are under way to develop and implement hospital accreditation programs in many more countries worldwide (appendix 4.C). Within the last few years accreditation has been spreading to many Western European countries (Scrivens 2001). The Netherlands, for example, is implementing a universal hospital accreditation program, and Belgium and France have introduced accreditation systems run by their national governments (box 4.16).

Accreditation is also being considered in most Central and Eastern European countries, as well as in several low- and many other middle-income countries. The approach taken in these countries has been to conduct an appraisal of local conditions and available resources and to modify another system's standards to reflect a level of

Box 4.15 United Kingdom: Health Facility Accreditation

The hierarchical control of the National Health Service (NHS) over Britain's health care system has traditionally obscured quality issues, since the issues were perceived to be handled internally. The interest in standards began to develop after the hospitals were made somewhat more independent following the 1991 reforms. In contrast to the North American experience, the changes were not driven by the medical profession, which has remained on the sidelines, and have not led to the creation of a single dominant accreditation body. Instead, progress toward accreditation has been halting, and a number of competing actors have taken part.

Britain's only comprehensive hospital accreditation system operates within one Regional Health Authority (South Western) and is directed only at small and community hospitals. This was derived from the Canadian model, has explicit standards, uses health service practitioners as surveyors, and awards a pass or fail. The standards focus only on organizational processes and make no attempt to incorporate clinical standards.

There is also a partial accreditation system developed as an independent foundation by King Edward's Hospital Fund in London. The fund, with a mission to improve quality in the NHS, has been testing JCAHO standards in pilot hospitals. Again, the focus was on organizational processes with no attempt to incorporate clinical audits or outcome indicators. Later, the fund established an Organizational Audit Scheme and is now moving toward grading outcomes and becoming a full-fledged accreditation system.

(Box continues on the following page.)

Box 4.15 (continued)

Last, the private health care sector is pushing for an accreditation system, which it sees as an advantage in competing for contracts in the NHS internal market—as well as substituting for potentially increased public regulation. Some hospitals are actually accrediting themselves, using a national system, designed for all service industries, that surveys the effectiveness with which participating institutions maintain the standards they set for themselves.

Sources: Scrivens, Klein, and Steiner 1995.

care that can be achieved, given environmental realities (box 4.17). The JCAHO, building on its experience in accrediting health care institutions in the United States, has established an international accreditation division to provide technical assistance to countries trying to introduce accreditation as a regulatory instrument (box 4.18; see also JCAHO Web site at http://www.jcaho.org/).

More electronically available resources are listed in appendix 4.D.

Educational accreditation. Above we discuss accreditation related to service provision. However, health care quality is also strongly influenced by the quality of education of health workers. Hence accreditation of educational programs and organization related to health care is another critical regulatory instrument for enhancing health care quality. Educational accreditation is the regulatory process whereby an external association or agency grants public recognition to a school, institute, college, university, or specialized program of study meeting preset criteria or standards, as determined through initial and periodic evaluations.

The purposes of accrediting educational institutions include:

- Establishing criteria for professional licensing

- Assisting prospective students in identifying acceptable programs

---

Box 4.16 Belgium and France: National Accreditation Systems

The Belgian system, introduced in 1987, is administered by local government. Participation is compulsory, and proof of accreditation is required for contracting with and reimbursement from the national insurance system. The national standards are based on planning requirements and are structural in nature; local government can add standards to reflect local needs. This is actually a form of inspection. Surveys of compliance with the standards are undertaken by full-time civil servants who visit every hospital at least once every five years.

France adopted accreditation in 1996, which requires all public and private health care organizations to participate in an external procedure of evaluation. Accreditation is intended to ensure continuous improvement in the quality and safety of care and to promote standardization of hospital and health care organization. The accreditation process is managed by an external agency called the Agence Nationale d'Accréditation et d'Evaluation en Santé, which is tasked with developing the standards and designing and implementing the accreditation process.

Source: Scrivens 2001.

- Stimulating higher standards among education institutions

- Identifying institutions and programs for investments of public and private funds and providing bases for determining eligibility for governmental assistance.

The accreditation process usually involves these basic steps:

- The accrediting agency, in collaboration with professional groups and educational institutions, establishes standards.

Box 4.17 Zambia: Designing Accreditation Programs for Developing Countries

In 1997 Zambian health policymakers identified as a reform priority the development of a mechanism for establishing standards and evaluating hospitals. To facilitate the design of an accreditation program, a multidisciplinary advisory group called the Zambia Health Accreditation Council (ZHAC) was established.

The ZHAC was actively involved in developing and field-testing a first draft of standards that identified 13 key functional areas for every hospital, as well as 49 performance standards and associated measurable criteria. The set of draft standards was distributed to all hospitals and health professional associations throughout Zambia as part of a consensus-building process known as a "field review." Following the field review, the standards were revised, and a draft survey process was developed and field-tested at hospitals of various sizes and types, ranging from a 100-bed mission hospital in a rural village to a 1,800-bed teaching hospital in a major city. Because of limited resources and the relative absence of formal written policies and procedures in most Zambian hospitals, much of the survey's emphasis is on evaluating processes and outcomes of care through observation and interview.

The monitoring and evaluation unit of the central board of health, operating under the direction of the ministry of health, administers the hospital accreditation program. Accreditation surveyors have been selected and trained. The group is comprised of doctors, clinical officers, nurses, dentists, pharmacists, and medical technologists. Each surveyor completes a three-day training course on the standards and survey process, as well as training on-location in several hospitals.

The accreditation program is designed to assist hospital management and staff in setting priorities for their resources, needed improvements, and funding. The program's success and cost-effectiveness in a developing-country context still must be evaluated.

Source: Maboshe, Tembo, and Rooney 1999.

Box 4.18 The JCAHO International Accreditation Service

Joint Commission International Accreditation

Building on its experience in accrediting health care organizations in the United States, the Joint Commission on Accreditation of Healthcare Organizations initiated the development of an international accreditation program in 1998. An international task force representing all regions of the world was convened to provide input into the standards development process. The task force distributed the draft standards to international reviewers to determine their applicability to an international health care setting; they were then pilot-tested in several hospitals in Latin America, Europe, and the Middle East.

Full implementation of the Joint Commission International Accreditation (JCIA) program took place in late

(Box continues on the following page.)

Box 4.18 (continued)

1999. Accreditation may be requested either by an individual hospital or by an accrediting body in another country that may wish to partner with JCIA to offer a joint accreditation, using a full or modified set of JCIA standards.

The final standards represent the important processes and functions of any hospital and are flexible enough to be adapted to meet the needs of a particular country with unique cultural or health care characteristics. The JCIA standards, organized according to either patient care functions or management functions, represent the following important hospital functions or processes:

Patient-Focused Standards

- Access to care and continuity of care
- Patient and family rights
- Assessment of patients
- Care of patients
- Patient and family education

Health Care Organization Management Standards

- Quality management and improvement
- Governance, leadership, and direction
- Facility management and safety
- Staff qualifications and education
- Management of information
- Prevention and control of infections

Further information about JCIA and the internal hospital standards can be obtained by contacting JCIA, One Lincoln Centre, Suite 1340, Oakbrook Terrace, IL 60181. Phone: 1-630-268-7400.

- The institution or program desiring accreditation prepares a self-evaluation study that provides a framework for measuring its performance against the standards established by the accrediting agency.

- A team selected by the accrediting agency visits the institution or program to determine first-hand if the applicant meets the established standards.

- Upon being satisfied, through the information obtained from the self-evaluation and the site visit, that the applicant meets standards, the accrediting agency lists the institution or program in an official publication with other similarly accredited institutions or programs.

- The accrediting agency periodically reevaluates the institutions or programs that it lists to ascertain that the standards are still being met.

In general, two types of accreditation apply to medical education institutions: institutional and specialized. Institutional accreditation applies to the entire institution and indicates that the institution as a whole is achieving its own validated and specified objectives in a satisfactory manner. Specialized program accreditation aims at protecting the public against personnel incompetence resulting from failure of their medical education and training to meet accreditation criteria. Because of the differing emphases of the two types of accreditation, accreditation of the institution as a whole should not be interpreted as being equivalent to specialized accreditation of each of its departments or programs (such as dental hygiene or physical therapy). Institutional accreditation does not validate a specialized program in the same manner and to the same extent as specialized accreditation. However, specialized accreditation usually requires that the program be housed in an accredited institution.

Governments usually undertake educational accreditation in close collaboration with self-regulatory (professional) bodies, since these entities are usually highly motivated to maintain high practice standards and to block practice by unqualified people.

In Canada and the United States no central authority controls educational institutions. Consequently, institutions vary widely in the character and quality of their programs. In both countries peer groups of educators and members of the profession conduct a voluntary self-regulation process. In the United States it is the joint responsibility of the American Medical Association and the Association of American Medical Colleges.[2] The only government influence is exercised by means of allocation of eligibility for receiving federal aid, which is performed by the U.S. Office of Education, in approving the private associations responsible for accrediting medical education institutions. In Canada it is the responsibility of the Royal College of Physicians and Surgeons of Canada and the College of Family Physicians of Canada.

In Western Europe educational accreditation arrangements vary across countries. However, in general, central governments exercise greater control over educational programs than in North America, and, as a result, accreditation has not really been an issue in the past. The United Kingdom differs slightly in requiring its medical schools and their examinations to be approved by the voluntary GMC, even though all the educational institutions are also approved and supervised by the ministry of education. The GMC also sets guidelines for curricula of the medical schools, both university- and hospital-based. This same process is in operation today in Australia. Just recently the Australian Medical Council was established to take over the GMC's role there.

In most of Eastern European central government health authorities typically control educational programs and institutions in the health sector. Only rarely are education authorities, or local bodies, involved. The professional societies are active only in the field of postgraduate or continuing education.

Personnel specialty certification. Certification is the procedure and action by which a duly authorized body evaluates and recognizes (that is, certifies) an individual as meeting predetermined qualifications. The certifying body is generally a nongovernmental agency or a professional association. While licensure is meant to establish the minimum competence required to protect public health, safety, and welfare, certification enables the public to identify practitioners who have met a standard of training and experience set above the level required for licensure. Accordingly, certification programs are usually voluntary and give certified persons special recognition or authorization to use a particular title or official designation, but the uncertified are not excluded from practice. One example is the optional registration of practical nurses, who are then awarded the title "registered nurse." The desire to raise nursing standards has led nursing associations to strive for compulsory registration in many countries.

The qualifications upon which certification is based may include:

• Graduation from an accredited or approved program

• Acceptable performance on a qualifying examination or series of examinations

• Completion of a specified length of work experience.

In some countries associations set minimum certification requirements for beginning workers that, in effect, attempt to prevent employment of uncertified persons. The certification process is helpful to potential employers who are not then obliged to evaluate each worker's education and experience subjectively. In addition, the prestige connected with certification makes the worker feel he or she is the best qualified to do particular work, which should result in a professional attitude and motivation to improve competence.

The procedures for certification of nurses, pharmacists, and other health personnel follow the general model of certification of physicians in each country. The degree of emphasis on certification and the mechanism whereby it is conducted vary from one country to another.

In both Canada and the United States most medical graduates seek specialty board certification, although it is not a professional or legal requirement. Hospitals may require specialty board certification as a prerequisite for obtaining certain privileges. In the United States 24 specialty boards certify specialty and subspecialty competence and establish training criteria. The specialty boards coordinate their activities through the American Board of Medical Specialties. In Canada two national certification bodies perform specialty certification: the Royal College of Physicians and Surgeons of Canada and the College of Family Physicians of Canada, which jointly certify 43 specialties and subspecialties. Although it is nationwide in operation and impact, the U.S. board certification regulatory program is not affiliated with the government. However, it is recognized by many government programs (such as Medicare) for participation and payment purposes and by most hospitals for staff appointments (Newble, Jolly, and Wakeford 1994).

Most other health science disciplines in the United States follow the model of medicine in their certification requirements, with only a few noteworthy variations that further demonstrate the differences among U.S. states. Dentistry, for example, has a statutory rather than a purely voluntary basis for specialty status in several states. Registration of trained nurses requires a formal examination in every state, but a national federation has established a uniform exam resulting in reciprocity in recognition of registered nurses' qualifications between the states. Examinations in pharmacy are also required in all states, and in many jurisdictions relicensure is periodically required on the basis of a minimum record of continuing education. Registration of laboratory technicians is mandatory in some states, where the candidate must pass an examination and have credentials from an approved school. In other states the laboratory technologist or technician may offer prospective employers voluntary certification by the American Society of Clinical Pathologists.

Specialty certification varies among Western European countries, although it is mostly left to professional bodies. In Norway the national medical association maintains a committee that regulates specialty-training requirements and administers certification examinations. In Belgium an especially rigorous sequence of training is required and is approved in advance by the national medical association. In addition, using the financial leverage of social insurance payments, specialty status must be registered with a government authority if the doctor is to be entitled to payments from the social insurance program at the higher specialist rates. In France specialists are registered with the ministry of national education after completing appropriate training and passing certification examinations given by the several specialty societies. The procedures for certification of nurses, pharmacists, and other health personnel follow the general model of certification of physicians in each country. There may be slight modifications in certain fields, such as in Norway, where the maintenance of nurse registration records has been delegated by the government to the voluntary nursing association.

In both Australia and the United Kingdom physician certification is done by the Royal Colleges of Physicians, which certify medical graduates first as Members (an interim qualification) and then as Fellows of the College. In addition, most colleges also employ strategies aimed at maintaining high standards of service by those already admitted to the professional group, including continued medical education (CME) and other professional development activities.

In Eastern Europe, as well as in most developing countries, entry licensing is governmental, with minimal attempts at certification or ensuring maintained competence is maintained. The role of the professional bodies is generally weaker than in North America or Western Europe.

Personnel recertification. The effectiveness of professional associations in controlling the quality of its members' performance after certification is often questioned. This has led to the emergence of recertification as an instrument to ensure continued competency.

Recertification is the process by which a professional body testifies periodically as to a member's competence, either with or without a period of formal retraining. Since a certificate issued to a practitioner cannot easily be withdrawn, recertification means that the validity of a certificate is limited in time, a condition that must be built into the certification system at the outset.

Recertification can be made contingent on meeting certain requirements such as:

• Continuing professional experience, for example, documenting a certain number of hours of professional practice each year

- Maintaining competence, for example, by undergoing periodic tests of clinical knowledge, clinical judgment, or surgical skill

- Demonstrating appropriate clinical performance or outcomes, for example, through assessment of a doctor's authenticated medical records of cases seen over a certain period.

The body that issues the initial certificate is usually responsible for recertification. The body usually also assumes responsibility for organizing educational and professional development activities that assist its members in maintaining competence for recertification. The structure of the body will vary across countries, and, to a lesser extent, across specialties within a country.

Maintenance of professional competence, which is emphasized only in industrial countries, is achieved through positive strategies, focusing on maintenance of competence, or negative strategies, focusing on identification of incompetence, or a combination of the two strategies. Positive maintenance strategies focus on encouraging continuous improvement by the average practitioner rather than on identifying and dealing with outliers (such as promulgation of practice guidelines, provision of continuing education activities, and the support of quality assurance activities). Negative maintenance strategies involve withdrawing certification because of major deficiencies in professional performance or in withholding recertification for failure to pass an exam. Most credentialing agencies worldwide have the power to use such negative strategies, even if they exercise it infrequently. Approaches vary among countries, and among certifying bodies in a given country, in the extent to which these two purposes are served. Some country experiences also show that the most successful approach to maintaining competence is participant centered, placing more value on the practitioner's intrinsic motivation than on external motivation from rewards or threats.

In the United States specialty boards have established voluntary recertification. In 1991, 16 of the 24 specialty boards either had instituted or had plans to institute time-limited certification and recertification.

In Canada, although the issue of recertification has long been discussed in professional circles, compulsory recertification is not yet required. In 1990 the two national certifying bodies, in collaboration with national specialty societies, established a pilot program for maintenance of competence. The program features voluntary enrollment, documentation of CME activities, and confidential summaries of aggregate clinical outcomes.

In Australia there is no uniformity in the recertification practices of the various professional bodies. Only one of the specialist colleges, the Royal Australian College of Obstetricians and Gynecologists, incorporated a system of mandatory recertification in its constitution. The system is dependent on the accumulation of a minimum level of participation in CME activities. The Royal Australian College of General Practitioners, while not insisting on mandatory recertification, expects its members to participate in professional development activities. Several other colleges are developing their own recertification programs. All are to be based on participation in CME but also include elements of audit and peer review.

Retrospective process-oriented regulation. Process-oriented regulation can be backward looking (retrospective) or forward looking (prospective). Retrospective methods include peer review, utilization review, and medical audits. Utilization reviews and medical audits were pioneered in the United States, where the mixed delivery system and fee-for-service reimbursement by private insurers led to a long-term escalation of costs. In the past three decades the inflation rate has been especially rapid. Largely in response to escalating costs, although also because of concerns about the quality of care, various payment organizations have put increasingly stringent controls on providers.

In the U.S. Medicare program, with its soaring costs, the federal government has introduced more and more constraints on both price and volume.[3] The rules for determining fees have become increasingly restrictive, and legal actions have been taken against doctors who are suspected of submitting fraudulent fee claims. In 1973 amendments in the federal law required establishment of professional standard review organizations (PSROs) to exercise peer review over all Medicare and Medicaid payment claims for services in hospitals. PSROs establish norms and standards for various diagnostic procedures and groups. Peer review organizations are the nation-wide and centralized replacement of PSROs.

Aside from governmental regulation, private payers, under the managed-care movement, have been imposing additional controls, primarily to contain costs by reducing inappropriate care and increasing coordination of care. Many of these techniques have achieved quality improvement as a by-product. The process of screening and grouping service utilization under different medical conditions is referred to as utilization review.[4] Managed care organizations and some fee-for-service plans are imposing utilization review procedures to screen and preapprove certain types of medical care or procedures such as hospital admissions, surgical interventions, long hospital stays, and referrals to specialists. Care that is determined to be unreasonable, inappropriate, or medically unnecessary can be denied. The utilization review posits the existence of optimal treatment levels and provides corrective feedback to physicians if over- or undertreatment is suspected. Health insurance programs also conduct payment claims reviews with an eye to ferreting out abuses, such as excessive diagnostic tests or surgical procedures of dubious value. This explicit health care rationing has been extremely contentious, however, and has generated much litigation, popular discontent, and pressure to legislatively establish greater access.

Other industrial countries have taken similar approaches to regulating provider performance. Canada uses both utilization reviews and medical audits. In medical audits in Germany health insurance funds conduct computerized reviews of each doctor's practice habits, as measured by such criteria as the number of medicine prescriptions, office visits, and laboratory tests per case, and the rates of certain surgical procedures. These measurements are compared with those of other doctors in the same specialty, and highly deviant individuals are identified. Such identification is an initial screening step, usually followed by a detailed audit of the individual doctor's work. If this audit reveals unjustified services the doctor may be reimbursed for only a fraction of his claims; in serious instances he or she may be denied eligibility for public reimbursement.

Prospective process-oriented regulation. Process-oriented regulation can be done prospectively by means of practice guidelines and clinical protocols. These instruments were pioneered in the United States, but their use is spreading to many countries. They represent systematically developed guidance to assist practitioners in decisions about appropriate health care for specific clinical circumstances and hence are the most "micro" of regulatory instruments. The methodology attempts to improve the quality, appropriateness, and effectiveness of care. There is evidence that process-oriented regulation often influences clinical decisionmaking in a way that improves outcomes and, in some cases, reduces costs. To be effective, guidelines must be well designed and credible (box 4.19).

The establishment of the National Institute for Clinical Excellence (NICE) in the United Kingdom is a recent quality regulation development.[5] NICE has introduced medical audits, clinical protocols, and benchmarks for treatment outcomes to regulate quality of care and address inefficiencies resulting from treatment variations in both the NHS and the private sector.

Outcome-oriented quality regulation. In recent years the emphasis in quality regulation has been shifting from asking, "Do providers have the capability to deliver quality care?" to asking, "Are they actually providing quality care?" There are two elements in this new approach to regulating quality. The first is the move from defining quality in terms of inputs and processes to defining quality in terms of outcomes. The second element is the range of mechanisms used to motivate health care practices that lead to better outcomes.

The study of outcomes and their measurement is a fast-growing science. It expands the application of cost-effectiveness evaluation to health services investment. Outcomes research has two defining characteristics. First, it emphasizes the study of patients and clinicians in real settings and focuses on effectiveness rather than efficacy. This implies that most outcome studies are observational rather than experimental. Second, outcome research employs a broader spectrum of outcome measurements than traditional clinical research, supplementing morbidity and mortality statistics with patients' reports

Box 4.19 Developing Practice Guidelines

The following basic principles for development of practice guidelines have demonstrated that they improve the effectiveness of those guidelines:

- Identify credible organizations to take on responsibility.
- Define clear goals with an explicit focus on values, ethical and legal issues, and costs.
- Make a formal selection of topics to ensure priority for those most relevant to the organization's needs. This may involve some form of needs assessment.
- Involve all the stakeholders (purchasers, patients, and clinical decisionmakers) in the key decisions that must be made, the outcomes to be considered, and the social, ethical, legal, and cost constraints within which the guidelines must operate.
- Agree on a formal guideline-development process and group decisionmaking approach (such as nominal group technique) and determine the different components required for the guidelines (this is known as a decision algorithm).
- If possible, start with existing guidelines from other places, where the institutional and development context is similar to your own.
- Institute an explicit, systematic, and critical review of the evidence relating to possible alternative decisions. Identify gaps in the evidence and explicitly acknowledge when guidelines must be temporarily based on inadequate evidence.
- Pilot-test guidelines with the end users and revise on the basis of that experience.

Source: Schneider and Wasem 1998.

of their symptoms, health-related quality of life, and satisfaction with their care. For example, outcome assessment facilitates the comparison of surgical as opposed to medical (nonsurgical) treatment for the same condition, different mixes of professionals, and hospitalization as opposed to ambulatory treatment (box 4.20).

Improved outcomes can be encouraged by tying funding to inputs or processes, when these factors can be directly linked to desired outcomes. The lack of research in this field makes it difficult to anticipate what types of initiatives for outcome-oriented incentives will work in different contexts.

Exercising pressure to improve outcomes is easier in some systems than in others. In most situations, independence of funders from providers makes it easier for funders to shift funds in accordance with performance on key outcome indicators. However, if a funder is a primary source of revenue for a provider, this leverage is often lower, since the funder will be unlikely to push a significant facility into bankruptcy. On the other hand, smaller funding organizations, such as individual health maintenance organizations (HMOs) in the United States, will find it easier to shift or renegotiate based on outcome results.

A number of outcome-oriented financial incentives are already in use in a variety of systems: in the United States bonuses for physicians in managed care settings achieving high degrees of patient satisfaction; in the United Kingdom targeted payments to general practitioners for improving immunization and pap smear rates; and in Germany a case fee that requires documentation of guidelines followed in antenatal care. Measuring exactly which changes in health come from a specific intervention by a provider is often difficult, for several reasons:

- *Practicability.* Trying to estimate or detect changes in health in routine care settings can be difficult and impractical.

- *Time.* The natural history of a condition and the duration of the likely treatment results must be taken into account. This is especially problematic in the measurement of health outcomes of chronic illness. The difficulty of routinely measuring positive out-

---

Box 4.20 Scotland: Use of Outcome Research to Regulate Quality

The average five-year survival rate of victims of ovarian cancer for Scotland is among the poorest in Europe, and rates vary geographically. The Accountants Commission for Scotland reviewed the arrangements for the management of ovarian cancer across a sample of regions. The findings led the Scottish Executive of the Royal College of Obstetricians and Gynecologists to set up a multidisciplinary steering group to produce a guideline for management of ovarian cancer. This guideline was published in 1995. It includes recommendations on referral patterns, surgery, pathological assessments, chemotherapy, and postsurgical management. Thus, outcome-targeted regulation can imply monitoring of activities and structures of health care provision (supply side) as well as consumption (demand side).

Source: Bundesminsterium für Gesundheit 1998; and Scotland: Use of Outcome Research to Regulate Quality.

---

comes of care has encouraged an interest, especially among health care purchasers, in measuring and minimizing negative outcomes. This involves monitoring the rates of undesired and avoidable outcomes, such as postoperative complications and deaths, as well as unplanned readmissions.

- *Attributability.* In order to tie financial or other incentives to the impact on quality of certain actions, it is necessary to connect the action to the outcome. Such attribution in health care is often problematic. Evaluation is especially difficult when too long a time has elapsed since treatment or when there are many intervening variables.

In addition, some services (such as immunizations) may benefit (that is, improve the health outcome for) persons who do not receive them. Evaluation also requires a health technology system that can monitor the impact of medical technology, in its broadest sense, on outcomes. In terms of influencing a provider's behavior, whether his or her performance can be attributed to monetary incentives is often unclear, since other factors also play a role. For example, HMOs are different from traditional private practice, not only in their use of capitation instead of fee-for-service payments but also in their greater use of practice guidelines. Monetary incentives are appropriate where feasible, if their use demonstrably improves health outcomes and makes care more patient-centered.

Patients' organizations. Most of the regulatory instruments discussed above are implemented under collaboration between government and professional, or provider, organizations. However, patients and community organizations also have an interest in ensuring health care quality. Governments can also create pressure to improve health care quality by legislating or creating institutions to strengthen the influence or leverage of such organizations.

There are several ways of strengthening the leverage of these organizations, including:

- To ensure wide dissemination of information regarding the existing standards and responsibilities of providers and facilities.

- To establish mechanisms for collecting information from patients, by means of surveys or complaint procedures in order to utilize patients' first-hand information about interaction with physicians and other health workers.

- To establish an ombudsman who handles complaints about public services or regulations that allow an appeal before an independent body.

- To collaborate with patients or community organizations on issues of particular interest to them. Such collaboration is most commonly seen with patients' organizations founded with an interest in treatment of particular, often chronic, diseases.

In certain settings malpractice suits are commonly used to enforce the rights of patients to take legal action against their doctor or health provider for injuries suffered due to negligence. The United States is one country where malpractice lawsuits have proliferated. Their frequency reflects patients' sophistication, lawyers' aggressiveness, the high cost of medical care (often not covered by insurance), and the tendency of insurance companies that provide coverage to doctors to settle claims, even of dubious merit, rather than risk court litigation. The amounts of malpractice awards and out-of-court financial settlements have risen so much that the cost of personal liability insurance, which nearly all U.S. physicians carry, has become astronomical—particularly for surgeons, anesthesiologists, and obstetricians.

Another mechanism that strengthens the leverage of patients to influence health care provision is the implementation of some form of patients' rights act. Several countries, or political jurisdictions within countries, have enacted a patients' bill of rights or issued some type of patients' charter. In some contexts, and depending on the legal system, a clear statement of patients' rights may merely raise consciousness. Patients' rights bills are likely to function more effectively in safeguarding citizens' rights if they—or existing laws and institutions—enable sanctions to be applied to providers or institutions that do not meet the established standards.

The range and specificity of entitlements, such as the right to receive a list of providers' fees, or the right to be provided with an interpreter, may affect the degree of compliance with patients' rights bills. Implementation of patients' rights bills may suffer if they are "neither enforced by statute, externally regulated, nor, as yet, monitored in any official way" (Silver 1997). Compliance can be encouraged by allowing institutions to determine their own standards while retaining governmental authority to sanction providers who fail to meet their own internal standards. Alternatively, the government can work with affected providers or facilities to establish standards that are achievable for the majority. The uniformity and potency of these standards may, however, be questionable. The legal status and specificity of possible sanctions, as well as the cultural context in which patients' rights are articulated, influence the extent to which they will be enforced. Community and consumer organizations can help enforce patients' rights (box 4.21).

Countries embarking on the development of a hospital accreditation program should plan to implement accreditation that is focused, first, on the structure of care, and later on process-based measures (WHO 1996). Outcome measures and clinical standards should be phased in later, because they are the most expensive and complicated to implement. These countries that are developing a hospital accreditation program also need to establish a body, charged with carrying out the survey and evaluation process (section 6). At the same time, the standards that are developed must be appropriate to local conditions. Until recently the only available accreditation model to imitate was the one developed by the U.S. JCAHO. Although this model provided a good structure-process prototype, the U.S. standards were not appropriate for countries with fewer economic resources. As international experience with accreditation increased, available models for standards and lessons learned from developing accreditation structures made the process less difficult for middle-income countries.

Section 5 Regulating Health Care Providers

In the previous section we discussed the regulation of various aspects of health care. In this section we shift to discussing the regulation of the providers of health care. While one could easily break down these categories much further, we focus on two general categories: primary care providers and hospitals.

Regulation of primary care providers. Primary care has been defined as first-contact care for new health problems, person-focused rather than disease-focused, comprehensive, and coordinated care (Starfield 1996). An effective system of primary care does not emerge spontaneously within a health care system. It must be financed, planned, and

Box 4.21 The Role of Community and Consumer Organizations

The emphasis on democracy, participation, and accountability of organizations responsible to the public is increasing throughout the world. As a result, the role of consumers and their representative organizations is seen as more and more critical to responsive and effective health services. Many types of community organizations are active in the health sphere, which reflects the interests of special groups of consumers as well as the wider community. These community organizations include hospital boards, patient organizations, family practitioner committees, consumer groups, advocacy and lobby groups, and residents' associations.

Community organizations are formed for many reasons. Often, groups of citizens wish to promote action toward an objective they believe is not getting adequate attention from the government. This applies to many agencies focused on a specific disease such as diabetes, cancer, and acquired immune deficiency syndrome (AIDS). Some voluntary groups are formed to focus attention on and advance the well-being of certain segments of the population, such as the elderly. Still other voluntary groups are promoted by government to mobilize private resources for a task that government hesitates to undertake. Humanitarian and religious objectives also play a part. Funds needed to support activities are always raised in part from voluntary donations. In many countries, however, patient organizations are subsidized by the government.

Consumer organizations may channel information and thus affect power relations between the state, consumers, and providers. For example:

• Hospital boards and family practitioner committees may present community perspectives and community needs to providers.

- Consumer organizations may provide consumers with information on different providers, thus assisting them in exercising their purchasing power, or they may provide government with information related to health care quality (from the patient's perspective).
- Local health committees may present community needs to government, for example, regarding the location of new private services.

India is one developing country where consumer organizations (such as Medico Friends Circle and the Association for Consumer Action on Safety and Health) are very active. In Mumbai, India, a private citizens' group helped reactivate the legislation that requires registration of private nursing homes. In a landmark case in 1995 the Indian Supreme Court ruled that Indian doctors could be sued for medical negligence in consumer courts. The consumer courts, composed largely of lay people, are an alternative to lengthy processes in the civil courts. Consumer groups had argued that medical services should be covered under the Consumer Protection Act. Consumer groups began this judicial process in the face of poor disciplinary action taken by the Medical Council.

The limitations of consumer and community organizations must be recognized. Although consumers may prove to be good judges of certain characteristics of health care, they are not fully able to judge clinical quality. Even if consumers can evaluate care received, they are frequently unwilling to complain, especially in low-literacy and low-democracy settings. In Ghana, Ministry of Health officials suggest that the social distance between Western-trained doctors and much of the population would prevent complaints from surfacing.

Source: Naylor and others 1999, p. 6.

regulated in such a way that primary care providers take responsibility for the health of the population under their care. Sufficient resources need to be allocated to primary care relative to secondary care in order to give people adequate access to primary care services. The supply and location of primary care staff, the quality of care, and access to care must be planned, monitored, and regulated. A recent reform trend has been to make primary care providers more independent (such as by giving them a budget for secondary care, as in the United Kingdom, or by effectively privatizing primary care, as in Central Europe, or Stockholm County, Sweden). As these providers become more independent, regulation becomes even more important.

In countries such as France and Germany that have social insurance systems, self-employed general practitioners (GPs) work under contract, while in national health care systems GPs can be either self-employed (as in the United Kingdom) or salaried (as in Finland and Portugal). In the Central and Eastern European countries GPs were state employees in the past but are increasingly becoming self-employed (Boerma and Fleming 1998).

Thus, in many health care systems, GPs are not only professional caregivers but also small-scale businesspeople. More generally, these doctors operate their practices personally, bearing the risk for any profits or losses. Hence, the realization of their personal goals will include an interest in the financial performance of their practice. Realizing financial goals is a common ambition, which is not restricted to self-employed doctors. Within employment contracts, salaried doctors also strive to achieve their individual financial goals (perhaps through overtime work, the receipt of performance bonuses, or the establishment of private practice on the side). Irrespective of employment status, economic gain may not be the first goal of health care providers. Health care providers also value their status in terms of approval, as professionals, by their patients and peers.

Regulation of general practice has different levels of application, from the level of the health care system as a whole, to intermediate levels of regional or local organization, to the microeconomic level of the individual GP practices. The overall health care system provides the context of the regulatory environment and the instruments for achieving objectives by means of regulation. National standards, rules, and incentives set at this level influence the GPs' broad scope of duties. For example, in some countries GPs serve the entire population. In others, primary care for children or for women is more specialized, carried out by pediatricians and gynecologists, respectively (Boerma, van der Zee, and Fleming 1997). In addition, in the administration of health care systems, there are usually intermediate structures, such as regional authorities or health insurance funds, that guide the behavior of health care professionals and organizations.

Explicit professional values and standards may also serve to regulate the behavior of GPs. Values can be influenced by professional bodies and, in some European countries, professional organizations of GPs, which also set formal standards of care. Through the mechanism of peer approval, professional standards are important for motivating GPs to work in the interest of their patients' health and well-being (which is not always in line with patients' preferences). Many countries, notably those in Western Europe, have strong, active professional associations of physicians, some of which are specifically for GPs. Because of the state's historical dominance in Central and Eastern Europe professional bodies are relatively weak, and those specifically focused on GPs are either absent or in their early development. Professional bodies' quality of leadership and activities are crucial in upholding professional values. Regardless of the effectiveness of their leadership and operation, however, the government clearly must oversee their structure and activities, especially in areas where professional interests are most at odds with social or patients' interests.

Additional types of behavioral incentives, usually applied by the government or by health insurance funds, are financial. These might motivate GPs to act as entrepreneurs in the narrow sense (to make a profit) and act in the best interests of patients at the same time, for example, by increasing vaccination rates (if a fee-for-service incentive for vaccinations is operating). They might also result in a GP's reducing the volume of care for a patient to preserve a budget or profit, or just the opposite, to overprovision of care, as might be the case in fee-for-service reimbursement of private providers.

At the microeconomic level social controls inside the practice group and the incentives provided by practice-level budgets influence GPs' behavior. General practice is organized in many ways, but one of the most obvious ways is in the number of GPs working in an organizational unit. The organization of the practice, especially team size, might influence the relative importance of personal interests and professional values, which probably have the strongest influence on GPs' behavior when they are working in small groups. For example, when GPs work in a solo practice, they are more dependent on their patients and are more inclined to give in to a patient's demands, even if not in the health interest of the patient (Freidson 1970). When GPs work in large groups the strength of group norms concerning professional values is usually weaker, primarily because the behavior of any individual is less visible. Thus, personal interests could influence GPs' behavior more when they work solo or in large groups than when they work in small groups. Depending on other incentives and regulations these personal economic interests may dominate, fostering excessive or inappropriate health care provision.

Across health systems, there are large differences in both the amount and content of regulation surrounding general practice—for example, in the types of rules and incentives used. To help develop an effective system of primary care—one that ensures everyone access to care; continuity and comprehensiveness of treatment; and integration within other levels of care—regulatory elements might include:

- Permits for new practices and incentives to work in underserved areas—to improve equity in the geographical distribution of GPs and primary care facilities

- Personal lists of registered patients for GPs—to encourage them to be responsible in an ongoing relationship for a defined population

- Elements of capitation in the payment system for GPs—to promote more cost-effective management of resources and greater continuity of care

- A gatekeeping role (where patients may see a specialist only if referred by the GP)—to prevent unnecessary specialist care

- Facilitation of peer review—to bring about effective external and internal monitoring of the quality of care provided

- Regulation to increase delivery of specific preventive and primary care services.

Regulation of hospitals (inpatient care). In many health systems private hospitals play a significant role, serving not only private but also public (or publicly funded) patients. In these instances, regulation of hospitals is a core responsibility of the government. Their responsibilities in this regard include: strategic planning, monitoring of services and facilities, and regulating and, where appropriate, designing particular subsector markets for service providers.

What needs to be regulated? Hospital activities need to be guided by regulations that steer hospital care toward fulfilling social objectives such as equality in access and service quality; capacity; and financial sustainability of public expenditure commitments, as well as protection of the health of the public (which includes hospital employees).

Enabling hospital care. Every country endeavors to provide its citizens with access to high-quality hospital care. As a first step, the right physical structures must be put in the right places. If the government provides hospital infrastructure through public hospitals no regulation in the initially described sense is necessary. In many countries public and private hospitals operate side by side, but only rarely does the planning process consider this when decisions are made on hospital location, capacity, and technology.

Countries that rely on a mix of public, not-for-profit, and for-profit providers, however, need to proceed differently to ensure the population's equal access to hospital care. Two main categories of regulation can be distinguished: an ex-ante approach, focusing control on the initial establishment of hospital facilities or capacity, and an ex-post approach, focusing on rationalizing existing capacities' inclusion in a public plan or reimbursement eligibility (box 4.22).

Specifying and rewarding hospital services. Once hospitals are established, key policy decisions must be made about access to them, about the types of services they should or may offer, about minimum

Box 4.22 Approaches to Regulating Hospital Capacity: Three European Examples

The ex-post regulatory strategy is used in Switzerland, where it is mandated that private hospitals should be "appropriately" taken into account when the cantons draft lists of hospitals. Listed hospitals, independent of their ownership, qualify for reimbursement of services under compulsory health insurance as well as for public subventions. Cantons' decisions of inclusion or exclusion can be challenged by submission to the federal government.

Variants of the ex-ante approach are exemplified in the Netherlands and Germany. In the Netherlands the Hospital Facilities Act of 1971 regulates the establishment of new hospital capacity. For this purpose, the country is divided into 27 planning regions, and hospital plans, using bed-need standards, are prepared by the respective provincial government. Hospitals may not be constructed or renovated without a license. Obtaining this permission is a four-step process: declaration of need, estimate of the area required, approval of the building plan, and receipt of the license.

In Germany the approach to hospital plans varies from state to state. In Bavaria the government stipulates that "[t]he hospital plan should . . . provide the conditions for hospitals to assure their services in efficient departments by mutual cooperation and division of tasks." The policy in Hesse is more interventionist, stating that "[t]he mutual cooperation of the legally required planning committees as well as cooperation with the state is not regulated in detail in the federal law; and in this respect further regulation is necessary." Bennema-Broos, Groenewegen, and Westert (2001) demonstrated that the Hesse approach led to a more equal distribution of hospital beds than the

Bavarian approach. However, lower costs both per bed-day (7 to 8 percent) and per case (4 to 5 percent) in the former state could point toward a possible trade-off between equity and efficiency.

Source: Busse, van der Grinten, and Svensson 2002.

quality standards that will or will not apply (section 4), and about reimbursement methods.

Access. Access poses three major issues: (a) Does the hospital have an obligation to treat any patient requiring care, irrespective of insurance status or potential profitability, or can it select its patients? (b) Is the hospital required to facilitate unscheduled admissions, for example, through an emergency room or similar arrangements? (c) Can a patient expect the hospital to be fully functional at any time of day, week, or year—with physicians always on site and available? These questions require regulatory standards, because leaving them up to individual hospitals may not result in positive answers.

The issue of patient choice has also drawn increased attention. As seen in the United Kingdom neither a purchaser-provider split nor hospital autonomization automatically widens choice—that takes separate regulation (or removal of regulations that prevent choice). Once again, increased regulation does not automatically mean fewer entrepreneurial opportunities for hospitals, as demonstrated in Sweden (box 4.23).

Types of services. Should hospitals be allowed to offer whatever services they want, or is regulation of services necessary? An oft-cited example of regulation that seemingly restricts entrepreneurial opportunities and innovation is the strict separation between ambulatory care and hospital care in Germany. The German Hospital Organization has long demanded a change in this rule. Since 1993 German hospitals have been allowed to offer patients ambulatory surgery and ambulatory care for a few days before and after their treatment as inpatients. The incentives for these services were ini-

Box 4.23 Sweden: Improving Patient Access

During the early 1990s Sweden's county councils took steps toward enhancing patient choice and creating incentives for public hospitals to improve their services. The county councils revised their budgeting arrangements so that "money follows the patient," instead of being budgeted to the hospital in advance. These reforms aimed at providing patients with prompt care and assuring their choice of providers (instead of being based on place of residence). Similar steps were taken in Denmark in 1993, and in Norway in 1999. Together with other concurrent developments such as the separation of purchasing and provision functions, the regulation enhancing choice also laid the groundwork for limited competition between hospitals, centering on access to care and, to a lesser degree, on perceived quality.

As a result, 2 to 5 percent of total health care resources shifted to different providers. As the national government sought to generate demand-led pressures for improving services it also took steps to create direct incentives for improving service quality. To guarantee prompt treatment for procedures with long waiting times, the central government granted hospitals extra funding but made these grants contingent on treating the patients within three months of diagnosis. Similar policies were implemented in Denmark, Finland, and the United Kingdom.

In Sweden patient choice and hospital competition appear to have led to substantial changes in the outlook and behavior of hospital administrators and medical staff. For the first time in their history these providers sought to compete with one another to provide prompt access to elective surgery. While service quality thus improved, the market mechanisms had no noticeable negative effect on existing clinical quality. To counteract the subsequent increase in total utilization (and therefore expenditure), new budgetary regulations were adopted.

Source: Busse, van der Grinten, and Svensson 2002.

tially weak, however, since remuneration was included in the hospital budgets. Giving legal monopolies to a group of providers (in this case the office-based physicians) constrains efficiency gains. If, however, hospitals were allowed to compete fully with office-based physicians, conditions such as reimbursement should be equal. This would necessitate the termination of public subsidies for capital investments, which could lead to a less equitable distribution of necessary technology.

Reimbursement. Financing hospitals is usually a major worry for regulators. While financing hospitals through line-item budgets does not stimulate entrepreneurial behavior, all other forms of financing—for example, by individual procedure, bed-day, case, or global budget—possess incentives to increase or reduce the number of cases, the length of stay, the number of procedures per case, and the like (Wiley 1998; and Langenbrunner and Wiley 2002). The question is: should payment be uniform by means of regulation, or should hospitals be allowed to negotiate different payment structures with their purchasers or third-party payers? There are good reasons for regulating certain aspects of individual payment systems—for example, to include case-mix adjusters in activity-based reimbursement systems to restrict adverse selection—but there appears to be no compelling evidence for mandating an equal payment system for all hospitals. Transparency, lower transaction costs, and ease of administration could be arguments for regulating reimbursement, but only if policymakers rank these objectives as highly as ensuring equal access or high quality. Whether a particular payment system induces the desired behavior—or the opposite—often depends on local circumstances.

Section 6 The Institutional Structure of Regulation

The design of any initiative to enhance the impact of health care regulation must take into account the relevant aspects of the country's institutions. As with any reform effort, such an initiative should be based on a thorough and detailed assessment of the conditions that determine the government's capacity for regulation (table 4.8). The government's success in its role as a regulator is contingent upon the existence of certain prerequisites, including:

• Technical capacity to perform the basic regulatory functions of standards setting, informing, enforcing, performance monitoring, and legislative review

• Ability to process information responsively

• Ability of the health care regulatory agency to work with other components and levels of government in other ministries and departments

• Political commitment to performing regulatory responsibilities.

The private sector's costs of providing information to the government are high. If the government simply receives information without acknowledging or using it, relations with the private sector suffer.

One or more of these prerequisites are absent in most LMC settings, where cases of government failure as a regulator are common (box 4.24). This has led to the widespread approach of focusing the governments' regulatory responsibilities on a limited range of functions, and to complement or supplement direct state regulation by other mechanisms. For example, the government can delegate or contract out some of its regulatory functions to private, self-regulatory agencies that have technical expertise in and intimate knowledge of the regulated sector. This technique is termed audited self-regulation (National Commission on Quality Assurance Web site; and Trubek 1999).

Table 4.8 A Framework for Comprehensive Regulatory Assessment

Overall country profile	Political economy	• Political ideology • Culture, values, and norms • Interrelationship or power balance between stakeholders • Per capita income level
	Demographic and health indicators	• Demographic data • Literacy rates • Health status
Existing or potential capacity for regulation	Overall health sector structure	• Provider mix and extent and forms of private provision • Breadth of insurance coverage: public, private • Health care utilization indicators
	Current regulatory system	• Status of current health care regulation • Effectiveness of current regulation in enabling private participation and ensuring desirable performance • Information systems, ease of data collection, and ability to process data efficiently
	Government capacity	• Organizational structure • Level of government • Technical capacity to perform regulatory functions (set standards, monitor, evaluate, and enforce) • Availability of trained personnel • Funding (public and private)

The Regulatory Regime

Regulations are not simply disembodied rules. They are elaborated and carried out within a certain institutional framework, or the regulatory regime (Altenstetter 1998). The regulatory regime derives from the interaction of government regulatory agencies and initiatives with relevant organizations and groups outside the public sector (see figure 4.5). The importance of specific organizations or groups

Box 4.24 India: Health Sector Regulation in a Developing Country

India's central and state governments have enacted laws to regulate:

- Health care facilities (an example is the Nursing Home Act)
- Medical practice (examples are the consumer protection act and the Indian Medical Council Act)
- Drugs (examples are the Dangerous Drugs Act, Drugs Price Control Act, and the Pharmacy Act).

In a survey of providers' perceptions of the effectiveness of these laws in influencing equity, efficiency, and quality, 76 percent of the doctors surveyed believed these laws were only moderately effective. The respondents attributed ineffectiveness to:

- Weak implementation and enforcement of rules and regulations
- Differences in enforcement of the laws from state to state
- Resistance from professional groups
- Failure of the medical profession to develop self-regulatory mechanisms and standards
- Irrelevance of some regulations because they have not been updated.

Source: Bhat 1996.

varies across health systems. For example, the national association of hospitals plays a significant role in Germany, where they have a statutory right to participate in sector negotiations on a range of issues. Because of the market orientation of service provision in the United States, health insurance organizations strongly influence compliance with standards through the process of selecting providers.

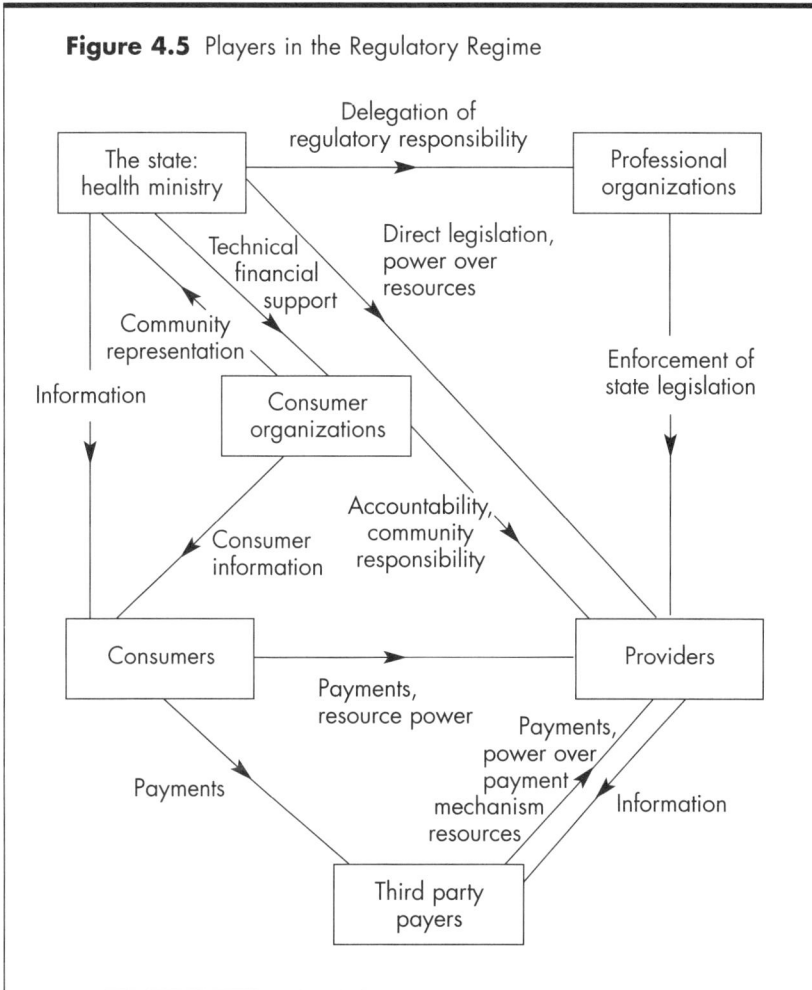

Figure 4.5 Players in the Regulatory Regime

Hence, to improve the effectiveness of the regulatory framework, governments must undertake specific legislative actions and take steps to bring about needed changes in the structure of the regulatory regime (Maor 1998). Table 4.9 provides some examples of questions that might be asked to assess existing regulatory structures and identify priority actions to improve the regulatory regime. Changes may be required to involve provider organizations in developing appropriate standards or benchmarks, for example. Actions may be needed

Table 4.9 Sample Questions for Assessing Existing Regulatory Structure

- What are the objectives of existing regulations: Do they seek to limit fees-for-service, stop excess provision, prevent poor practice, or a combination of these?
- Does the regulation deal with basic infrastructure and staff training, or does it consider the outcome of care?
- What is the balance between incentive options (carrot) and restrictive regulations (stick)?
- Who are the agents responsible for setting rules and incentives, monitoring implementation, and enforcing sanctions if rules are transgressed?
- Are the regulatory agencies active, seeking out low-quality providers, or are they passive, awaiting presentation of complaints?
- What is the formal regulatory role of the government relative to capacity (congruence)?

Source: Bennett and others 1994.

to involve consumer organizations in monitoring compliance and other aspects of enforcement. The advantage held by these organizations with respect to critical information makes them important partners in many regulatory initiatives. Decisions regarding collaboration and consultation with these actors have a significant impact on the degree to which such initiatives are successful.

The scope of a regulatory regime can be seen in the extent to which regulation is comprehensive—how much of the regulated provider's activities it encompasses. The safety of medicines is regulated, but medicine prices are not usually regulated, and neither are the earnings of pharmaceutical companies. The scope of regulatory control can also vary according to the number of providers that are regulated and the extent to which they are regulated.

One element of the regulatory regime is the extent to which regulations serve to inform consumers about the regulated provider's activities rather than dictate which activities will be allowed. The key distinction between informing and enforcing regulation is the discretion afforded consumers. Informing regulation supports consumers in making rational, knowledge-based choices. Enforcing regulation makes choices for consumers. The choice between informing and enforcing regulation is partly determined by the relative costs of acquiring and processing information for the regulator and for consumers. Consumers' relative leverage in dealing with providers is also important. Informing regulation is less effective in instances where the impact of a bad outcome is severe, as is the case with the side effects of some pharmaceuticals. Informing regulation also works poorly when the degree of understanding required to comprehend the information is very high, as is the case with radiation doses of imaging technologies.

The role and organization of regulatory players is a crucial aspect of the regulatory regime. Policymakers need to understand the politics, organizational relationships, and power balance between the various regulatory players. These players are the regulators (state agencies, self-regulatory bodies, and professional associations); the consumers (patients, insured persons, and consumer organizations); the providers; and third-party payers (insurance funds). Figure 4.5 illustrates the dynamics of these relationships. It is clear that policymakers need to think strategically about the players, the information they possess, and the motivation and interests they have relative to the government's goals.

Designing Regulatory Institutions

The literature on designing regulatory institutions that are specific to the health sector is sparse. However, based on the experience from other sectors, a standard prescription for designing good regulatory institutions typically includes the words "independence," "transparency," "accountability," "expertise," and "credibility." These words convey important principles, while implementation must be sensitive to different countries' legal and political institutions.

The concept of an independent regulatory agency operating with transparent procedures, making rational decisions based on its statutory responsibilities, and subject to judicial review is a familiar one in Canada, the United States, and a few other countries. Even in the United States, however, where the concept of the independent regulatory commission was born years ago and has had nearly a century to evolve, regulatory agencies are not completely free of political pressures. The concept may be alien in many countries. This is particularly true in countries where governments are accustomed to making policy decisions behind the closed doors of ministries and government departments, and citizens have limited opportunities for due process, transparency, or judicial review. Moreover, it takes time for regulatory institutions to be created and then to mature; their independence and credibility are established on the basis of both their legal foundations and their behavior when confronted with difficult decisions involving substantial interest group controversy (Gilbert and Newberry 1994). Finally, the issue of the independence of regulatory agencies, though correct in principle, is not effective in the absence of other pillars of regulatory institutional design, particularly accountability and transparency.

In light of these considerations, we offer only some general guidelines regarding the attributes of good regulatory institutions. These guidelines are applicable in a variety of ways to individual countries according to their economic situation and legal and political institutions (box 4.25).

Governance: Intragovernmental as opposed to a separate agency. In organizational design, should the regulatory agency be placed within the ministry of health or should it have a separate identity as an independent or quasi-independent agency? Conventional wisdom suggests that regulatory agencies should be independent entities. It has been argued that independence may reduce corruption and political interference. In any case, the separation of jurisdictions between the ministry and the regulator should be clear and not arbitrary.

In general, the structure of regulatory bodies in the health sector is related to the country's overall administrative structure. For intragovernmental structures most countries have one agency with major responsibility for general regulation in health care. It may be a discrete body in the central government, concerned exclusively with health, or it may be combined with other social functions such as population control, welfare, social security, education, environment, or culture. The U.S. Department of Health and Human Services is a good example of such an agency. When the population's health protection is the sole function, the agency is usually designated as a ministry or department of health. As noted above, the government may choose to delegate regulatory tasks in various areas to other bodies (within and outside government).

Box 4.25 The Kyrgyz Republic: Designing an Accreditation Agency

In 1995 the Kyrgyz Republic embarked on an effort to establish a facility accreditation program. It was decided that the program would be administered by an accreditation council jointly run by the mandatory health insurance program, the ministry of health, and the physicians' association. It was perceived that the council could benefit from the technical responsiveness of a peer organization, the financial incentives of an insurance system, and the enforcement power of a governmental organization.

The council's terms of reference included the development and updating of facility standards and the monitoring of hospital and polyclinic compliance with those standards. In the future this organization's role could expand to cover the practice of individual doctors and the operation of rural ambulatory centers. The accreditation council would grant the authority to inspect hospitals and polyclinics and to impose penalties and sanctions for noncompliance with facility standards. Withholding insurance payments is a major sanction that could be imposed in case of serious noncompliance.

Options for funding the accreditation council include (a) hospitals and polyclinics pay for inspections in order to become accredited; (b) hospitals and polyclinics pay an annual fee; (c) the government provides start-up funding; and (d) the government pays operational costs.

Source: Becker 1995, pp. 2–4.

Terms of reference. Any regulatory agency needs a clear statement of its mandate and functions. The agency's terms of reference (TORs) should cover at least information gathering and the dissemination of sector-specific performance indicators. Such information would

allow assessment of the sector's evolution and the creation of incentives for transparency, compliance, self-monitoring, and efficient
performance. TORs could also include assessment of provider performance against indicators and enforcement of compliance.

Agency funding. Conventional wisdom and incentive theory suggest
that effective regulation requires a predictable and adequate level of
funding in order to limit the opportunities for undue influence.

Agency staffing. To fulfill its obligations a regulatory agency needs
staff with the necessary qualifications and skills to support its regulatory responsibilities. Among the relevant specialties that may be
required are law, accounting, quality control, and price and payment
controls. Analytical and information management capabilities are also
essential.

Developing adequate staff resources and skills can take several
years. The likely availability or unavailability of experienced staff
should be taken into account in the selection of instruments to be
used in regulating providers. These considerations imply that use of
relatively simple regulatory mechanisms may initially prove more effective in practice than theoretically superior mechanisms that are
more complicated. Opportunities to evaluate, adapt, and enhance
regulatory procedures as experience is gained can be built into the
program at the outset.

Public representation on the regulatory body has been supported
in some settings. Experience with public representatives is mixed,
because it is difficult to find appropriate representatives who are well
informed yet truly independent. An alternative is to set up a public
advisory board to the body, which can have a totally open information and deliberation process. It can solicit complaints, help resolve
disputes, and provide advice.

Regulatory discretion. Statutes can convey responsibilities to the regulatory agencies in two ways. The first is to give the regulatory
agency substantial discretion by defining a general set of policy ob-

jectives that the regulatory agency is directed to pursue and leaving it to the agency to develop the specific regulatory mechanisms it will use to achieve these objectives. Legislative authority, procedural requirements, and judicial review regulate the agency's discretion. The second approach is to give the regulatory agency much less discretion by defining more precisely what it is supposed to do and how it is supposed to do it.

In developing countries that lack a strong history of regulatory independence and enforcement of property rights and contractual obligations, allowing the regulatory agency less discretion often makes sense at least in the beginning. Decreased agency flexibility is the down side. As experience and credibility are gained and administrative and judicial review procedures are developed, the agency can be given more discretion. The regulatory agency cannot do an effective job, however, if it lacks the minimal authority needed to require the providers in its jurisdiction to submit outcome, quality cost, price, and other information necessary for assessing their services and performance. Moreover, it must have the authority to audit regulated providers.

Accountability and regulatory oversight. Accountability of a regulatory body is important, and checks and balances such as budgetary reviews and supervisory oversight provide ways to control regulators. Discretion can be granted only when the right incentive and accountability structure ensures that the regulatory agency will behave appropriately. Part of regulation in any health system is to provide for evaluation of a regulatory body's performance by another at a higher level of authority or by a body from a different sector.

Procedures and judicial review. The choice of administrative procedures and opportunities for judicial review involves striking a balance between fairness to the regulated entities and excessive due-process obligations that would create significant risk of administrative delays.

In developing countries that have a history of poor infrastructure performance and arbitrary government intervention, opportunities for judicial review are especially important in order to guard against decisions by a regulatory agency that exceed the scope of its statutory mandate or that fail to follow established guidelines.

Operationalizing regulation. After selecting instruments and the providers on which regulatory changes will focus, policymakers still need to ensure that the design and implementation plans are realistic, can be implemented, and are worthwhile.

Balancing Conflicting Regulatory Roles and Goals

Balancing and integrating various forms and objectives of regulation are key regulatory challenges. Government health authorities may have a compelling interest in sustaining and developing the provider network. On the other hand, their efforts to identify and deal with poorly performing providers may generate strong pressure to close or otherwise reconfigure facilities.

Attempts to constrain prices may encourage providers to skimp on quality where possible. Attempts to ensure access to health care, regardless of the patient's ability to pay, may undermine the operation and sustainability of the provider network. Strengthening the authority of professional bodies to enforce standards for licensing may enable them to engage in cartel-like behavior in keeping out qualified providers on inappropriate grounds. These conflicts must be taken into account and dealt with proactively for efforts to enhance the impact of regulation to be successful.

The Political and Cultural Context of Regulation

Regulation is an inherently political process in which individuals and groups with vested self-interests attempt to influence the success or failure of regulatory intervention. Regulation is also influenced by social values. For example, some societies may be characterized by a preference for organizing activities through government instead of the market. For historical and internal organizational and anthropological reasons, some cultural groups may prefer a more centralized, hierarchical way of organizing various realms of social interaction over the more autonomous, decentralized style of markets. Moreover, the review of international experience shows that health systems are not converging toward a similar regulatory model. Instead, they are sharing in new regulatory innovations while maintaining their own unique structures (Saltman 1998).

Weighing the Costs and Benefits of Regulation

Most countries find that the design of appropriate regulatory mechanisms and the enforcement of these mechanisms impose high administrative costs on both the regulator and the regulated. For example, regulating private health insurance to avoid adverse selection requires complicated regulatory mechanisms with very high transaction costs. In the context of health sector reform, experience with regulation is especially problematic. Reform has often begun in the context of resource-poor and weak public sectors, and the additional requirements of the regulatory reform initiative are often nearly impossible to achieve.

It is essential to have a realistic assessment of the costs and benefits of regulation. In addition to the costs of establishing the new bodies and procedures the ongoing costs of operation must be considered, including the cost of maintaining the regulatory body; the cost of administering regulatory processes; the cost of disseminating information; the cost of adjudicating disputes; and the compliance costs of the regulated entities.

The review of literature on regulation of other sectors demonstrates that the costs and benefits of regulatory activity can be assessed by using standard economic analysis.

An analytic framework for cost-benefit analysis of government regulation that could be adjusted for use in the health sector is presented in figure 4.6 (Guasch and Spiller 1999).

However, the thresholds for considering harm "minor" as opposed to "major," and "low" as opposed to "high," may vary considerably

Figure 4.6 Framework for Cost-Benefit Analysis of Government Regulation

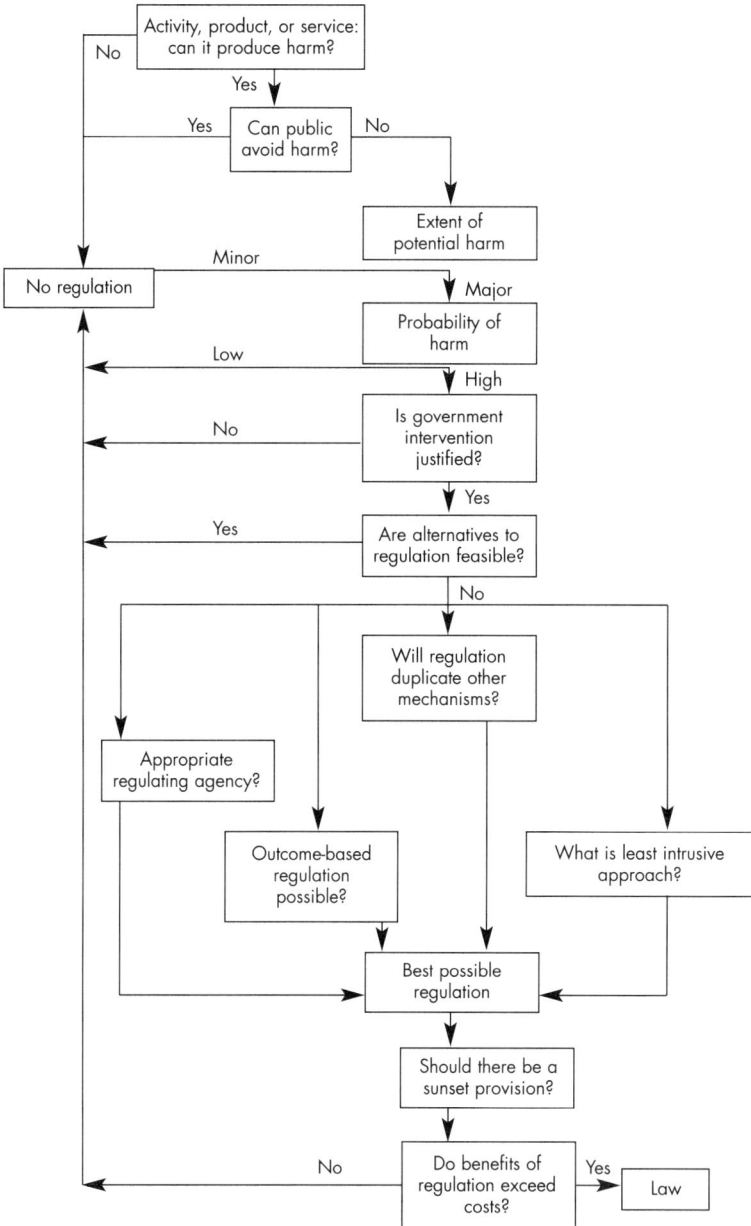

compared to other sectors. An example of this is regulation requiring pharmaceutical companies to disclose even very rare side effects.

Viewing Regulatory Design as an Ongoing Adaptive Process

Regulation is not a once-and-for-all designing of rules, incentives, and constraints. Instead, it is an ongoing process of reacting to developments in the regulated sector and dealing with problems as they emerge (Wildavsky 1979; and Brennan and Berwick 1996). The evolution of regulation in the health sector, therefore, is not a matter of linear progression from one mechanism of control to the next, but rather a constant mixing and remixing of regulatory tools that accumulate through the years as the health system develops.

Regulation must be viewed as a dynamic, responsive, and even opportunistic process. Some policies include provision for the regular review and updating of the regulatory instruments, based upon changing market conditions. One approach is to write a "sunset clause" into every regulation, requiring its reconsideration every few years. This, however, can be very resource-intensive and time-consuming for the government, especially in countries with voluminous regulations. Sunset clauses can also be resource-intensive for the regulated entities. Because such a clause makes planning difficult for the regulated entity it may hold back certain investments or other activities, or it may be required to plan for a quick change of course if the regulations change upon this review.

The goal in designing regulations and implementation processes is to design and incorporate flexible rules into a system that restrains arbitrary administrative action, and that therefore does not discourage expansion and development of the regulated activities.

Conclusions and Recommendations

Because of market failures encountered, private provision of health services must be accompanied by the regulation of access to medical services and goods as well as their effectiveness, quality, and efficiency. Regulation is among the most challenging of government's responsibilities in the health sector.

International experience offers several practical considerations that should be contemplated in designing and reforming regulatory regimes.

- Regulation is an inherently political and cultural process and must fit the context of each health system. The choice of a regulatory model should fit the country's overall political economy. Country experiences show that the appropriateness of regulatory practice in a particular country setting is a major determinant of its successful implementation. For example, choosing a self-regulatory model for health care in an environment where independent entities are unfamiliar with delegating and fulfilling delegated decisionmaking powers might not be appropriate. It would at least require much more careful preparation and implementation than in a country accustomed to decentralized decisionmaking, and coordination among government and individual professional bodies.

- Regulation should seek to complement and enhance ethical values as a means of influencing health care provision.

- National and regional regulatory policymaking is essential to ensuring access to health care providers and services as well as controlling national health care expenditures.

- Effective regulatory initiatives require strategic collaboration with a range of other regulatory actors.

- The role and structure of regulatory bodies are crucial aspects of the regulatory regime. Key challenges are balancing and integrating various forms of regulation, such as monitoring the financial performance of health payers and providers with the assessment of quality of health services. If financial regulation and quality assurance are not integrated, both are undercut and increase stress between the regulated and the regulators. At the same time, excessively detailed regulation may undermine the effective operation of the regulated organizations, even causing them to reduce or discontinue their operations.

- Regulatory instruments applied to one aspect of the health system cannot be viewed or dealt with in isolation. For example, standards such as capacity limits, quality measures, or price regulations that are imposed on one part of the system alter incentives and behavior in other parts of the system. Each subsector has intricate direct and indirect linkages to other subsectors, requiring multiple initiatives to achieve a set policy objective. Examples of the perverse consequences of narrowly drawn regulatory efforts are numerous.

- Regulation of both the private and public sectors should be carried out within the same institutional framework.

This review of international experience with health care regulation has identified a set of factors that can be regarded as prerequisites for successful implementation and enforcement of a health care regulatory system.

- Good regulation in the health sector should always have a clear, long-term purpose. Just as all large, private, for-profit corporations use strategic planning to maximize their ability to achieve their objectives, so too should public regulators use strategic planning, particularly in dealing with a sector as complex and with as many powerful actors as the health sector (Walt 1998).

- Political commitment is a primary requirement for initiating or reforming health care regulatory policy. Without this commitment a national policy cannot be formulated or, above all, implemented.

- Health sector regulation is not a straightforward matter of setting and enforcing standards. The validity of standards and the determination of whether they have been achieved are likely to be subjected to challenges, engendering costly enforcement efforts.

- Learning from and copying the experiences of other countries, with adaptation to local circumstances, may be a useful approach for countries embarking on health care regulatory reforms. For example, accreditation provides a case study in the international propagation of models—the U.S. model directly shaped the systems in Australia and Canada and indirectly influenced developments in Britain. In each case the model was adapted to fit national circumstances, however.

- Badly instituted regulation and regulation without systematic monitoring and enforcement may be worse than no regulation at all, in that such regulation invites disrespect and ultimately undermines state authority. This situation requires a balance that preserves adequate cooperation between actors without sacrificing public accountability. In many LMCs regulation is thus not only a matter of designing good regulations but of building administrative capacity to ensure that those regulations are respected and enforced. This finding is equally true in a self-regulatory context.

- Regulation of capacity, prices, market structure, and entitlements needs to be coordinated. Otherwise, incentives and constraints imposed by different forms of regulation are likely to interact in a dysfunctional way (Saltman, Busse, and Mossialos 2002).

- The appropriate regulatory package for each country must attempt to balance conflicting goals and to combine the right mix of "sticks" and "carrots" to complement each other.

- The costs and benefits of any regulatory intervention must be weighed in determining whether or not to proceed with implementation.

- Without reasonable institutional capacities in ministries of health, independent regulatory agencies, professional associations, and provider associations, the efforts to regulate the health sector are likely to fail.

- Cooperation and coordination among regulatory agencies should be encouraged. Failure of government agencies to coordinate with each other in implementing regulatory policies can result in redundancy, conflicts, excessive costs, and regulatory failures.

- Regulatory agencies should seek public input in addressing health care regulatory reforms. The opportunity for public input frequently minimizes legal challenges to the reform by industry and individuals and enhances compliance.

- Involvement of members of the medical profession and the health provider community in establishing and reviewing regulation is crucial to success.

- Regulation is a continuing process of public management and requires flexibility. Any regulatory initiative should therefore be seen as an ongoing process of adapting to changing needs, behavior, and competence of those regulating and those being regulated, as well as changes in the broader social and political environment.

Appendix 4.A Regulatory Instruments Summarized by Regulatory Strategy and Target of Regulation

TARGET OF REGULATION/REGULATORY STRATEGY	CONTROLS	INCENTIVES
Indirect regulatory instruments (aimed at the input-provider interface)		
Capital and funding	• Regulation of capital markets • Mechanisms for allocating public funds (such as contracting, prospective/retrospective reimbursement	• Government low-interest loans • Government guarantees for borrowing on private markets
Manpower	• Control of medical school admissions • Pay scales for public managerial personnel	• Accreditation of educational institutions
Facilities, equipment, and supplies	• Import restrictions • Global budgets • Testing requirements and quality controls on production of equipment and supplies	• Duty-free imports of medical equipment and supplies
Technology/knowledge	• National health technology agencies/advisory panels	• Research funding
Direct regulatory instruments (aimed at the provider-consumer interface)		
Price of services	• Rate setting and price controls	• Government subsidies
Health system capacity (quantity and distribution of services)	• Certificate of need programs • Health maps	• Bonuses to serve in underserved areas
Quality of services	• Registration/licensing requirements • Practice guidelines • Medical technology/equipment safety acts	• Voluntary facility accreditation • Personnel credentialing
Combinations of the above targets	• Fines, penalties, and sanctions • Antitrust law (to control prices and quality of services) • Professional standards review organizations and peer review organizations (to control cost and quality of services)	• Tax laws (to influence volume and price of private provision) • Provider-payment arrangements (can influence volume and quality of services)

Appendix 4.B Summary of Control-Based Regulatory Instruments

AREA	METHOD OF REGULATION	APPLICATION	TARGET	DESCRIPTION	COUNTRY
Health care facilities	Facility licensing	Operation of new facility	Minimum facility structure	Allows only facilities meeting minimum quality and safety standards to operate.	Universal
	Certificate of need programs	New facility construction or facility expansion	Community need for service Resource allocation	Ensures that any new facility construction is based on local social need.	United States
	Health maps (carte sanitaire)	Health planning and distribution of health facilities	Efficient distribution of health facilities	Plans diffusion and geographic distribution of government hospitals and other provider organizations.	France
	Health system agencies	New facility construction or facility expansion	Rationalization of capital investment	Reviews hospital expansion and modernization plans to determine eligibility for capital reimbursement from federal government.	United States
	Antitrust regulation	Relationship between providers	Price and quality of services	Safeguards against provider monopolies and enhances competition.	United States
	Facility accreditation	Facility structure and performance	Quality of services	Evaluates health facilities according to standards for optimal structures and processes.	Australia, Canada, Czech Republic, Kyrgyz Republic, Lithuania, New Zealand, South Africa, United States, Zambia

(Table continues on the following page.)

319

Appendix 4.B (continued)

AREA	METHOD OF REGULATION	APPLICATION	TARGET	DESCRIPTION	COUNTRY
Health care personnel	Licensing	Minimum qualifications	Quality of services	Restricts entry into medical practice to personnel meeting minimum qualifications.	Universal
	Primary and specialty certification	Specialized competence	Quality of services	Recognizes higher or more specialized levels of professional competence.	Most countries
	Recertification	Maintained competence	Quality of services	Ensures maintained professional competence.	Canada, United States
	Practice guidelines and outcomes research	Clinical practice	Quality of services	Assists physicians in decisions about appropriate health care for specific clinical circumstances.	United States
	Professional standards review organizations	Utilization review	Quality of services, Cost of care	Establishes norms for various procedures and applies them to individual cases of hospital use (such as length of stay) so as to identify noncomplying practitioners.	United Kingdom, United States
	Peer review organizations	Utilization review	Quality of services, Cost of care	Like professional standards review organizations but nationwide and centralized in nature.	United States
	Fines, penalties and sanctions	Provider compliance with regulation	Varied	Punishes provider personnel and organizations for faulty behavior or noncompliance with regulations.	Universal

Appendix 4.C Status of Accreditation Systems Worldwide

COUNTRY	ACCREDITING BODY	TYPES OF STANDARDS	NUMBER OF ACCREDITED HOSPITALS	DEVELOPED INDICATORS	FUNDING SOURCE	LIMITED SCOPE?
Australia	Australian Council on Healthcare Standards	Structure and processes	203 (1994)	Yes	Survey fees, publications, and education	No
Canada	Canadian Council on Health Services Accreditation	Processes and outcomes	502 (1996)	Proposed for 2000	Member fees and survey fees	No
China	Hospital Grade Appraisal	Processes and outcomes	1,086 (1991)	—	—	Yes, hospitals and teaching hospitals
Czech Republic	Joint Committee on Accreditation	Structure, processes, and outcomes	13	Yes	Survey fees	Yes, hospitals
Japan	Council for Quality Health Care	—	79	—	—	Yes, community hospitals
Kyrgyz Republic	Ministry of Health	Structure, processes, and outcomes	—	No	Survey fees, board member organization support, other	Yes, hospitals
Lithuania	State Accreditation Services by Ministry of Health	Structure and processes	53	No	Ministry of Health and survey fees	Yes, nursing rehabilitation, and medical care hospitals

(Table continues on the following page.)

Appendix 4.C (continued)

COUNTRY	ACCREDITING BODY	TYPES OF STANDARDS	NUMBER OF ACCREDITED HOSPITALS	DEVELOPED INDICATORS	FUNDING SOURCE	LIMITED SCOPE?
Netherlands	National Organization for Quality Assurance in Hospitals	Structure and processes	—	—	—	Yes, medical specialists
Netherlands	Netherlands Institute voor Accreditation van Ziehenhuiren	Structure and processes	18	No	Survey fees	Yes, hospitals
New Zealand	Health Accreditation Programme for New Zealand	Structure and processes	115 (1997, all services)	Proposed	Member fee (1998)	No
Republic of Korea	Joint Commission on Accreditation of Hospitals	Structure and processes	131	Yes	Survey fees	Yes, teaching hospitals
Republic of Korea	Hospital Performance Evaluation Program	Processes and outcomes	96	—	—	Yes, hospitals
South Africa	Council for Health Service Accreditation of South Africa	Structure, processes, and outcomes	40	Proposed	Survey fees	No
Taiwan, China	Ministry of Health	Structure, processes, and outcomes	525	Yes	Government	Yes, hospitals

Country	Organization	Focus	Number	Mandatory	Funding	Links
United Kingdom	Health Services Accreditation	Structure, processes, and outcomes	Unknown	Yes	Survey fees or grants	Yes, hospital departments
United Kingdom	Kings Fund Organizational Audit	Structure and processes	79 (1994)	No	Survey fees and publications	Yes, hospitals
United Kingdom	Southwestern Hospital Accreditation Program	Structure and processes	67 (1994)	No	Grants, survey fees, consulting, and publications	Yes, community hospitals
United States	Joint Commission on Accreditation of Health-care Organizations	Structure, processes, and outcomes	5,155	Yes	Survey fees, publications, education programs, and consulting	No
United States	American Osteopathic Association	Structure, processes, and outcomes	400	No	Survey fees	Yes, hospitals
United States	Commission of Accreditation of Rehabilitation Facilities	Structure, processes, and outcomes	700–800	Proposed	Survey fees, publications, and education	Yes, rehabilitation services

— Not available.
Source: Vincent and Rooney (pp. 9–10).

Appendix 4.D Electronic Accreditation and Quality Assurance Resources

QCI International—http://www.qci-intl.com

This full-service consulting, training, and publishing firm is a source for products and services related to total quality management. It focuses on teams such as employee involvement teams, with special emphasis on building facilitator and team-leader skills.

Medical Quality Assurance—http://www.doh.state.fl.us/mqa

MQA is responsible for planning, developing, and coordinating programs and services of 18 regulatory boards, six councils, and five professions directly administered by the Florida Department of Health. MQA develops policies to regulate medical professionals while protecting the health and safety of Florida residents. Many links are available, including health care provider license look-up and information on regulated professions.

HQHQ—http://www.hqhq.org

This Web site provides online training for health care professionals. The training is certified as fulfilling the requirements in the United Kingdom for continuing medical education. An "Evidence of Learning" section gives participants a chance to check their own progress (including their responses to text questions) via an e-mail review.

International Society for Quality in Health Care— http://www.isqua.org.au

This international nonprofit organization, based in Australia, provides a forum for individuals and institutions with a common interest in health care quality, to share expertise via a multidisciplinary forum. ISQua is supported by members, including leading quality health care providers and agencies in just under 70 countries. ISQua runs the Agenda for Leadership in Programs for Health Care Accreditation, which: assesses and endorses the standards of national organizations against internationally approved principles for health care standards; surveys and accredits national accreditation bodies to international standards for performance excellence; and assists countries to develop health care accreditation programs. ISQua publishes the International Journal for Quality in Health Care. http://www.isqua.org.au/isquaPages/Journal.html

IQMA Classifieds—http://www.openhouse.org.uk—E-mail address: iqma@openhouse.org.uk

This site is a clearinghouse for people interested in all aspects of quality assurance. Individuals may post classified ads in these categories: quality-training courses, recruitment, articles for sale, articles wanted, research, publishing, and general classifieds. This Web site is not specifically oriented to health care.

AddVal Inc.—http://www.addvalinc.com

AddVal Inc., founded by nurse executives, specializes in credentials and primary verification, quality improvement, and accreditation consultation. Its mission is to add value to health care. It creates products and services for physicians, managed care companies, and hospitals. Its nurse consultants create specific work plans for organizational needs and resolve issues in a timely fashion.

Appendix 4.E Case Studies

Germany: Regulating Technology Capacity and Diffusion

Evaluating the success of CON-type regulation is difficult. This can be demonstrated using the example of Germany, which experiences continued conflict regarding the diffusion of expensive medical devices and their distribution between the ambulatory and hospital sector (Bruckenberger 1998). This judgment is a result of assorted attempts by corporatist and legislative bodies to improve planning of expensive medical devices in light of increasing costs and new types of devices such as extracorporal shock-wave lithotripsy. Until 1982, when expensive devices came under hospital planning requirements, they had not been regulated. Since then, devices that were not part of an agreement could not be considered in the per diem charges, and thus their costs could not be covered in social insurance payments (the Swiss use a similar regulatory approach). Between 1989 and 1997 diffusion and regional distribution of expensive medical equipment for supply to the population covered by social health insurance were controlled intersectorally through joint committees involving both the hospital and ambulatory sector. Site planning was accomplished by state-level committees, made up of representatives of hospitals, doctors' associations, health insurance funds, and a state representative. They negotiated aspects of the joint use of devices, service requirements, the need for the technology based on population density and structure, and operators' qualifications (Perleth, Busse, and Schwartz 1999).

Though abolished in 1997, the regulation appears to have been relatively successful in containing excess technology diffusion and related cost escalation during the period it was utilized (Jakubowski and Busse 1998).

Maryland, United States: Combining Competition with Regulation for Cost Containment

Price regulation and competition are traditionally viewed as alternative cost containment mechanisms. The U.S. state of Maryland has successfully combined price regulation and competition in the hospital market to contain costs. In the United States the lack of comprehensive cost control programs, encompassing all payers and providers, frequently leads to cost shifting. In the early 1990s the growth of managed care made costs more difficult to shift, resulting in reductions in care to the uninsured or underinsured. Maryland is one U.S. state where the success of an all-payer system in containing hospital costs coincided with substantial growth in enrollment in health maintenance organizations (HMOs) over the last decade. Some inferences can be drawn from Maryland's experience about the compatibility of all-payer systems and managed competition.

In 1971 Maryland was the first U.S. state to implement an all-payer hospital rate-setting system. The system uses a quasi-public utility approach to hospital rate regulation. The principle of rate setting is to base hospital reimbursement on the reasonableness of the relation between costs and charges across all the payers. Each Maryland hospital has had at least one full rate review. Most hospitals also have their rates revised each year. The revision process takes into consideration inflation adjustments, volume adjustments, and changes in payers and case mixes.

If a hospital's revenues per admission are less than (more than) its cap, it will receive additional (reduced) revenues through higher (lower) updates of the service rates the next year. The rate-setting commission adjusts each hospital's data in several ways to ensure fair comparisons, and then sets a statewide limit on hospital revenue per admission.

The Maryland all-payer system has successfully contained hospital costs. Maryland's growth in per-admission hospital costs was less than the national average for 17 consecutive years. The success of the all-payer system in controlling hospital costs coincided with substantial growth in the number of HMOs in the last decade. The Maryland experience suggests that regulatory and competitive strategies can be compatible (Wallack, Skalera, and Cai 1996).

Notes

1. A special licensing is required for graduates of medical schools outside North America and is administered by the Educational Commission on Foreign Medical Graduates in the United States and by the Medical Council of Canada in Canada.

2. The same approach is adopted by the National League of Nursing regarding professional nursing schools.

3. Medicare is a federal program that provides comprehensive health insurance to individuals 65 and older in the United States.

4. Utilization reviews study retrospective service utilization patterns and use them as a basis for preapproval (or denial) of future service provision. Medical audits are postservice reviews and are thus purely retrospective in nature.

5. Visit at http://www.nice.org.uk.

Bibliography

Altenstetter, C. 1998. "Implementing the EU Regulatory Policy on Medical Devices." In D. Chinitz and J. Cohen, eds., *Governments and Health Systems*. Chichester, U.K.: John Wiley.

Anderson, G., R. Heyssel, and R. Dicker. 1993. "Competition vs. Regulation: Its Effect on Hospitals." *Health Affairs* (Spring): 70–79.

Anderson, G., D. Halcoussis, and L. Johnston. 2000. "Regulatory Barriers to Entry in the Health Care Industry." *Quarterly Review of Economics and Finance* (Winter): 485–502.

Asiimwe, D., and J.C. Lule. 1993. "The Public/Private Mix in Financing and Provision of Health Services in Uganda." In S. Bennett and A. Mills, eds., *Proceedings from the Workshop on the Public/Private Mix for Health Care in Developing Countries*. Health Policy Unit Report. London: London School of Hygiene and Tropical Medicine.

Ayres, I., and J. Braithwaite. 1992. *Responsible Regulation*. Oxford: Oxford University Press.

Baldwin, R., and M. Cave. 1999. *Understanding Regulation: Theory, Strategy and Practice*. Oxford: Oxford University Press.

Becker, G. 1995. *Strategy for Health Facility Accreditation*. Bethesda, Md.: Abt Associates Inc., Zdrav/Reform Project.

Becker, G. C., B. Ente, and Standards Development Committee, Republic of Kyrgyzstan. 1995. *Licensing and Accreditation Manual for Hospitals*. Bethesda, Md.: Abt Associates Inc., Ministry of Health, Republic of Kyrgyzstan, and Zdrav Reform Project.

Bennema-Broos, M., P. P. Groenewegen, and G. P. Westert. 2001. "Social Democratic Government and Spatial Distribution of Health Care Facilities." *European Journal of Public Health* 11: 160–65.

Bennett, S., and E. Ngalande-Banda. 1994. *Public and Private Roles in Health: A Review and Analysis of Experience in Sub-Saharan Africa.* Geneva: World Health Organization.

Bennett, S., G. Dakpallah, P. Garner, L. Gilson, S. Nittayaramphong, B. Zurita, and A. Zwi. 1994. "Carrot and Stick: State Mechanisms to Influence Private Provider Behavior." *Health Policy and Planning* 9 (1): 1–13.

Berg, O. 1999. "The Organization of the Norwegian Health Care System: The Rise and Decline of a Public Iatrocracy." In O. Molven, ed., *The Norwegian Health Care System.* Oslo: University of Oslo.

Bhat, R. 1996. "Regulation of the Private Health Sector in India." *International Journal of Health Planning and Management* 11: 253–74.

Boerma, W. G. W., and D. M. Fleming. 1998. *The Role of General Practice in Primary Health Care.* London: Stationery Office.

Boerma, W. G. W., J. van der Zee, and D. M. Fleming. 1997. Service Profiles of General Practitioners in Europe. *British Journal of General Practice* 47: 481–86.

Brennan, T. A., and D. M. Berwick. 1996. *New Rules: Regulation, Markets and the Quality of American Health Care.* San Francisco, Calif.: Jossey-Bass Publications.

Bruckenberger, E. 1998. "Vernetzte Versorgungsmodelle mit Kliniken, Praxen und Kassen." *Zeitschrift für Allgemeinmedizin* 74: 259–62.

Bundesministerium für Gesundheit, ed. 1998. *Leitlinien in der Gesundheitsversorgung* [Guidelines in Health Care]. *Vorträge und Berichte von der WHO-Konferenz zu Leitlinien in der esundheitsversorgung* [Papers and Reports of the WHO Conference on Guidelines in Health Care Practice]. Baden-Baden: Nomos.

Busse, R. 2000. *Health Care Systems in Transition—Germany.* Copenhagen: European Observatory on Health Care Systems. http://www.euro.who.int/eprise/main/WHO/Progs/Obs/hits/TopPage

Busse, R., and F. W. Schwartz. 1997. "Financing Reforms in the German Hospital Sector—From Full Cost Cover Principle to Prospective Case Fees." *Medical Care* 35 (10): OS40–OS49.

Busse, R., T. van der Grinten, and P.-G. Svensson. 2002. Regulating Entrepreneurial Behaviour in Hospitals: Theory and Practice. In R. B.

Saltman, R. Busse, and E. Mossialos, eds., *Regulating Entrepreneurial Behaviour in European Health Care Systems*. Buckingham, U.K.: Open University Press.

Cassels, A. 1995. "Health Sector Reform: Key Issues in Less Developed Countries." *Journal of International Development* 7 (3): 329–48.

Data for Decision-Making Project. 1993. *Consultation on the Private Health Sector in Africa: Summary of Proceedings*. Washington, September 22–23, 1993. Draft. Cambridge, Mass.: Data for Decision-Making Project, Harvard School of Public Health, Cambridge, Mass.

Evans, R. 1976. "Does Canada Have Too Many Doctors? Why Nobody Loves an Immigrant Physician." *Canadian Public Policy* 2: 147–60.

Freidson, E. 1970. *Profession of Medicine: A Study of the Sociology of Applied Knowledge*. New York: Harper & Row.

Gilbert, R. J., and D. M. Newberry. 1994. "The Dynamic Efficiency of Regulatory Constitutions." *Rand Journal of Economics* 25 (4): 538–54.

Guasch, J. L., and P. Spiller. 1999. "Managing the Regulatory Process: Design, Concepts, Issues, and the Latin America and Caribbean Story." World Bank, Washington, D.C.

HEW (U.S. Department of Health, Education and Welfare). 1977. "Report on Licensure and Related Health Personnel Credentialing." Washington, D.C.

Hughes, D. 1993. "General Practitioners and the New Contract: Promoting Better Health through Financial Incentives." *Health Policy* 25: 39–50.

Hursh-César, G., P. Berman, K. Hanson, R. Rannan-Eliya, J. Rittmann, and K. Purdy. 1994. *Summary of Country Studies: Private Providers' Contributions to Public Health in Four African Countries*. Conference Report, November 28–December 1, 1994, Nairobi, Kenya, Data for Decision-Making Project, Boston, Mass. http://www.hsph.harvard.edu/ihsg/publications/pdf/No-21-1.pdf

Jakubowski, E., and R. Busse. 1998. "Einflußfaktoren für Großgeräteanschaffung lassen einen deutlichen Anstieg der Großgeräteanzahl erwarten." [translation] *Gesundheitswesen* 60: A56.

Kenney, G. 1993. *Assessing Legal and Regulatory Reform in Family Planning: Manual on Legal and Regulatory Reform*. Washington, D.C.: Futures Group International, OPTIONS Project.

Kessler, D., and M. McClellan. 1999. "Designing Hospital Antitrust Policy to Promote Social Welfare." Working Paper 6897. Cambridge, Mass.: National Bureau of Economic Research.

Knowles, J., A. Yazbeck, and S. Brewster. 1994. "The Private Sector Delivery of Health Care: Senegal." Major Applied Research Paper 16. Health Financing and Sustainability (HFS) Project, Abt Associates Inc., Bethesda, Md.

Kumaranayake, L. 1997. "The Role of Regulation: Influencing Private Sector Activity within Health Sector Reform." *Journal of International Development* 9 (4): 641–49.

Laffont, J., and J. Tirole. 1993. *A Theory of Incentives in Procurement and Regulation*. Cambridge, Mass.: MIT Press.

Langenbrunner, J., and M. Wiley. 2002. "Paying Hospitals in Eastern Europe and the Former Soviet Union." In M. McKee and J. Healy, eds., *Hospitals in a Changing Europe*. Buckingham, U.K.: Open University Press.

Maboshe, M., J. Tembo, and A. Rooney. 1999. "Development of a Hospital Accreditation Program: The Zambian Experience." *QA Brief* 8 (2): 15–17. URL http://www.qaproject.org/

Maor, M. 1998. Choosing a Regulatory Regime: The Experience of the Israeli Electricity Market. Draft.

Mujinja, D. Urassa, and K. S. Mnyika. 1993. "The Tanzanian Public/Private Mix in National Health Care." In S. Bennett and A. Mill, eds., *Proceedings from the Workshop on the Public/Private Mix for Health Care in Developing Countries*. Health Policy Unit Report. London: London School of Hygiene and Tropical Medicine.

National Commission on Quality Assurance Web site. URL http://www.ncqa.org/

Naylor, C. D., P. Jha, J. Woods, and A. Shariff. 1999. *A Fine Balance: Some Options for Private and Public Health Care in Urban India*. Washington, D.C.: World Bank, Human Development Network.

Newble, D., B. Jolly, and R. Wakeford, eds. 1994. *The Certification and Re-certification of Doctors: Issues in the Assessment of Clinical Competence.* Cambridge: Cambridge University Press.

NHS (National Health Service) Executive. 1994. *The Operation of the NHS Internal Market: Local Freedoms, National Responsibilities.* HSG (94) 55. London: HMSO (Her Majesty's Stationery Office, U.K.).

Norton, E. C. 1992. "Incentive Regulation of Nursing Homes." *Journal of Health Economics* 11: 105–28.

Perleth, M., R. Busse, and F. W. Schwartz. 1999. "Regulation of Health-Related Technologies in Germany." *Health Policy* 46: 105–26.

PHR (Partnerships for Health Reform Project). 1999. *Health Reform and Priority Services.* Bethesda, Md.: Abt Associates Inc., Partnerships for Health Reform Project. URL www.phrproject.com

Porter, J. D. H., and J. Grange, eds. 1999. "Involving Private Medical Sector in Tuberculosis Control: Practical Aspects." *Tuberculosis: An International Perspective.* London: Imperial College Press.

Ravenholt, B. B. 1996. *Potential for Increased Involvement of the Commercial Sector in Family Planning Service Delivery in the Philippines: Assessment and Initial Strategies.* Washington, D.C.: Futures Group International, POLICY Project.

Rodwin, V. G. 1997. "Managed Care in the US: Lessons for French Health Policy." In C. Altenstetter and J. W. Bjorkman, eds., *Health Policy Reform, National Variations, and Globalization.* London: MacMillan.

Roemer, M. I. 1977. *Comparative National Policies on Health Care.* New York: Marcel Dekker, Inc.

———. 1991. *National Health Systems of the World.* Vol.1. Oxford: Oxford University Press.

Saltman, R. B. 1998. "Convergence, Social Embeddedness, and the Future of Health Systems in the Nordic Region." In D. Chinitz and J. Cohen, eds., *Government and Health Systems.* Chichester, U.K.: John Wiley.

Saltman, R. B., and A. de Roo. 1989. "Hospital Policy in the Netherlands: Parameters of a Structural Stalemate." *Journal of Health Politics, Policy, and Law* Winter, 14 (4): 773–95.

Saltman, R., R. Busse, and E. Mossialos, eds. 2002. *Regulating Entrepreneurial Behavior in European Health Care Systems*. Buckingham, U.K.: Open University Press.

Saltman, R., and R. Busse. 2002. "Balancing Regulation and Entrepreneurialism in Europe's Health Sector: Theory and Practice." In R. B. Saltman, R. Busse, and E. Mossialos, eds., *Regulating Entrepreneurial Behaviour in European Health Care Systems*. Buckingham, U.K.: Open University Press.

Schneider, M., and J. Wasem. 1998. *Regulating Private Markets and Insurance*. Flagship Course on Health Sector Reform and Sustainable Financing. Washington, D.C.: World Bank, Economic Development Institute.

Schut, F. T. 1995. *Competition in the Dutch Health Care Sector*. Ridderkerk: Ridderprint.

Scrivens, E. 2001. "Accreditation and the Regulation of Quality in Health Services. In R. B. Saltman, R. Busse, and E. Mossialos, eds., *Regulating Entrepreneurial Behaviour in European Health Care Systems*. Buckingham, U.K.: Open University Press.

Scrivens, E., R. Klein, and A. Steiner. 1995. "Accreditation: What Can We Learn from the Anglo-Phone Model? *Health Policy* 34 (3): 193–204.

Silver, M. H. 1997. "Patients' Rights in England and the United States of America: The Patient's Charter and the New Jersey Patient Bill of Rights: A Comparison." *Journal of Medical Ethics* 23: 213–20.

Slater, S. R., and C. Saade. 1996. *Mobilizing the Commercial Sector for Public Health Objectives. A Practical Guide*. Arlington, Va.: BASICS, and New York: UNICEF.

Starfield, B. 1996. "Is Strong Primary Care Good for Health Outcomes?" In J. Griffin, ed., *The Future of Primary Care*. London: Office of Health Economics.

Trubek, L. G. 1999. "Informing, Claiming, Contracting: Enforcement in the Managed Care Era." *Annals of Health Law* 8: 133–45.

Vincent, D., and A. Rooney. 1999. "Improving Health Service Delivery with Accreditation, Licensure and Certification." *Quality Assurance Brief Project* 8 (2): 9–10.

Wallack, S., K. C. Skalera, and J. Cai. 1996. "Redefining Rate Regulation in a Competitive Environment." *Journal of Health Politics, Policy, and Law* 21 (3): 489–520.

Walt, G. 1998. Implementing Healthcare Reform: A Framework for Discussion. In R. B. Saltman, J. Figueras, and C. Sakellarides, eds., *Critical Challenges for Health Care Reform in Europe.* Buckingham, U.K.: Open University Press.

Weill, T. P., and R. M. Battistella. 1998. "A Blended Strategy Using Competitive and Regulatory Models." *Health Care Management Review* 23 (1): 37–45.

WHO (World Health Organization). 1996. *Continuous Quality of Care Development: Outcomes and Quality of Care.* Copenhagen, Regional Office for Europe.

Wildavsky, A. 1979. *Speaking Truth to Power: The Art and Craft of Policy Analysis.* Boston: Little, Brown.

Wiley, M. M. 1998. Financing Operating Costs for Acute Hospital Services. In R. B. Saltman, J. Figueras, and C. Sakellarides, eds., *Critical Challenges for Health Care Reform in Europe.* Buckingham, U.K.: Open University Press, p. 218–35.

Wilsford, D. 1995. "States Facing Interests: Struggles over Health Care Policy in Advanced Industrial Democracies." *Journal of Health Politics, Policy, and Law* 20 (3): 571–614.

Wooldridge, M. 1996. Opening in AMA Summit proceedings. Competition in Health: a brave new world? Canberra: Australian Medical Association.

Yesudian, C. A. K. 1993. "Behavior of the Private Health Sector in the Health Market of Bombay." *Health Policy and Planning* 9 (1): 72–80.

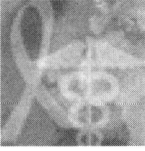

About the Editors
and Contributors

The Editors

April Harding is a Senior Economist in the Health, Nutrition, and Population Department of the World Bank. Since arriving at the World Bank Ms. Harding has provided technical assistance to governments in more than 13 countries, primarily on issues related to private sector development and privatization. She currently manages the analytical work, operational support, and training related to private participation in the health sector. She speaks and publishes in numerous forums on public-private partnerships, private participation, privatization, and reform of health services. She has recently edited a volume on hospital reform in developing countries, *Innovations in Health Service Delivery: Autonomization and Corporatization of Hospitals*.

Prior to joining the World Bank Ms. Harding was a Research Fellow in Economic Studies at the Brookings Institution. From 1987 to 1991 Ms. Harding was a Fellow of the Russian and East European Center at the University of Pennsylvania, where she also received a Ph.D. in Economics, with a concentration in Comparative Economic Systems and Public Finance.

Alexander S. Preker, Chief Economist for Health, Nutrition, and Population and Editor of the HNP Publication Series, is responsible for coordinating the World Bank's Health Systems Development team and overseeing its analytical work on health financing and service delivery. He coordinated the team that prepared the Bank's 1997 Sector Strategy on health care in developing countries, was one of the authors of the World Health Report 2000 on Health Systems, and was a member of Working Group 3 of the WHO Commission on Macro-Economics and Health which reported in 2001. Mr. Preker has published extensively on topics related to health systems development and is a frequent speaker at major international conferences. He is on the editorial committee of several journals and on the scientific committee of the International Health Economics Association Conference in San Francisco, 2003. Mr. Preker has an appointment as Associate Professor at the George Washington University, is on the External Advisory Board for the London School of Economics Health Group and is a member of the teaching faculty for the Harvard/World Bank Institute Flagship Course on Health Sector Reform and Sustainable Financing. His training includes a Ph.D. in Economics from the London School of Economics and Political Science, a Fellowship in Medicine from University College London, a Diploma in Medical Law and Ethics from King's College London, and an MD from University of British Columbia/McGill.

The Contributors

Reinhard Busse, Ph.D., is a professor of health care management at Technische Universität Berlin, as well as the associate director of research of the European Observatory on Health Care Systems. The primary focus of his research is comparative European health systems and health technology assessment. He has degrees in public health as well as in medicine.

Sarbani Chakraborty is a Health Specialist in the Europe and Central Asia Region of the World Bank. Since joining the Bank in 1999 Ms.

Chakraborty has been involved in Bank projects and analytical work in several countries (Georgia, Lebanon, Mongolia, and Oman). This has involved technical work in areas such as decentralization of health services, public-private mix, provider payment systems, poverty and health, and primary health care.

Prior to joining the Bank she was involved in health sector research and project work in South Asia. Ms. Chakraborty has a Masters of Public Health and a Ph.D. in Health Services Research from the Johns Hopkins School of Public Health. Her Ph.D. dissertation focused on measuring and understanding the determinants of technical quality of care for childhood illnesses among informal private providers in rural India.

Nihal Hafez Afifi is a health policy and management consultant. Her training includes, in addition to an M.D., a Masters of Business Administration from the American University and a Masters of Public Health, with a concentration in International Health, from Harvard University. Dr. Hafez Afifi has worked with the U.S. Agency for International Development, the World Bank, the Harvard Institute for International Development, the Data for Decision-Making Project of the Harvard School of Public Health, the Partnership for Health Reform Project, and Abt Associates. She provides technical assistance in health care regulation, cost recovery systems, health sector institutional development, analysis of the political environment for health policy change, and designing health care reform programs for developing countries.

Robert J. Taylor has served as a manager, educator, and consultant in hospital and health services management in more than 25 countries. After receiving an MHA in Health Services Administration from the University of Minnesota, he served as an administrator in a number of private hospitals in Minneapolis. In 1977 he was appointed chief executive officer of Hennepin County Medical Center, a public teaching hospital in the same city. While there he was a founder of the Health Futures Institute, established to examine the potentials of public-private cooperation in health care. In 1981 Mr. Taylor moved with his family to Karachi, Pakistan, where he served four years as Director General for Commissioning at the Aga Khan University Hospital. In 1985 he founded Taylor Associates International, a consulting firm specializing in organizational development and management strengthening in developing countries. He is an instructor and lecturer and has written extensively on health care management, change management, medical specialty services, and trends in health care.

Index

5572 020000 048572